PE

St John Greene grew up in the West Country, where he met his teenage sweetheart, Kate. A qualified paramedic and lifeguard, St John, known to his friends as Singe, founded Training Saints, which specializes in teaching extreme sports to young people. Since Kate's death Singe has devoted his life to raising their two young sons, Reef and Finn. He continues to run Training Saints and is chair of governors at the boys' school. He spends all of his free time teaching them the things he loved to do with Kate: sailing, scuba diving, jet skiing and power boating near their home in Somerset. *Mum's List* is his first book.

Mum's List

ST JOHN GREENE

with RACHEL MURPHY

PENGUIN BOOKS

PENGUIN BOOKS

Published by the Penguin Group
Penguin Books Ltd, 80 Strand, London WC2R 0RL, England
Penguin Group (USA) Inc., 375 Hudson Street, New York, New York 10014, USA
Penguin Group (Canada), 90 Eglinton Avenue East, Suite 700, Toronto, Ontario, Canada M4P 2Y3
(a division of Pearson Penguin Canada Inc.)
Penguin Ireland, 25 St Stephen's Green, Dublin 2, Ireland (a division of Penguin Books Ltd)
Penguin Group (Australia), 250 Camberwell Road,
Camberwell, Victoria 3124, Australia (a division of Pearson Australia Group Pty Ltd)
Penguin Books India Pvt Ltd, 11 Community Centre,
Panchsheel Park, New Delhi – 110 017, India
Penguin Group (NZ), 67 Apollo Drive, Rosedale, Auckland 0632, New Zealand
(a division of Pearson New Zealand Ltd)
Penguin Books (South Africa) (Pty) Ltd, 24 Sturdee Avenue,
Rosebank, Johannesburg 2196, South Africa

Penguin Books Ltd, Registered Offices: 80 Strand, London WC2R 0RL, England

www.penguin.com

First published 2012

001

Set in 12.5/14.75 Garamond MT Std
Typeset by Palimpsest Book Production Limited, Falkirk, Stirlingshire
Printed in Great Britain by Clays Ltd, St Ives plc

ISBN 978 1 40591 325 6

www.greenpenguin.co.uk

MIX
Paper from responsible sources
FSC www.fsc.org
FSC™ C018179

Penguin Books is committed to a sustainable
future for our business, our readers and our planet.
This book is made from Forest Stewardship
Council™ certified paper.

ALWAYS LEARNING

PEARSON

For Kate.
These memories should have been for us when we were old and grey. I wrote this book for you, to preserve our memories for ever. It is a testament to our love.
Infinity acres and acres, Singe, Reef and Finn.

Contents

Acknowledgements

This book would not have got off the ground if it weren't for South West News Service, who interviewed me after Kate's death and wrote the very first story about Mum's List for the media.

Literary agent Jonathan Conway of Mulcahy Conway Associates also played a pivotal role, introducing me to my publishers, Penguin Books. Thank you, Jonathan, for your professionalism, excellent advice and guidance throughout the process. I also want to thank my editor, Katy Follain, and her assistant, Tamsin English, at Penguin for being so welcoming and enthusiastic, and for showing the boys such kindness.

Rachel Murphy, who wrote *Mum's List*, has been awesome. Rachel, you are patient and caring, and I'm sure it helped that you are a parent yourself, but how you got into my head in such a short space of time and wrote this book so skilfully is beyond belief. You have written it *exactly* as I would love to have been able to write it myself, and I can't thank you enough.

I also want to say a heartfelt thank you to Kate's parents, Christine and Martin, and her brother Ben. You have all given me an incredible amount of love and support, and continue to do so. I know I can always count on you, and Reef and Finn love you dearly.

Thanks also to my own family for being there for me. My dad's Sunday lunches deserve a special mention, as at times they were the only home-cooked meals we had. My brother and sisters helped keep my chin up too, and I am so grateful to you all for showing me how much you care, and encouraging me to move on. Matt, your support has been fantastic, and I will never forget how you kept me company in the long evenings after Kate's death, phoning me up or calling round for a coffee when the boys were in bed and the house was so quiet.

To all my close friends – you know who you are. Kate would have been most impressed with all your help and guidance. You were always on the end of the phone when things went wobbly and I needed to talk. Kate would be proud of you all.

Prologue

'What d'you want to drink?' my brother asked.

He was standing at the bar, smiling, clearly pleased to see me. I instinctively looked over my left shoulder, turning to Kate.

'What d'you fancy?' I asked her.

It was noisy in the nightclub, and lights were flashing all around us. I could see Kate's outline against the backdrop of disco lights and dry ice. She looked beautiful in the half-light, but then again Kate always looked beautiful. Her pale-blue eyes twinkled back at me, and I felt her squeeze my hand. A split second later I felt a squeeze around my heart, as the penny suddenly dropped.

Kate wasn't actually there beside me. It was just a shadow of her, a hazy illusion of what I desperately wanted to see. I was so used to having Kate at my side that my mind had played tricks on me.

I felt my face flush as I turned back to my brother, who was staring at me, open-mouthed.

'Oh my God, Singe, are you all right?' Matt asked nervously.

It was his girlfriend's eighteenth birthday party, and he'd been delighted I'd accepted the invitation so soon after

Kate's death. It was my first big night out with members of my family since losing her, and I wanted it to go well for everybody's sake.

'Don't worry, I'm fine,' I said, meaning it.

'Are you sure?'

'Yes, I'm sure. Don't worry, I'm not going mad! Some habits die hard, that's all. Let's have a drink.'

Matt gave me a relieved smile, and I beamed back at him. It was good to see Kate again, I thought, though I didn't say it out loud. She had died less than a month earlier, and seeing her was a little reminder of just how fresh my grief was and how much I missed her.

As I worked my way around the party, doing my best to put other people at ease who didn't quite know what to say to me, I felt comforted by the fact that Kate was still so close to me. She was dead, but it didn't mean she had stopped being a part of my life. How could she? She *was* my life, even though I now had to carry on without her.

I stood on my own for a while, watching the teenagers on the dance floor. They were so full of fun, just as Kate and I were at that age, and in fact for most of our lives together. The buzz in the air and the youngsters' laughter made me remember our early dates. I pictured Kate in her teens, dancing in skin-tight jeans, without a care in the world. She looked older than she was and never had any trouble getting into the nightclubs, even at sixteen. She always strutted up to the doormen, giving a confident giggle and a wiggle that never failed to impress, and it was often me who was challenged about my age instead of her, despite the fact that I was five years older. Kate always looked stunning, and through the blinking lights and lasers

I couldn't see anyone but her on the dance floor. Her eyes were locked on mine, and I felt like I was the only other person in the room.

After we'd been clubbing, Kate and I would often take a midnight picnic up to Priddy in the Mendip Hills. I could see her aged seventeen, sitting on blankets under the stars, looking for satellites and listening to the choirs of frogs and mini-beasts. It was Kate's favourite place in all the world. There was no light pollution, and the stars burned so bright it felt like we were inside a massive planetarium, just the two of us. I breathed in the smell of Kate's perfume mingling with the sweet scent of damp grass, and we talked and melted away together for hours and hours.

The memory warmed my heart. Kate and I were soul mates, and we stayed that way for more than twenty years. How lucky was I? Looking around at the teenagers at the party, with all their lives ahead of them, I felt so grateful I had met Kate when we were both so young, and that we had had the chance to spend so many happy years together. That was something cancer could never take away.

Kate's diagnosis took the wind out of our sails, to say the least. It came literally weeks after our little boy Reef's own recovery from an incredibly rare and aggressive form of cancer, and so it felt even more unbelievably cruel and unlucky. I remember how I scrabbled around for positives. At least my feisty Kate would fight like a tigress, I thought. Reef had survived against far worse odds, so Kate would beat it too, no question. Reef's cancer had left him with a slightly withered left leg, which upset his balance, but he had adapted remarkably well, and most people had no idea he was registered disabled. I knew Kate would show the same resilience, whatever cancer threw at her and took from her.

We'd always lived life to the max. We'd travelled the world and made the most of every day together. We had no regrets about the past, and that was a huge blessing. The most positive thing of all was that I knew for certain that, however ill Kate became, she would continue to squeeze the most out of every minute of every day.

As I begin to write this book, a year after losing her, I can tell you that Kate certainly didn't let me, or the boys, down. She did us all proud until her dying day, and beyond. Even when she was desperately ill in her final few months she took the boys on trips to Disney World and Lapland and insisted on taking them to see the *Snow White* pantomime in Bristol just days before she died, even though getting her there in a wheelchair with oxygen tanks proved to be more of a pantomime than the show itself!

She also produced Mum's List, which she added to right up until the end of her life. Kate wasn't trying to be immortal and she'd have been humbled by the huge media interest it attracted, which led to people asking me to write this book. The list was for us, not for her, and it was I who unwittingly prompted her to write it when I cuddled her in bed and asked: 'What if you leave me?'

Kate was a devoted mother and loving wife, and she wanted to give me a helping hand to make sure I raised our boys as best I could without her. When I read the final list after she was gone, I felt less alone. Kate's spirit lived on, and I was so grateful to her for the massive effort she put into completing it on her deathbed. I still had a link to my fantastic wife and I took great comfort from that.

I think some people worried about the impact the list might have on my life. What if it made Kate's presence live on so powerfully my grief would never end? What if it tied me to the past so closely I could never move on?

For me, there was never any doubt in my mind. Kate's list was an incredible gift, no question. I felt sure it would guide me and reassure me and help me build a fantastic future for our boys.

I still have no idea how long it will take me to fulfil all of Kate's wishes, or even if I ever will. Some may take a lifetime. Only one thing is certain. I am taking every step as best as I possibly can, in memory of my wonderful wife Kate.

Chapter 1

'Kiss boys two times after I have gone'

'We made it!' Kate giggled. That giggle. That blonde hair. Those cornflower-blue eyes. I looked at my beautiful wife and laughed. She had a knack of making me laugh. Even just hearing that cheeky giggle of hers set me off. That day, once I'd started laughing I just couldn't stop. I lay back in the wet sand and pulled Kate down with me, cracking up laughing. It reminded me of the day I proposed to her more than twenty years earlier. Then, I'd deliberately made her crash off her skis into a mound of powdery snow. I dived in on top of her and produced an engagement ring from my pocket. She giggled, and we kissed, just as we did now. Back then I laughed with relief that she wanted to be my wife, and with excitement at the prospect of spending my life with such an amazing woman. Now I laughed with relief and excitement again, but for different reasons.

I could feel worry seeping out of me, through my back and into the sand, and I felt a surge of joy and optimism about the future, something I hadn't felt in a long while. A wave washed over our feet, and Kate and I shrieked and huddled tighter together. As the water ebbed away I felt the terror and the darkness of the past three years wash into the sea and drift away from me. The sun beamed brilliantly, shining light and warmth back into our lives.

We lay back on the sand, holding hands. I thought about how life had changed in so many ways for Kate and me; but in so many other ways it hadn't. We had two children now, our precious little boys, Reef and Finn, but at heart we still felt like two giddy teenagers, on the lookout for the next adventure. Now, I felt sure, nothing could hold us back.

Propping ourselves up on our elbows, we watched the boys chase each other along the beach. It was summer 2008, and Reef's fourth birthday was just weeks away. 'We are very sorry, but Reef may not survive for more than a few days.' I remembered the shocking chill those words brought when he was eighteen months old, and we were given the devastating news that Reef had cancer. It felt like a bucket of ice had been tipped on to my chest, freezing my heart and crushing my lungs. When I tried to come up for air, I was winded with yet more unbearable news. Doctors warned that, if he did survive, our little boy would be disabled. 'We are very sorry, but Reef may never walk again.'

Thinking about it now was like remembering a script from a film or a story about somebody else's life. It was incredible to think that the child we'd held close and cried over each time he needed a blood transfusion or another dose of chemotherapy was this same, carefree little boy running along the beach. He was our miracle.

I smiled at Kate. I could tell from the look on her face she was thinking similar thoughts. I was surprised by how young she looked, relaxing on the water's edge beside me. The two lines I'd grown used to seeing carved deep between her eyebrows had melted into her soft skin. She looked like a girl again, like the carefree Kate I knew before our world was ruled by fear and worry and the aching, helpless sorrow you feel for a sick child.

'Look at Reef run!' Kate giggled. 'He made it!' Even her voice sounded younger and freer. 'We made it!' Her eyes were flashing the way they used to when we scuba dived on holiday. I always looked forward to the moment Kate pulled off her mask because her face shone like a rainbow, as if she'd stolen the glittering scales and electric stripes from the tropical fish. That's how she looked that day, lapping up the sight of Reef and Finn playing chase.

'Singe, it's incredible. We're so lucky.' I nodded and grinned. My old Kate was back. Lucky was not a word other people might use, but it was the word Kate chose that day, and it's one of the reasons I loved her so much. Other people might have felt bitter or badly done by, but not Kate. She embraced life and always tried to look on the bright side.

'Can't catch me, can't catch me!' I heard Finn tease. My eyes flicked from Reef to his little brother. For a two-year-old Finn was an awesome little runner, and he was giving Reef a run for his money. Everyone said Reef was the thoughtful one like Kate, which I had to admit was true, but Finn was my 'mini-me', cheeky and sports-mad and boisterous. He was our miracle too. I remembered the moment I heard that Kate had gone into premature labour with him, and my chest tightened just as it had done when I answered the phone on the night of Finn's birth. The discovery of Reef's abdominal lump had sent Kate's stress levels through the roof. Her contractions began as we waited for the results of tests to tell us exactly what sort of lump Reef had. Kate was just seven months pregnant; it was way too early for her to give birth.

Watching Finn scamper about on the beach, I thanked God that the madness of those hospital days was over. Both boys had been in danger of losing their lives. One in a special care incubator, one with cancer in his pelvis. What were the odds? What was the point of thinking like that? It was insane. It was only a couple of years before, but it suddenly seemed a lifetime ago.

I exhaled deeply, blowing out the memory of fear and anguish into the sea air. The boys were whooping and skipping without a care in the world, and I marvelled at them. Friends nicknamed us 'The Incredibles'. 'You're such an amazing family,' they told us, before and after our misfortune. In that moment, with Kate smiling by my side and our boys playing happily together, I felt it was true. We'd had our run of bad luck but we'd come through it smiling triumphantly. My family was truly incredible.

I recalled that sunny day when we sat in the car overlooking the pebbled beach at Clevedon less than two years later. Now it was 20 January 2010, and instead of sunbeams, dark-grey barrels of cloud pointed down from the sky. The boys were buckled into their car seats, and I decided to get in the back and sit between them. As I stepped out of the car I shivered as the wind bit my face. I wished I could push back the clouds and pull out the sun. I patted my coat pocket to make sure the bubble gum was still there. It was something Kate and I had talked about. The boys had been nagging us for ages to try some gum, and we'd both decided this was a good time to give them a treat.

'Boys, I have something really, really important and really, really sad to tell you,' I said, pulling them in close to my sides. I felt a little ear dig into my ribs on either side of my chest. My heart was thrashing around so wildly in there I was worried the sound of it might frighten the boys, and I took a long deep breath to try to steady the thud.

I'd picked the boys up from pre-school and school and driven straight to our favourite spot near the beach at Clevedon, trying to keep things as normal as possible on the short journey. 'How was your day?' I asked, immediately regretting the question. Whatever they said, it was going to get a lot worse. I don't know what they replied, it took all my energy just to drive the car safely and pretend to be like any other parent picking up their children on a cold Wednesday afternoon.

This morning I'd written 'Oh my God, my darkest hour' in my diary. Now this hour felt even darker. Reef and Finn listened intently, waiting for me to tell them the important and sad news. They were dressed neatly in their uniforms, and my heart went out to them. They were such good boys, always eager to please, and I instinctively gave them a little smile and ruffled their fair hair. I think I'd done a good job so far of hiding my feelings and I wished I didn't have to tell them what had happened earlier that day. I wished I could be like other parents on the school run, chatting about friends or homework and telling the kids what they were having for tea. I didn't know what to say or how to say it, so I just squeezed the boys tight for a moment while I tried to control my breathing and hold back my tears.

'Say what you mean,' I imagined Kate whispering gently to me. Her voice was soft and encouraging but it cut straight into my heart. I remembered her saying exactly the same words just a few weeks earlier, as she lay in bed writing her list. 'I think it's really important to say what you mean, and I want the boys to learn that,' she had explained, before writing instruction number four in her diary: *'Please teach them to say what they mean.'* The school and hospital had reiterated this in their advice to me. I was not to beat about the bush or use vague language, as it might give the boys false hope or confuse them.

I cleared my throat and shifted position so that I could look at both their faces while I spoke. I had to tell them straight. 'I'm sorry to have to tell you this, boys,' I said, my voice cracking. Four soft blue eyes looked into mine. In that moment I saw Kate in the boys' eyes, and I could feel her watching me. I remembered her crying and saying she wished she could swap places with Reef when he was suffering, and I knew exactly what she meant. If I could have shouldered both boys' pain for them I would have, but it was impossible to shield them from this.

Their little eyes were scanning my face now like miniature flashlights, looking for clues through the fading light. They were only four and five years old, too young for this. I swallowed uncomfortably and felt my face redden as I tried and failed to hold back the tears.

'Mummy has died. She won't be coming home from hospital again. She died this morning.' Hearing the words come out of my mouth made me gasp and break down. The boys clung to me, and the three of us cried in each other's arms, spluttering out hot white breath into the cold winter air.

'Has Mummy gone to heaven?' Reef sniffed eventually.

'Yes,' I said.

'Is she on a cloud?' he gulped.

'Yes,' I said, before quickly adding: 'You can imagine her to be on a cloud if you like.'

I'd been told not to say things like 'Mummy has gone to sleep' because it might make the boys afraid to go to sleep in their beds at night, or they might imagine she could wake up one day. I didn't want them to really believe Mummy was on a cloud, because she wasn't, but I thought it might be all right for Reef to imagine her there, if that's what he wanted.

Nobody spoke again for a while. We just sat and cuddled and cried until a loud engine noise overhead made us all turn around and look out the misty back window of the car. Through watery eyes we watched two aircraft fly diagonally across the heavy grey blanket of sky above us, leaving a perfect white cross in their wake.

'Look, Mummy just blew us a kiss,' Reef said, and we all carried on crying.

It was just the three of us now. I felt that very acutely as we huddled in our own white cloud together, sharing the same oxygen and pain. We sobbed solidly for at least half an hour, oblivious to the dark and cold descending on us. The salt from my tears stung my face, and the boys' cheeks turned from their usual rosy pink to blotchy red. I could have cried for hours and days, but when the boys' soft sobs and panting cries lessened a little, I sensed it was time to stop.

'Would you like some bubble gum?' I asked them. Their faces brightened a bit as they unwrapped the pink parcels of gum, but Finn still had tears coursing down his cheeks.

'Thank you, Daddy,' he said politely as he stuffed the

gum into his mouth. 'Why has Mummy died?' He sniffed loudly and looked straight into my eyes.

'Well, you know she has been very ill, don't you? And when you saw her last night in hospital and she gave you a big cuddle she was very, very ill. She was so ill, she died.'

'I want to see her,' Finn said. 'Can I see Mummy again?'

'I'm sorry Finn, but you can't see her any more.'

He chewed his gum miserably, and I watched him helplessly, unable to think of a word I could add that would possibly make my answer any better.

'I like this,' Finn said after a minute or two. 'It tastes nice, Daddy.'

Reef nodded. 'Thank you for getting us the bubble gum,' he said, wiping the tears off his face with the sleeve of his coat.

'Can we have it again?'

'I think we should always have bubble gum on special occasions. Mummy thought that was a good idea too. Let's go home now.'

Buckling myself back in the driving seat I felt strangely calm. I'd successfully completed a task on my own, and a very major task at that. I felt Kate would have approved of how I handled the situation, and that she would have done exactly the same if she were in my shoes. It was comforting to think that.

As we pulled away from the empty beach I looked at the boys in the rear-view mirror. Both were staring out of the windows with swollen eyes, chewing noisily on their gum and filling the car with the smell of sweet strawberry flavouring.

Those two innocent little passengers were now my sole

responsibility. My stomach muscles contracted, and I tightened my grip on the steering wheel as I thought about the enormity of that responsibility. They had no mummy any more; it was all down to me. I was suddenly a widower, and I was suddenly a single dad. Even hearing those words in my head shocked me and made my blood ebb and flow uncomfortably around my body.

Part of me wanted to run away and pretend none of this had happened, yet I also felt a powerful urge to do everything in my power to protect my boys and make Kate proud. I still wanted to be her Mr Incredible; it was the very least I could do.

I drove slowly and carefully. I couldn't take any chances now. I'd have to slow down on every journey. If something happened to me, who would look after the boys? Besides, there was no rush to get home. The house would be exactly as I had left it earlier. Nobody would be burning dinner in the oven like Kate used to. My lips curled into a weak, involuntary smile as I thought about Kate's attempts at cooking. If you couldn't put it in the microwave and wait for it to go 'ping' it was beyond Kate. That's what I always said to tease her.

Ruth, who was Kate's best friend, helped her out when we got married, teaching her how to cook half a dozen simple dishes. Tagliatelle, lasagne, Mexican fajitas, curry and spaghetti Bolognese became her 'specialties', but Kate never really did master the art of cookery. Now Ruth had another role. *'Ruth good for parenting advice'* Kate instructed, *'as she has two boys same age gap – if conflict between grandparent views'*. Remembering that little word 'if' made me smile. Our parents are so different and, like most couples, we'd had our issues trying to keep both sides of the family happy. Now Kate's parents, Christine and Martin, had a son-in-law but no daughter. Everything was messed up. I hadn't even thought about that until now, and it made my head throb. It must have made Kate's head throb too, but she was one step ahead of me, thinking up ways to make life easier for me after she was gone.

I like Ruth a lot. She used to be married to my friend Chris, whom I met twenty-odd years ago when I was learning to scuba dive. Eventually Chris signed Kate off when she took her scuba diving qualifications too. Ruth is divorced from Chris now, and she lives a short walk away from our house. I call her my 'pet Rottweiler', as she's one of those friends who speaks their mind and tells you when you're being a prat. I admire that, and I thought how clever it was of Kate to set Ruth up to give me parenting advice.

I flicked a glance over my left shoulder. 'Don't swallow the gum, boys,' I said. 'Remember, that's why we didn't give it to you before. Please be careful. Promise me you'll be careful.'

'OK, Daddy,' Reef said. 'I can blow bubbles, look!'

With that he blew a broken bubble, making a loud raspberry sound that made Finn giggle. They were still chuckling as we pulled into the drive and piled through the front door.

I missed Kate's familiar cry of 'Hello boys!' as the front door opened. I missed not seeing her handbag strewn in the hall or her shoes kicked off at the bottom of the stairs, but to my relief and surprise the house didn't seem half as empty as I'd feared. The phone was ringing, our terrier,

Coral, was barking, and before I'd even got my coat off someone was knocking on the door.

It was Paula, one of the mums from school. She was crying her eyes out, and my immediate reaction was to try to comfort her. 'I'm sorry, Singe,' she blurted out. 'I just had to come round and I had to do something.'

'It's OK, don't worry,' I told her, giving her a hug. 'I'm touched you came.'

It felt good to be the one offering support instead of receiving it. It was a role I was a lot more comfortable with. She held out a huge cake tin. 'I have to bake when I'm upset. Here's about 240 brownies. I'm so sorry!'

I laughed as she ran off down the path, apologizing, leaving me standing there with the overflowing tin.

Over the next few hours lots of other friends and neighbours arrived with bowls of curry, cottage pies and lasagne. Some popped in for a few minutes, others scuttled away and left wonderful goodies on the doorstep. I felt like a one-man disaster zone, like I'd become a mini-Haiti overnight, and I needed food drops and emergency rations to survive. Kate's parents came round and played with the boys for a bit while I listened to all the phone messages, answered the door and slipped off into the conservatory to allow myself a little cry in private.

Kate was everywhere, but she was nowhere. Some of her favourite clothes lay crumpled on top of the ironing basket, and I noticed one of her brightly coloured life jackets had fallen off its peg by the back door. We had a garage full of life jackets and every piece of survival gear you could imagine. The irony of it had never struck me until that moment. Irony didn't even seem the right word; sheer rotten luck was more like it. Why had Kate not survived? She was fit and healthy. She never smoked and hardly drank, and she followed all the health advice going. The only thing she wasn't great with was eating vegetables, but she did her best with them. She didn't deserve to die. Why had this happened to Kate?

I could hear other people's wives and mothers coming and going, offering words of comfort. My wife, my soul mate, was gone. Our boys had lost their mummy, but other lives carried on. Other people cared and loved and shared. Other people breathed and talked and hugged, and other people walked out of my front door and went home to their children and their other halves.

At 7 p.m. I was alone, and it was time for the boys to have their bath. Kate and I always stuck to the same routine. One of us would run the bath, and Kate would get the boys washed and tucked up calmly in their pyjamas and kiss them goodnight. Then it was my turn, and I'd read them a story and invariably wind them up again. I would tickle them and make them giggle, and Kate would come and stand at their bedroom door, hand on hip and shaking her head disapprovingly.

She secretly loved it, and she knew I knew it. She was full of fun, and nothing pleased her more than seeing her boys laugh. She was also a brilliant mum, though, and rules were rules and bedtime was bedtime. 'Come on, you three naughty boys,' she scolded, eyes glinting cheekily. 'Time to settle down.' She kissed the boys goodnight, and then I kissed the boys goodnight, usually giving them one last little tickle when Mummy wasn't looking.

Where did I start tonight? Now I had to be Mummy and

Daddy, an impossible task. 'Come on, boys, bath time,' I called. I'd said the same thing a thousand times, but now it seemed new and different, like I'd said it for the very first time. The three of us went upstairs together like we had done so many times before, except it wasn't the same. Nothing would ever be the same again now Kate was gone.

My eyes were drawn to the doorframe of the boys' bedroom. Their heights were notched up in pencil on the white frame where Kate used to stand, pretending to be cross. I remembered her balancing books on the boys' heads and telling them not to wriggle as she recorded their heights. There wasn't a lot between them, despite the eighteen-month age gap. Reef's illness meant he wasn't as tall as he might have been, and he and Finn looked incredibly close in age. *'Need to measure me on door frame – Mummy was 5ft 1in,'* Kate had carefully added to her list. That was a job the boys could help me with. That would be something good to do together.

I turned on the bath taps and noticed Kate's favourite milky bubble bath standing on the side of the tub, half empty. 'Half full,' Kate corrected me. I'd heard her say that so many times. She was a half full sort of person. Kate's glass was never half empty, even when sickness sapped her life away.

I held that thought in my head as I bathed the boys and got them into their pyjamas, forcing myself to think positively. I would never get over losing Kate, but I was so lucky to have these two cracking little lads. They were a part of her and a part of us. I had so much to live for despite Kate's death.

'Can we sleep in your bed tonight?' Reef asked. 'Of

course you can,' I said. They bounded into our bedroom and launched themselves on to the bed like a couple of little rockets. Kate had bought an absolutely massive king-sized bed when she got ill. She had wanted to create a cosy nest when she was too weak to get up so the boys would have plenty of space to cuddle in with her. Sadly, she died in hospital before the bed was delivered, and now they had so much space it was ridiculous. They looked marooned in the middle of the huge cream leather frame, a cloud of fluffy white duvet surrounding them.

'Snuggle in now, boys,' I said. 'Time to settle down.' They wriggled under the covers obediently, perhaps expecting a little tickle, but it wasn't the right time for that. I was using up all my energy just going through the motions of being normal and not breaking down in front of them. 'Now be good, sleep tight,' I said. I bent down to kiss them both goodnight. As I did so the scent of Kate's perfume on the pillows mingled with the soapy smell of the boys' heads. *'Kiss boys two times after I have gone,'* Kate said, but I didn't need reminding. 'Night-night, Reef,' I said, kissing one cheek and then the other. One kiss from me, one from Kate. I did exactly the same with Finn, then I gave them both a massive cuddle, grateful I could bury my head between them so they couldn't see my tears.

I felt Kate's presence very powerfully. Her perfume was so evocative I could feel her wrapping herself around me, around all three of us, and I half expected her to whisper a 'thank you' in my ear after she watched me kiss the boys as she had instructed.

I quietly closed the bedroom door and let out a stream of silent tears, pressing my hands over my mouth so the boys didn't hear me. As I did so I glanced in the open bathroom door and noticed the school uniforms still littering the floor, exactly where the boys had left them. That's how life was now. There was nobody to pick up where I'd left off, and certainly nobody to finish my sentences or read my mind like Kate used to.

I stooped to pick up the clothes and froze as I heard an unfamiliar noise. It sounded like footsteps coming up the stairs, but that was ridiculous because I was all alone in the house. I held my breath and strained my ears, frantically trying to remember if someone still had a key or if I'd forgotten a visitor. I didn't want to shout out and frighten the boys, but something wasn't right. Nobody had called my name, and there'd been no knock at the door. It wasn't Kate. The footsteps were too heavy to be Kate's or, rather, for me to imagine them being Kate's. I straightened my back, instinctively heading to the bedroom to guard the boys. As I stepped across the landing a sudden gush of water in the pipes around the bathroom replaced the sound of the footsteps.

I dissolved in tears. It was just the central heating creaking. I sat on the edge of the bath and sobbed as silently as I could. I'd never noticed how noisy the house was before. When Kate was here I guess I always assumed she was making the noise, but now she wasn't. Even the bath was squeaking under my weight, making a grating 'eee-aww' sound as my body shook with heavy, muted sobs.

When I eventually stopped crying I went downstairs, not quite sure what to do next and looking for jobs to do to keep me busy. There were more messages to listen to, the dog to feed and a sink full of teacups to wash. The fridge was full of all the food prepared by friends and relatives. I had no idea who had brought what, and whose crockery was whose. I'd have to sort that out.

Tomorrow was Thursday, and I was glad the boys could go to school as normal. I thought it was best to maintain their routine and I was glad of the distraction as I sorted out their school bags and made their packed lunches. Still, I couldn't wait for the day to end. At least if I was asleep I wouldn't be able to burst into tears.

The boys were fast asleep when I eventually crept into bed, but they both wriggled in close as my head hit the pillow. I didn't sleep well, nodding off and waking frequently with a foot in my ear or a head in my armpit. *'Mummy loved Reef's cuddles at night.' 'Finn's cuddles were always very special.'* They were on Kate's list. It was almost impossible to believe she had written those words just weeks earlier, yet she would never cuddle the boys again.

It was so unfair. I could see Kate propped up with her diary, in this very spot where I lay. She was wearing a pretty white cotton nightshirt, which was typical Kate. When we first met I used to call her the 'Timotei girl' because she wore a floaty white linen gypsy skirt and a white cotton sleeveless top, exactly like the girl in the shampoo advert. Except, of course, Kate's hair was much more beautiful than the model's, that's what I always said.

It had been pretty traumatic for Kate when she lost her hair. She had always been very proud of her blonde hair, and she cried when it came out in clumps on the pillow and blocked the plughole when she showered. She never really complained, but I knew she was heartbroken. She was a very beautiful woman, and her hair had always been a big part of her beauty.

I remember being angry about her hair. Losing a breast was bad enough. Why did she have to go and lose her hair too? It was just so cruel, and I hated seeing her upset about it. She still looked bloody fantastic to me, even when she was bald as an egg. When we went to the rugby I told her that her head was perfectly shaped, like a rugby ball. 'I'll take that as a compliment,' she laughed. 'You should, you look gorgeous,' I replied, and I really meant it. Kate was always stunning.

We were watching the England v. France match at Twickenham, and England won. Kate was ecstatic, jumping up and down like she did as a teenager when she watched me play rugby for a local team. It was a great boost seeing her like that in the midst of her chemotherapy.

'We have just *got* to take the boys to see the rugby,' she said excitedly.

'We'll take them to see Ireland v. England in Dublin,' I suggested.

'Brilliant idea!' she said, clapping her hands.

Now losing a head of hair seemed minuscule in comparison to the enormous loss of Kate. There was nothing left of Kate, or at least nothing physical. She had ice-blue eyes. They shone out of her face, giving her a beautiful glow. As for her figure . . . well, don't get me started. The first time I saw Kate she was wearing bleached jeans that looked like they'd been sprayed on. She looked incredible then and she still looked incredible twenty-five years later. I know she would have carried on looking incredible for another twenty-five years and more, had she been lucky enough to grow old.

Instead, Kate lost everything. First her breast, then her hair. Now her eyes had stopped shining, and her gorgeous body was gone. I'd never be able to make love to my beautiful Kate again. I wouldn't even be able to take the boys to the rugby with her. Instead, that was another item on the list. *'Take the boys to see an international rugby match.'* At least that could be arranged, I'd see to that.

The alarm clock rang out at 7.30 a.m. the next morning, jolting me into a half-awake panic. My body seemed to know before I did that this wasn't a normal day, and I immediately tensed and my heart raced as my mind caught up. I looked at the boys curled up like two little dormice beside me. They were lying on Kate's side of the bed. Kate was dead, I remembered. I felt like someone had just given me the news and it was sinking in all over again. The boys started fidgeting and stirring. Their mum was dead. That was all I could think about. My wife was dead and their mum was dead, and here we all were, about to get up for school and start the next day of the rest of our lives without her.

Another alarm sounded, this time on my mobile phone. It startled me because I didn't remember setting another alarm, and I instantly worried I'd already made a mistake and missed something important, something Kate had booked in or wanted me to do. The words 'Reef's medicine' flashed on the phone screen. I smiled and let some tears leak from my eyes, remembering how Kate had asked me for my mobile phone when she lay in her hospital bed towards the end. She had diligently set the alarm so I would never forget to give Reef his daily medication.

Reef sat up in bed and caught me wiping tears from my face. 'Oh, for goodness' sake stop cryyyy-ing, Dad!'

he said, his little face twisted with frustration. He must have thought I'd cried all night, and maybe he was right. Finn sat up now, looking forlorn. Reef put his arm around his shoulder and said firmly, 'Come on, we'll be all right.' The boys' eyes met, and they gave each other a knowing look and a half-smile, a couple of brothers hatching a plot. 'Course you'll be all right, boys,' I said, pulling on a cheerful smile. It was only half fake, because their bravery gave me the will and strength to face the day.

'OK, boys, take turns in the shower, please,' I said, turfing them out of the bed. We had a routine in place on school days, and I was determined to stick to it, as I figured it would help me cope. I needed the boys to pull their weight now and do things for themselves a bit more, and it wasn't going to help any of us if I started molly-coddling them or rewriting the rules.

While the boys showered, I laid out their school uniforms and made the bed; then, while I showered, they got dressed as usual, with Reef helping Finn into his black trousers and green sweatshirt. The pair of them went downstairs to feed Coral and the guinea pigs, and I got the boys' breakfasts ready and gave Reef his medicine.

Everything went to plan. 'Teeth, please, boys,' I said, and they scampered back up the stairs just like they always did after breakfast, jostling for pole position. 'It's my turn first,' Finn said. 'Just a minute,' Reef replied as they reached the landing. 'How about you brush your hair while I do my teeth . . .'

I shuffled around the kitchen, clearing up the breakfast dishes. As the boys disappeared behind the bathroom door, it fell silent downstairs.

The dog was statue-like in the conservatory, watching some birds forage for crumbs in the frozen yard. I could hear myself breathing as I stood and watched her in silence. Kate's breathing had been so laboured towards the end. When we lay together adding to her list she was fighting for every breath, dependent on the ugly oxygen tank she was attached to. I despised it and welcomed it. I didn't want Kate to need it. In the past the only times I'd seen Kate breathless were in happy times, when she laughed so hard she had tears rolling down her cheeks, when we made passionate love or when her heart was racing with exhilaration as she pulled off her mask after a dive.

In the end the oxygen tanks weren't enough, and Kate had to go into hospital. I thought she'd get better in hospital. I thought her lungs would have a rest and she'd catch her breath after the exertion of Lapland and Christmas. It didn't happen like that. Instead, Kate got worse. 'Singe, I want to write a last letter to the boys,' she said. It was 19 January 2010.

Doctors had told me just weeks before, on our return from Lapland, that they hoped Kate had eighteen months to live. I clung on to that hope every single day, even when I saw it fading away before my eyes. Eighteen months would take her through to Reef's seventh birthday, and Finn would be five and a half. Kate herself would turn forty in March 2011. Surely she could make it to her fortieth, at the very least?

I couldn't help Kate, or even watch her write her last letter to her boys. It was way too soon, and it was something I felt should be private between Kate and her sons. From the hospital, I called Lois, a lovely friend of ours who's an English teacher. 'Can you help?' I asked. 'Kate mentioned you, if you don't mind. I know you've talked about it. I just couldn't do it.' I kissed Kate goodnight in her hospital bed, leaving her with Lois. 'I'll see you in the morning. I love you. Acres and acres,' I said.

'Thanks, Singe,' Kate said gratefully, and I felt a flash of anger. Why did my wife have to be grateful for this? No mother should have to write a goodbye letter to her two little boys.

'Good luck,' I said, kissing Kate again on the cheek. 'Acres and acres,' she said quietly.

Driving home, I was visited by images of patients I'd treated when I used to work as a paramedic. I'd saved dozens of lives. I saw the faces of young women who'd abused their bodies and poisoned themselves with drugs and alcohol. I could see them clearly under the blue flashing light, convulsing, vomiting and falling unconscious, then surviving against the odds, against their will in some cases. Life was so unfair.

I lay in bed that night feeling cold without Kate by my side, and I thought about her letters to the boys for what felt like hours. Reef and Finn were sleeping soundly, and I was grateful for all the help I was getting from family and friends that meant the boys' routine was unaltered when I needed to go to the hospital to see Kate.

What would she write to the boys? How would she cope with such a difficult job when she was already so frail? What was I thinking? This was Kate, my Kate. She was a powerhouse of a woman inside that tiny little body. She would do a magnificent job, I was sure. I was also sure she was just being cautious, and that there was no mad panic to write the letters so soon. She still had time.

I slept eventually, or rather my body collapsed into a series of short, confused naps. I had dreams filled with images of Kate smiling and laughing and then fighting for breath. I couldn't see in the dreams why she was fighting for breath. Was it the old Kate, refuelling her body after an exhilarating dive or coming up for air after kissing me passionately, as she did so often? Or was she struggling to fill her broken lungs?

It was pitch-black in the room when the phone by my bed rang out. I looked at the luminous hands on the clock. It was nearly 4 a.m. on the morning of 20 January, and I knew it was bad news before I heard the nurse speak.

'Kate's taken a very bad turn for the worse.'

I had to see Kate before she went. This was it, there wasn't a moment to spare. Throwing on clothes as I ran down the stairs two at a time, I lurched out of the house and banged on the door of the house next door. Jane, our kind neighbour, was amazing. 'Kate's dying,' I told her, and left her to do the rest, shouting instructions about staying with the boys and taking them to school in the morning.

It was a forty-minute drive to the hospital in Weston-super-Mare. Too long, too far. Missing Kate was unthinkable. I pressed my foot hard on the accelerator and tore up the roads. Fifteen frantic minutes later I slammed the car across four parking spaces in front of the hospital and headed to the nearest door. It was a fire exit, but I ripped it open and bolted down the corridor towards Kate's ward. Two security guards shouted 'Oi!' and started to give chase, but I didn't look back.

Kate was in a private room and a nurse opened the door ready for me when she heard me thundering along the corridor. Clearly, every second counted. Thank God I wasn't too late. There were five nurses surrounding Kate in the bed. I noticed she wasn't attached to any drips or drains any more. It was too late for that.

'We have made her comfortable with morphine,' one nurse explained. Kate's eyes looked at me as I cuddled her small body. Her mum and dad were on their way, and I desperately wanted Kate to hang on until they arrived to say goodbye. She was taking very shallow breaths now, and the nurses were whispering about giving her more morphine. Christine and Martin arrived just as one last big dose went in.

'Sorry,' Kate said to me, and I grabbed her hand.

'Don't be stupid! You have nothing to be sorry for,' I said. I cuddled her and held her left hand, the hand I'd placed her engagement ring on, and then, in later years, her matching wedding band and finally her eternity ring.

Her parents sat together, holding Kate's right hand. We kept talking, offering reassurances, even when Kate's breath stopped coming. I knew from my paramedic training that the brain is still active for a couple of minutes after breathing stops. A nurse had gently reminded me of this, and I kept talking to Kate. 'You were the most wonderful wife and mother,' I told her. 'I will do everything I can to carry out your wishes. I will tell the boys how much you loved them, and what a wonderful mum you were.'

'We're ready!' Reef shouted. Coral started barking loudly, scattering the birds from the back garden, and Finn bounded into the kitchen and asked, 'Is it swimming tonight, Daddy?' I was back in the moment, but it felt surreal, like I wasn't quite there. Kate had died just the day before, and here we all were getting ready for school, carrying on with our lives. It felt somehow wrong, yet I knew it was exactly the right thing to do. Without a shadow of a doubt, I knew it was what Kate would want us to do, and so we put on our coats and shoes, and I drove the boys to school.

Chapter 2

'Mummy wants Daddy to use the phrase "acres and acres"'

'Can you read us a story?' Reef said, scampering on to his bed.

Finn followed his brother into their bedroom.

'Can you read us *Captain Flinn and the Pirate Dinosaurs*?' he asked.

There had been no discussion about them sleeping in their own room tonight; both boys had just done it, seemingly without thinking. It was less than a week since Kate had died, but I suppose even a few days is a long time when you're a small boy. Besides, they knew they could always come and snuggle in with me if they changed their minds.

'Come on then, pirates,' I said, throwing in a little 'ooh –aaargh, me hearties', which made them giggle.

I could have told the story off by heart, we'd read it so many times. The boys cuddled in on either side of me, and I smiled as I saw their expectant little faces, waiting to hear the story as if for the first time. There was something reassuring about reading an old favourite, knowing exactly how the boys' eyes would widen in wonder when little Flinn (who Finn firmly believed was a cartoon version of himself) went through a secret passage into the magical pirate world. I made sure I did a few blood-curdling sound effects when the T Rex, stegosaurus and triceratops pirates battled on the high seas, and the boys squealed with delight.

'Can we have a secret passage?' Reef asked.

'Ooooh, can we?' Finn chimed in.

'Pleeeeasssse, Daddy? That would be just soooo cool.'

Kate would have loved the idea, and I did too.

'We'll see,' I said, my mind already thinking about one of Kate's wishes, to build a playroom for the boys. It was so important to her it was mentioned on the list twice. '*Please use the money for a playroom for the boys . . .*' she wrote. '*Would like them to have a playroom and climbing wall,*' she added, just to make doubly sure.

I kissed the boys goodnight. 'Acres and acres,' I told them as I did so. 'Acres and acres.' they both replied comfortably. Four kisses, and my two little pirates were already drifting off. Lucky boys, I thought. I knew I would find it hard to sleep tonight, all alone in bed.

I wandered across the landing, realizing that this was the first time I'd had the opportunity to potter round our bedroom alone in peace and quiet since Kate's death. Closing the door softly behind me, I felt glad of the time to just look and think, but I was daunted too. I would have to start moving Kate's clothes out of the room, I thought. We had several wardrobes, all fit to burst. Glancing round, I could see the corner of one of Kate's favourite crocheted Roxy tops trapped in the door of one, a baby-blue sweat jumper spilling out of a drawer and several pairs of trainers and ballet pumps peeping at me out of shoe boxes.

I called Kate my 'mini-mermaid'. I loved buying her clothes, especially what I called her 'surf chick' gear. I knew her body and shape so well I didn't have to worry about buying the wrong size. Her friends thought it was really funny that I bought her more clothes than she bought for herself, but I knew what would look good on her. She had such a lovely figure she looked fantastic in everything, whether it was casual sports wear or slinky little black dresses.

I opened one of the wardrobe doors and ran my hands through Kate's clothes. It upset me to see everything there, all clean and ironed and ready for Kate to wear again. I didn't know the end would come so fast, that item after item that went back in the wardrobe would never come out again, or at least never be taken out again by Kate.

I saw a Voodoo Dolls cotton dress I'd bought for her the summer before. She loved it and it looked amazing on her. I saw her padding along the beach in it, barefoot, pretty as a picture. There was a lovely white cotton Weird Fish shirt I had pictured Kate in the moment I saw it in a shop window, and I could picture her in it now, giggling as she ate a rapidly melting strawberry ice cream, sitting in the sunshine. Next, I spotted a pair of sexy high heels she'd worn once with a black French Connection dress that had bright flowers up the side. The shoes were stacked on top of a pair of pink and white Heelys. Typical Kate, I thought. A siren in killer heels one minute, a nutty speed queen the next, whizzing along the pavement on trainers with wheels fitted under the heels, still looking like the teenager I first met at the roller disco.

Kate loved dangly earrings. I could see a couple of her favourite pairs lying on the dressing table where she had left them, but I knew there were hundreds of others stashed in drawers and jewellery boxes. She adored them, and I'd bought loads for her over the years. I loved seeing her wear them. I loved the way Kate cherished them all, whether they were cheap ones picked up from a street trader on holiday or white gold and aquamarine ones, bought as special gifts for her birthday or our anniversary.

There was a piece of white card on top of the chest of drawers, a discarded piece of packaging, and I picked it up and pinned the two stray pairs of earrings from the dressing table carefully through it. I picked out several more pairs from a little jewellery pot and pinned them up too, in neat lines, until the card was filled with flashes of silver dolphins, lovers' knots, dancing turtles and shiny shells.

It reminded me of being a boy, painstakingly pinning dead bugs and dragonflies out on pieces of stiff card, so that I could marvel at their structures and skeletons. I remembered the pang I sometimes felt when I held them under my schoolboy microscope, feeling slightly guilty about my morbid fascination, knowing they would never fly again. Kate had jokingly scolded me about my childhood hobby, because on the other side of the moors she was busy collecting insect eggs and trying to breed moths and butterflies in a vivarium. That was her schoolgirl hobby, and her love of moths and butterflies endured.

'So after all my hard work, once I set them free across the fields, are you telling me you were standing there with a net, ready to catch them and kill them and pin them on a piece of card?' she said with mock indignation.

'Sorry!' I said. 'Had no idea the trouble you'd gone to!'

'Murderer!' she accused.

I picked up a black leather handbag off the floor beside Kate's side of the bed. It was one of her recent favourites, the one she had taken to hospital with her the last time she went in. I'd brought it home and instinctively placed it by the bed, where Kate often used to leave it herself. It had a simple black clasp which I gently opened before peeping tentatively inside. I felt a bit uncomfortable, as if I was prying, but I knew this sort of thing had to be done, even though admin and organization were certainly not my strong points. Kate's bank cards and driving licence had to be cancelled for a start. She would have wanted me to sort things out properly, like she would have done, and I didn't want chores to pile up and paperwork to descend into chaos.

I took out her purse and pulled out a handful of plastic cards and old receipts. Next, I carefully tipped the rest of the contents of the bag on to the bed. Before me was a snapshot of Kate's life, in bits. A photo of me and the boys in Disney World, grinning, faces pushed together, was partly covered by an old passport photograph of me and Kate. It showed the pair of us as fresh-faced teenagers, cheek to cheek, laughing our heads off in one of those old-fashioned photo booths where the flash always went off when you weren't quite ready, catching you unawares.

There was a laminated photograph of Kate and me with Reef and Finn, nuzzling up to a dolphin in Florida, and a four-leaf clover that Kate had covered with Sellotape so it looked laminated too. Beside the clover was a thick, black hair band that had some of Kate's mousy-coloured hair wrapped around it. I had mourned Kate's soft blonde hair when it grew back darker and coarser after her treatment. Mourning a head of hair seemed so trivial now.

It was upsetting to look through Kate's personal possessions, but also strangely cathartic. Once I'd started I didn't want to stop. I was touching things she had been the last person to touch and I liked the thought of that.

I picked up one of Kate's favourite pink lipsticks, a mascara and a face powder that had been in her handbag too. They were all Clinique, her favourite brand. She didn't wear much make-up, she didn't need it. Even a tiny bit could make her look very glamorous, very quickly. Still, Kate had a wonderful girly streak, and I knew she had drawers full of the stuff too. An old Swiss Army knife and a boat shackle – a sort of hook – were mixed up with the make-up. They were not items a typical woman might have in her handbag, but Kate wasn't a typical woman. I felt a burst of pride. I absolutely loved that she wasn't a typical woman.

How would I ever be able to find another soul mate like her? Kate was a one-off, my dream woman. She threw herself headlong into life. She bungee-jumped off bridges with me. She soared high in helicopters, dived the oceans deep and sailed the sea like a professional sailor. Afterwards, it was often Kate who took *me* to bed. I could hardly believe my luck. When she got dressed up for a night out she made my eyes pop out of my head. She was jaw-droppingly beautiful, and I always felt like the cat who'd got the cream when she was on my arm.

Even just curled up on the sofa reading a book in jogging pants and without a lick of make-up, Kate still looked bloody fantastic. She had a radiance about her you just can't get from a bottle. Motherhood, with all the stresses and strains it brought, didn't take the shine off

Kate. She lit up the room wherever she walked in and she lit up my life, in every department. She kept her figure, and her sexual energy. We were besotted with each other, always kissing and cuddling like a couple of teenagers, even after so many years together. She was simply irreplaceable.

'Find a woman to settle down with so the boys can have a female influence and stability in their lives.' When Kate wrote that, and told me that wish, her courage devastated me.

'How can I ever find another soul mate?' I sobbed gently, not wanting to argue with Kate, but not wanting to agree to something so unthinkable. I was shaking with tension and had tears dripping down my face, and Kate squeezed my hand, which took a huge amount of her energy.

'You should try,' Kate wept. 'I want you to be happy, Singe. It's best for the boys, too.'

'I will try my best, with everything,' I promised. I'd need time for that one – lots of time, I thought.

I opened Kate's glasses case and lifted out the pink and black designer specs I'd picked out for her when she needed them for driving in recent years. I held them up and looked through them, watching Kate's belongings distort through the lenses. Everything went blurred, and I blinked. I was used to seeing Kate's eyes looking back at me through those lenses. I'd have given anything to see her eyes again, instead of these fuzzy-looking fragments of a life left behind.

I wandered over to the computer on the table by the window and switched it on. Kate had always been the one who sorted out the emails, and she was much better at things like Facebook than me. She was good with photos too, filing them neatly in albums in the old days, complete with notes and dates sometimes. More recently, Kate whacked everything on to the computer, and when she was ill she made me buy a gigantic Apple Mac so we could manage our videos and pictures better, and enjoy looking back on happy memories.

I think I was on auto-pilot that night as I clicked on to her Facebook page and uploaded a few recent photos – images of Kate playing with the boys at home, stroking the dog – simple, ordinary stuff. It was something she often did, once the boys were in bed. I'd hear her busily tapping away even before I'd finished reading to them some nights. I wanted to keep other people's memories of Kate as fresh as mine were. It was a kind of therapy, I think. It gave me some sort of connection to Kate as well as to the world outside our bedroom.

I'm not good at being alone. I hate it, in fact. That night made me realize just how much I hated being alone, because the computer made me feel a tiny bit less lonely. I clicked on my own Facebook page next. I'd posted up a hastily composed message the day Kate died, to let as many people know as quickly as possible. My sister Kaye had been the first person to spread the word, sending out a text from my phone. 'Really sad news. Kate passed away in the early hours. Please pass this on to anyone who knew Kate and Singe,' she wrote. My phone had gone mental. I didn't know what 'OMG' meant before that day, but, 'Oh My God', I certainly did afterwards.

We have friends all over the world, and I had to let everybody who didn't get the text know. I could barely remember typing the terrible news on Facebook, and I read my words again, as if for the first time.

> To all my friends and family, I am afraid I have very sad news; Kate has passed away this morning peacefully. My thoughts are with Kate and the boys. Thank you for all your kind words and support. It is Kate's wish not to receive flowers or cards but to have the money donated into a trust for the boys. Details to follow regarding funeral arrangements at a later date. I will be in contact in due course. Singe xXx.

It didn't seem real at all, and I think I read it two or three times over, trying to digest it.

I wanted to write more now, to express my feelings. I typed quickly, wanting to unload and share my emotions as genuinely as possible.

> I would like to thank all our family and friends for their love and support. Kate was truly an extraordinary woman: an amazing, awesome partner and soul mate and an incredible mum and friend. She loved us all with such intensity and we described these feelings by saying 'Acres and Acres,' something which the boys use now. Nobody knows what the future holds for us but with all your love and support, we will make it !!!
>
> Life will be different without her but I am confident Kate will be proud of what we have achieved together so far, and what HER boys will in the future. (Watch this space!!!)
>
> I miss her desperately BUT, my boys remind me of

Kate every day . . . a look, a smile or a flash of their eyes keeps me strong. Many friends and family members who knew how much we meant to each other have quoted . . . 'It's better to have loved and lost, than to have never loved at all,' and I guess that's something that won't ever fade away. Thinking of Kate and how lucky I have been to know her. All my love, Acres and Acres Singe xXx :)

Before I logged off I looked at my Facebook profile, which was created long before Kate was ill. Under the section for 'favourite quotations' I'd written in bold lettering:

WORK HARD! PLAY HARDER!!
FEEL THE FEAR AND DO IT ANYWAY!
IF YOU'RE NOT LIVING ON THE EDGE YOU ARE A WASTE OF SPACE!
LIFE IS TOO SHORT AND YOU CAN'T TAKE IT WITH YOU.

I let the words bounce around my head as I logged off. Kate couldn't take me with her. Her life was too short, and I was still here, without her. I was so glad we had lived on the edge, and Kate's death only made me more determined to work hard and play harder. I would instil those philosophies we both shared in our boys.

When the hum of the computer disappeared I looked around the silent bedroom and wondered what to do next. The whole house was eerily quiet, and it felt like midnight, but the clock told me it was still only just gone 9 p.m. What should I do? I couldn't face going downstairs and eating on my own, even though the fridge was still bulging with home-made cottage pies and apple crumbles.

I was drawn to a small, pretty box on my bedside table. Kate's matching wedding ring, engagement ring and eternity ring were in it, and when I took off the lid I saw them slotted together, like a completed puzzle. That's how it felt when I put the eternity ring on Kate's finger, several years after our marriage and many years after our engagement. It was the finishing touch; a declaration of my undying love, of 'infinity acres and acres'. When I gave it to her I imagined our future panning out, perfectly. I saw us growing old and grey together, sitting side by side in a couple of rocking chairs, knitting and reading. That's how I dreamed and pictured it would be, no question.

My own wedding band, which also matched Kate's, had become too tight and was digging into my skin. I'd put on lots of weight in my forties. I blamed hospital food, as it had formed a large part of my diet on and off for five years now. When Reef was ill I drank litre after litre of Red Bull to keep me awake through the long nights in hospital, when I needed to stay alert and watch over him. If I fell asleep he tossed and turned and wrapped himself up in knots inside all the tubes attached to his body, and I was afraid he might pull one of them out.

I'd been saying for ages I would have to lose weight or get my wedding ring enlarged, but now there was another choice, of course. I could take it off. In that moment it felt like the right thing to do. I had to face it: I wasn't a married man any more. When I married Kate it was 'till death do us part', and that time had come. I eased off the ring painfully, placed it alongside Kate's three rings and instinctively picked up the black hair band I'd tipped from her handbag, which still lay on the duvet.

Taking Kate's Swiss Army knife, I carved a delicate lover's knot through the thick band and placed it on my ring finger. It fitted perfectly in the smooth groove left by my wedding band, and I started to cry. I decided I would give all the wedding rings to Kate's mum to look after for the time being, as she had a really secure safe. They were far too precious to leave lying around in a jewellery box.

I had a sense I was making some progress now, making decisions and sorting a few things out, but I also realized that I was totally unprepared for this aftermath. I had not believed Kate was dying, even when she was slipping away and writing her list. When the truth could no longer be avoided, I hadn't thought about *what* she would leave behind, my focus had been on *who*: the little boys she could no longer bring up, and myself, of course.

It was only just dawning on me what a big job I had on my hands simply dealing with Kate's possessions, let alone anything else. Her personal belongings filled the room. I couldn't clear them out wholesale and give them to a charity shop. I'd have to do it all properly, giving special items to friends and family so they all had a bit of Kate too. I remembered Kate telling me to give some clothes to Ruth. 'She's the same size as me. Make sure she wears them. Someone might as well get some wear out of them,' she instructed coolly.

'Stop that!' I'd laughed rather uncomfortably. 'How can you say that?'

'You can give those boots to Amanda from work too,' she went on, regaling me with the details of a shopping trip they'd been on together, when they'd jokingly fought over the cute pair of black boots.

Kate was always one step ahead, and she was always thinking of others, of maximizing other people's happiness. I would also have to pick out what I wanted to keep, but I wasn't daunted by that task. I reckon Kate knew that, because she hadn't given me any specific instructions about what to keep for myself. I had the pick of so much, a lifetime of shared memories, and the thought suddenly energized me: instead of getting rid of Kate's possessions, I would start by saving the ones I could never let go of.

I crept on to the landing and hooked open the loft hatch. I'd need a big suitcase for this, I thought. Unfolding the ladder and climbing into the darkness, I felt around for the light switch. I clicked it on and immediately spotted a couple of large, faded keepsake boxes sitting side by side, unexpectedly, right under my nose.

'Shit!' I blurted out.

My legs turned to sand, and I grabbed hold of the ladder to stop myself falling. I'd been in the loft just a few weeks earlier, putting away Christmas decorations, and the boxes definitely weren't there then. I hadn't seen them for decades and I stared at them in shock and disbelief, recognizing them but not quite believing what I was seeing. A powerful wave of nostalgia washed through me, the sort you get as a child when a long-lost toy turns up out of the blue, sparking a maelstrom of memories.

I knew exactly what was inside the boxes; they were love letters, scores and scores of them, written from Kate to me. As a teenager she bombarded me with letters and poems, especially when she was very young and her parents tried to keep us apart. I kept every single one, and when we moved in together she took them back and carefully boxed them up. That must have been over twenty years ago. So much had happened since then. I certainly couldn't remember the last time I'd seen them. We'd moved house six years earlier for a start, and I didn't remember seeing them in the move. Now here they were, staring me in the face, daring me to read them all over again.

Trust Kate to pull a stunt like that, I thought, once the initial shock had subsided. She was organized yet sentimental, practical but unashamedly romantic. Now, even after her death, she was still dazzling me with the same irresistible qualities. I admired her style.

Kate liked to get one over on me whenever she could, and she'd certainly done me over a treat this time, that's for sure. She must have predicted what I'd do and had planned this moment carefully, making sure she placed the letters where I couldn't fail to find them. She probably even knew I'd come out with a few choice words and almost fall off the ladder when I spotted the boxes, and she'd have loved provoking my gobsmacked reaction. How on earth she had managed to find the letters after all these years, let alone struggle around in the loft while attached to an oxygen cylinder to help her breathe, was mind-blowing.

I carefully carried the boxes down the ladder and placed them ceremoniously in the middle of our bed. Next, I sat beside them and stared at them for a few minutes before touching them again. I wanted to savour the moment, but I was trembling with anticipation by now. Taking the lid off would set me on an emotional journey back in time. I knew that once I started reading, I wouldn't be able to stop.

It would open up so many old memories stretching back over so many years. 'Are you sure you are ready for this, Singe?' I asked myself silently. 'Too right,' I thought, suddenly grinning widely.

I thought how lucky we were that our memories were overwhelmingly happy. What was I afraid of? What was I waiting for? Suddenly I felt like a child on Christmas morning, desperate to see what was inside the boxes. I took off the lids excitedly, my heart racing. My eyes fell on the lipstick kisses on the pink and yellow pages before me, and I instinctively lifted the notepaper to my lips and kissed Kate's kisses. The sweet pink shade of the lipstick and Kate's girly handwriting catapulted me back to the 1980s, and my eyes greedily devoured a poem, just as they had decades earlier.

A poem is hard to write
The words never come off right,
Once the rhyme is found,
No words with that sound,
Spring to your mind,
To express what you find in love.

I felt surrounded by Kate. In my hands I had a direct link to the teenage Kate, the passionate, loved-up Kate who eagerly pursued me from the first time she saw me, refusing to listen to her parents, promising she'd love me for ever. She was a gorgeous girl, and I was flattered she'd fallen for me in such a big way. I could hear her reading the poem to me, giggling her sexy giggle, and I could taste and smell the sugary, sweet gloss of her lips on mine.

Kate was convinced we were made for each other, right from the moment she set eyes on me. She told me so over and over again, fixing her seductive eyes on mine, intent on making me believe her, and making me hers. I have to be honest. I didn't share her vision of the future, not in the very early days anyhow. Kate was too young when we first met, and I was too much of a player to think long-term. No wonder that was one of Kate's dying wishes: *'Please teach them to respect women and not double date.'* She knew what men could be like, and she didn't want Reef and Finn to follow my teenage footsteps in that respect.

'Don't let them ride a motorcycle or scooter especially on the road,' was another request borne out of my misspent youth. 'Singe, I know what boys are like,' Kate told me as she wrote those wishes. 'I know what you were like. You were lucky you never got hurt, but they might not be so lucky. It's not worth the risk. Please keep them safe. Buy them cars, teach them to drive, keep teaching them to drive the boat, but don't let them ride motorbikes.'

'I promise,' I told her, looking deep into her eyes, which were locked on mine, leaving me in no doubt how passionately Kate felt about this.

I used to tear around on my Suzuki Katana with its flash silver tank, wondering what all the fuss was about when Kate's parents didn't want her to ride on the back. Now I was older and wiser, and I knew exactly what all the fuss was about. Life is precious, and you have to put safety first. I didn't think long-term at the start of our relationship, but Kate did, and she made sure she told me so in many of her letters.

I picked up a poem and read the first page before my tears forced me to take a break.

> We are tight knit,
> Never to be split,
> Even once married,
> On we shall still carry on,
> In love.

Kate was sixteen when she wrote that, and even though we'd known each other for a year or so we'd only just started properly dating. I was flattered and thought she was endearingly naive. In fact, it turned out she knew a heck of a lot more than I gave her credit for; her vision was spot on.

Now, here she was in 2010, no longer here yet still one step ahead of me. I couldn't get over it, and I couldn't stop the tears from falling even though I felt thrilled and buoyed by the memories. Kate had carefully planned for me to sit here and read these letters in the days and weeks following her death. It was amazing. She knew that even though my emotions would be all over the place, the old memories would cheer me up, and they did.

My heart was beating with anticipation each time I read another page, and warm feelings of love and tenderness loosened the cold, tight grip of grief inside my chest. This wasn't a way of holding me back, locking me back in time by reminding me how loved-up we were together. Kate wanted me to meet someone else, I knew that. This was a gift of unashamed romantic nostalgia for old times' sake, and I silently thanked her for it.

I could just imagine Kate's face if she was looking down

on me now. She would be giving me a knowing smile of encouragement, a little nod to say it was OK to feel elated and distraught, excited and bereaved all at the same time. 'Dive in!' she would say. 'Enjoy the memories!' The more I read the more I wanted to read, and I greedily devoured page after page after page, gorging on the next before the full pleasure of the last one had sunk in.

I lifted one of Kate's poems to my nose and sniffed. She had a habit of spraying flowery perfume on her love letters, and I remembered the sweet clouds that floated from each envelope the first time I opened them. The smell always sparked a powerful reaction in me, making me count the hours or the days until I could see her and touch her and smell her again. As a teenager Kate always wore Le Jardin by Max Factor. I could see the bottle so clearly in her dainty white handbag, as if it were in the handbag I'd just emptied out. I could smell it on her neck, all fresh and feminine, just like Kate. Now I thought there was still the faintest trace of scent buried deep in the fibres of the faded paper, but I couldn't be sure.

I lay back on the bed and turned my head into Kate's pillow, to smell her again. Recently she'd worn Charlie Red, which she adored. One of the young nurses at the hospital wore it, and Kate asked her what it was and asked me to buy her a bottle. It became Kate's favourite perfume, and I loved it too. I expected to breathe in a satisfying, familiar fix of the lingering scent on the pillow, as I had done when Kate was here, and as I had done every night since she was gone. She never got the chance to sleep in the big new bed, but I had kept the pillow from the old one. It helped me get to sleep, feeling her so close I could smell her, but I was dismayed to find there was nothing there.

I sniffed again, this time more urgently. I picked up the weakest smell of her perfume, almost as faded as the one on the love letter. I looked at the poem in my hand again. The handwritten date on the top was June 1987, and I had an upsetting thought. How could the thirty-eight-year-old Kate, who had lain in this room just weeks before, have already started to fade as much as the sixteen-year-old Kate?

It was a depressing moment, and it made me confront an unpalatable truth; every version of Kate was a memory now, and there would be no new memories to make with her. At least I had a heck of a lot of reminders of the past, I thought, turning back to the boxes and picking out a piece of A4 paper. It was the sort with the old-fashioned red-ink margin you used to get in school, and Kate had set out a kind of lover's list of commandments on it. I remembered it well. The 'Contract of Toad Ship', as she had called it, cast me as the toad-like villain and herself as the princess in our own little fairytale world. With a fountain pen Kate had neatly written:

> You need to:-
>
> Phone at least twice a day
> Flatter me (remember flattering can get you everywhere)
> Supply a flower once a week
> Complete fidelity, soul ownership
> Take me out Saturday evenings
> Be loved and to love
> Tell no lies, and give straight answers
>
> Sign and return contract of mate-ship.
> Sign here:- ....

Her last commandment made me fill up, and I read it again and again. 'Tell no lies, and give straight answers.' 'Tell no lies, and give straight answers.' I reached over to my bedside table. Kate's diary was in there. It took me several minutes to find what I was looking for, but I knew it was there somewhere. I eventually found it on one of the pages she had scribbled on when she had stayed up through the night, jotting down the list of things she wanted me to pass on to the boys. There it was, the entry Kate's teenage commandments had just reminded me of. *'Please teach them to say what they mean.'*

Those words were etched on my brain. They had helped me when I had to tell the boys Mummy was dead, but I wanted to see them in black and white, in Kate's pretty handwriting. I started to cry, but they were happy tears. Values Kate had wanted in me all those years ago were now being instilled in her boys. I'd make sure I brought Reef and Finn up to be truthful and give straight answers, especially to the women in their lives, and I would make sure I taught them to always say what they meant.

I really hoped they'd be as lucky in love as we were.

I remembered the first time I ever saw Kate. For me it was business as usual at the Robin Cousins roller disco rink near Bristol, where I worked on a Saturday night. The place was teeming with teenagers. Hot, excited bodies whirled round the skate rink, pulsating to the beat of eighties hits like 'Part-time Lover' by Stevie Wonder, Duran Duran's 'Wild Boys' and Madonna's 'Like a Virgin'. When the girls fell over I picked them up as quickly as possible to stop them causing a pile-up. If they were injured I took them to the first aid room and sorted them out.

It was a dream job for a red-blooded nineteen-year-old, and I did my utmost to live the dream. With my spiky bleached blond hair and black headband I fancied myself as Billy Idol. I also had the coolest skates on the planet, covered in designer graffiti, plus I had a six-pack to die for. Needless to say, I loved my macho nickname, 'Rambo', and I thought I was God's gift to women. To my delight, lots of girls seemed to agree with my high opinion of myself. I lapped up the attention when they flirted with me, and I flirted back outrageously.

One night I spotted a veil of ultra blonde hair shimmering under the disco lights as it danced towards me. Moments later its pretty owner stopped in front of me. She was wearing incredibly tight jeans, and it was impossible not to notice her amazing figure.

'My friend Anna has hurt her wrist,' the girl said.

She was looking at me intently through two blonde curtains, which framed her face. I stopped and looked straight at her, and that's when I realized she wasn't just pretty, she was very, very pretty – stunning, in fact. What stood out the most were her eyes. They were a gorgeous pale ice-blue and were absolutely captivating.

'And there's a gang of girls over there who've been picking on us . . .'

The girl's pink-glossed lower lip wobbled slightly, and I was afraid she might cry. I didn't want those pools of blue to spill down that exceedingly pretty face.

'Come on, show me where Anna is, and we'll sort this out,' I said. 'I'm Singe.'

I put my arm around the girl's shoulder.

'I'm Kate,' she said.

I could feel her trembling slightly, poor girl.

'Don't worry, everything will be fine,' I reassured her, puffing out my chest and enjoying playing the knight in shining armour.

'Thanks,' she smiled. It was a dazzling smile that seemed to light up her whole face, and I couldn't believe she'd cheered up so quickly.

It didn't take long to strap up Anna's sprained wrist. I was aware of Kate looking at me, and I enjoyed the buzz of being eyed up by such a good-looking girl, even though she did look several years younger than me.

'Are you working next weekend?' she asked unexpectedly.

'Yes, I am.'

She had a confident tone in her voice now and was standing with her shoulders back and head held high.

'That's good. It's my birthday, and I want a birthday kiss.'

Kate then winked at me, one luminous blue eye disappearing momentarily behind a sparkling blue eyelid.

'All right,' I said, smiling.

Kate didn't look like a girl who was going to take no for an answer, and I didn't want to say no even though I should have. I already had a girlfriend and was dating a string of other girls, but Kate was very pretty, not to mention insistent, and it was only a kiss, wasn't it? It was a perk of the job, I figured.

I also worked as a lifeguard and taught trampolining at leisure venues all around Bristol. I was paid to have fun, and the girls seemed to like me. I think, if I'm truthful, I was seeing a total of eight girls at that time, and I kept up with them all by roaring between dates on my motorbike, dressed in cool black leathers.

'Can you teach me to skate backwards?' Kate asked when she turned up the following week, moments after the rink doors were open.

It was good to see her, and she looked even more stunning than I remembered. She was wearing the same spray-on jeans and the fantastic view from the rear was definitely worth giving a few backwards skating lessons for.

'How about that kiss then?' she asked almost as soon as we got started with the lesson.

'I can't kiss you here!' I laughed.

'I want my birthday kiss. You promised!'

'There's too many people around,' I said, surprised by how seriously she seemed to be taking this.

'Where, then?' she insisted.

'Meet me by the fire doors when I lock up at the end.'

I did wonder whether she'd actually bother to hang around that long just for a kiss, but I had a funny feeling she probably would.

Sure enough, at 9 p.m. Kate was standing there with the same confident look I'd seen before, her eyes shining expectantly.

'Wish me happy birthday, then,' she said excitedly

'Happy birthday!' I beamed, and leaned in to kiss her.

It turned out to be a surprisingly erotic kiss. I hadn't expected Kate to kiss me back so passionately, but I certainly didn't complain, and it was extremely enjoyable.

'Do you know how old I am?' she said cheekily when we pulled apart.

‘Sixteen?’

‘No, fifteen . . . in a few days,’ she said jubilantly.

I felt a little quiver in my stomach. I was about to turn twenty. This wasn’t right; she was a full five years younger than me.

‘You’re a very pretty girl but you’re also a very bad girl,’ I scolded gently. ‘You’re too young for this.’

Kate’s face fell.

‘No I’m not!’ she said indignantly.

I laughed and said goodbye. She was a lovely girl but was far too young for me.

I thought that would be the end of that, but I didn’t bank on Kate’s determination. Unbeknown to me, when we kissed Kate had decided I was ‘the one’. Years later she would relate to me how she went ‘all peculiar’ the first time I put my arm round her shoulder, when I told her Anna would be OK. That’s why I felt her tremble: it had nothing to do with her being upset by the skate-rink bullies. Kate told me she decided there and then that I was going to be hers, and the kiss sealed her decision. She was most definitely not going to take no for an answer; I was her man, and that was the end of it.

Thank God she didn’t give up, I thought, my eyes flicking between the love letters and Kate’s diary. We had all those years together, thanks to my feisty Kate never giving up. When I’d told her she was too young for me at fifteen she had insisted that at least we could be good friends ‘for the time being’.

She persuaded me to go to her house for coffee after the roller disco one Saturday night, and her dad reluctantly agreed that I could follow his car back to their house when he picked her up. Like an idiot, I couldn't resist showing off on my motorbike, overtaking Kate's Dad and looping round his family saloon. I'd got my racy Suzuki engine from Silverstone and I revved it up noisily, thinking I looked the business with my pointy winkle-picker shoes and Alien II bike helmet.

By the time we pulled up at their extremely smart suburban house in Portishead, Kate's dad Martin practically had steam coming out of his ears. I don't think Kate's more tolerant but protective mum Christine was too impressed either, especially when she saw me strutting up the drive in my black leathers, Kate's eyes feasting on me. My reputation preceded me, too. It didn't take Kate's savvy parents long to find out I already had a steady girlfriend, not to mention a string of other girls in tow, and they banned Kate forthwith from the roller disco.

Looking back, I can't blame them being concerned about their only daughter. Kate had never had a serious relationship before, and I was hardly ideal first boyfriend material – in fact I was every parents' worst nightmare. I was prepared to accept the situation, because even though I fancied the pants off Kate she was simply too young. Precocious Kate had other ideas, of course, and she told me to 'watch this space' as she was not giving in without a fight.

She was certainly true to her word. Kate played badminton and started to turn up at the leisure centres where I worked all over town. I enjoyed the attention – what bloke wouldn't? But she was still so young, and I still had a lot of other pretty girls around me. I told her I really wanted her to be my friend, but I didn't want any hassle about her age and her parents, and I couldn't see how we could separate the two.

'Will you wait for me?' she asked over and over again. 'Will you be my boyfriend when I am sixteen?'

'We'll have to see,' I told her. 'You're a stunning girl. You'll probably go off with somebody else before then.'

'I don't want anybody else but you, Singe,' she said. 'I want to marry you. I want to be with you for ever and ever.'

I smiled and laughed and lapped up the attention, but Kate was deadly serious, bless her.

I thought it was cool at the time to wear thin silver bangles right up my arm, and lots of the girls I knew used to give me a bangle as a gift. One day Kate turned up out of the blue and gave me a silver bangle too. It was thicker than the rest, and I thanked her for it and put it on alongside all the others. Every time Kate turned up she'd ask me if I still had the bangle.

'It's right here,' I told her. 'I wear it every day.'

'Good,' she said, giving a secretive smile. 'Don't lose it. You never know when you might need it.'

Over the months we became good mates, chatting over a Coke or a coffee at various leisure centres, whenever Kate managed to sneak out of the house. Kate's intentions were always clear, but we fell into a comfortable friendship, chatting like old mates, and Kate would actually give me advice about how to handle girls. She was open and honest, and talking to her gave a Romeo like me a real insight into the workings of the female brain.

'I shouldn't tell you all this, because one day I'll be your girlfriend and you'll be able to read me like a book,' she joked.

'Well, wouldn't that be fun,' I teased.

Even though I fancied Kate and she knew it, going out

with her before she was sixteen was simply non-negotiable. I lost count of how many times I told her that, and over time she accepted it. Nevertheless, there was always a lively spark between us, fizzing away close to the surface of our skin.

One night, months and months on, I found myself sitting alone in my dad's house, having fallen out with my steady girlfriend. I'd just got back from work and I took off all my silver bangles and put them on the coffee table in front of me. The one Kate gave me rolled across the glass and performed a little spin, circling the others and stopping noisily in front of me. I picked it up and examined it, because I noticed there was something engraved on the inside. 'Katie Johnson' it said, followed by her phone number and the words 'Call me! x' I laughed out loud. How cheeky was that? I dialled Kate's number immediately, and thankfully she answered straight away. She was breathless with excitement when I asked her how she was.

'Fantastic! I'm sixteen at last!' she replied, trying to keep her voice down so her parents didn't hear. 'You can take me out now, Singe!'

'It's a date,' I told her. 'When can we meet?'

'I don't know. My mum and dad still won't be happy about us seeing each other,' she whispered. 'We'll have to meet up in secret.'

I agreed, even though this wasn't ideal, and Kate met me outside one of the leisure centres I worked at after a coaching session. She'd told an elaborate tale to put her parents off the trail, and over the coming weeks we managed to meet at several other leisure centres, coffee shops and even bus shelters for a kiss and a cuddle before her parents inevitably rumbled us. This time they banned Kate not only from skating, but from contacting me or ever seeing me again.

She sobbed hysterically down the phone. 'Singe, I can't bear to not see you,' she said dramatically.

'Don't get in a state,' I told her. 'We'll work something out. We'll just have to have a bit of a break, that's all.'

I wasn't fobbing her off. I really did want to date her, but I thought it was best to let the dust settle.

'Give it a little bit of time, Katie, it's not the end of the world. We'll get back together somehow, I'm sure.'

Kate was gutted, more than I realized, and I was quite miffed too. I was dating several other girls, but things had changed. Kate was always in the back of my mind. I found myself thinking about her often, wondering how she was and hoping I was right, that maybe we would get together properly one day.

A few months passed before we met again by chance, on the day a travelling fairground came to Clevedon. I was with a girlfriend and another couple on the Waltzers. The sun was belting down, and 'Come on Eileen' was thumping out of the speakers so loudly I could feel the beat of the music drumming on my ribcage.

Everyone was laughing, full of fizzy drinks and candyfloss. As we span, I watched my world turning all around me. One minute I was looking out along the rippling water of the Bristol Channel, the next I was facing the town with its busy seafront cafés and crowds of excited kids and teenagers. I didn't know which way I'd face next. There was so much fun and so many opportunities in my life. I wanted to keep on spinning, taking a bit from here and there, never slowing down.

I spotted the back of her head first. That veil of ultra-blonde hair was unmistakable, and it took me back to the very first time I saw her at the roller disco. Now a gentle sea breeze was making that blonde hair dance seductively in the sun. I leaped straight out of the Waltzers and slammed the safety bar shut so my girlfriend couldn't get out. I then made a rapid beeline for Kate, pushing though the crowds with my eyes fixed on the back of her head.

When I finally reached her I put my hands over her eyes from behind, before she had a chance to turn around and see me.

'Hey, who's that?' Kate giggled.

I grinned and said nothing, enjoying the thrill of the chase.

'Who is it?' she asked again, tugging at her friend Rachel, who was standing beside her.

Rachel grinned and said boldly: 'Who would you most like to see in the whole wide world?'

'Singe!' Kate sang loudly, without any hesitation. 'I'd love to see Singe!'

I couldn't believe she knew it was me. I dropped my hands and she span round and gave me the biggest smile ever. I saw there were tears welling in her eyes, and I felt my heart swell in my chest. Something big had just happened. I fell in love with Kate right there and then. And I fell in love big time. I wanted her, and she wanted me. That was the end of it, or should I say the beginning. Inevitably, it was also the start of another battle with Kate's parents, who were still unhappy about their daughter's choice of boyfriend.

*

I looked down at several pages of green and yellow notepaper in my forty-four-year-old hand and let Kate's letters remind me of the next part of our love story. Scanning the pages, I picked out phrases I could almost hear Kate whispering to me.

> I really do love you and want to share the rest of my life with you . . . My love for you, Singe, will never die . . . This is not an endless battle we are fighting. We can win in the end, and God do I want to . . . Words cannot express how much I am missing you and nothing, not even making love can prove how much I love you . . . PLEASE PLEASE, PLEASE come back and win me back. I will stand up for you.

The letter ended with the words: 'I love "U" 4 ever and 2gether 4 ever. Lots and lots of love, missing you greatly. Katie xxx.'

I felt the pain all over again. I missed her too, then and now. I missed her when her parents found out we'd finally slept together, after Kate went on the pill and didn't make a very good job of keeping it secret. Her dad went absolutely ballistic, and once again we were banned from seeing each other. I can see it from his point of view now, but I couldn't then. We were two young people in love, and we were being sensible and careful underneath all the incredible passion.

'I love you so, so much,' Kate told me when she lay in my arms one evening.

'How much?' I asked.

'Yards and yards,' she giggled.

'I love you miles and miles,' I replied.

'I love you more,' she said.

'How can you love me more?'

'I love you acres and acres.'

'Acres and acres,' I nodded. 'I like that.'

I kissed her, looked deep into her dreamy eyes and told her: 'Acres and acres' over and over again. It became our secret code for 'I love you', one we used countless times in hushed phone calls when Kate didn't want her parents to know who she was talking to or what she was saying. The phrase stuck, and we carried on using it when we finally managed to convince Kate's parents nothing could keep us apart, when we eventually moved into our first flat together a year or two later, then got engaged a few years after that, and, of course, when we married, nearly a decade on.

Now Reef and Finn used it too, and Kate wanted to make sure they would carry on using it when she was gone. *'Mummy wants Daddy to use phrase "acres and acres".'* It was on her list; it was going to be used for ever more.

I stayed up most of the night reading the love letters and enjoying old memories. Before I went to bed I put my head round the boys' bedroom door. 'Acres and acres,' I whispered to them both.

Back in our bedroom I picked up Kate's bottle of Charlie Red and sprayed it on my pillow. I was very grateful to Kate for being so thoughtful and leaving the letters for me to find and I felt glad I could reread them now whenever I wanted to. I wasn't going to live in the past, but I needed to remember the past to help me move on.

The letters made me realize how important it is to treasure memories, and I decided I would gather together all the bits and pieces of Kate's list and get everything typed on to one neat page, so I could use it as a sort of guide, to help me through. Kate would have done the same had she had the strength and the time; she told me that.

Kate had started writing the list in her diary when she was in bed at home, but she had also left scribbled instructions on scraps of paper and, when she was too weak to write in hospital, she texted me items to add to the list. Stupidly, I deleted some texts. Even in her last days, when her life was ebbing away, I wouldn't quite allow myself to believe she was leaving me. I remembered tutting and sighing when my phone beeped.

'In the summer, take the boys to Llantwit Major, the beach in South Wales where Mummy spent holidays as a child . . .'

'You'll be here in the summer, silly bag!' I thought, pressing delete.

I'd remembered most of them, if not all, and now I wanted to make sure nothing was lost or forgotten.

The next morning I took out Kate's diary again and looked for what I knew to be the opening item on her list. '*Kiss boys two times after I have gone*' was the very first thing Kate had come out with when we talked about writing down her thoughts and wishes. She was very clear that instruction had to be top of the list, and when she said it I realized she'd obviously been thinking about this long before she mentioned it to me.

I felt a bewildering mixture of admiration and pity for Kate as I watched her bravely write those words down, starting her list. They were words no mother should ever have to write; that's what I thought. Perhaps I would never need the list, I told myself. Perhaps we would look back one day and laugh and say: 'Can you *believe* we wrote that list?' Kate clearly didn't share my optimism. It was too late for hope, and she knew it. She drew in a deep breath of oxygen so she could say the words out loud as she wrote them, and so the list began.

Now I took a new sheet of A4 paper from the printer in my home office and began to copy Kate's list out neatly, in full. When I'd exhausted the items in her diary, I scoured the scraps of notepaper she'd written ideas and instructions on in hospital and added those too. Finally, I copied out wishes she'd texted to me from her hospital bed, and I added a few things I had deleted when I was in denial about Kate's condition, but had not forgotten.

This is what I wrote:

Kiss boys two times after I have gone
Go to as many school activities as possible – praise assemblies etc.
Please teach them to be on time
Please teach them to say what they mean
Don't fill outside with your boats, give boys space to play
Go caravanning with cousins or let boys go for long weekends
Singe's pepper sauce
Joint bank accounts into your name – Dad to help with finances
Mum arrange funeral etc
Christen boys – Noel
Professional memory scrapbooks/boxes/video
Did not like windy weather

Did not like tomatoes unless in sauce or soup

Would like Reef to learn recorder or guitar, Finn the drums and electric keyboard

Mummy loved Finn's laugh and how he sucked his thumb and folded his ear in

Mummy liked walks down the riverbank

Mummy liked catching crabs

Mummy wants Daddy to use phrase 'acres and acres'

Mummy liked learning butterfly and bird names and would have loved to have hand-fed a wild robin like she used to feed the squirrels

Would love the boys to find their own four-leaf clovers

Don't leave Finn out – try and have quality game time with him too

Please don't go on off-the-beaten-track holidays as I strongly believe vaccinations in Reef and me triggered the cancer

Need to measure me on door frame – Mummy was 5ft 1in with size 5 feet and usually weighed about 8st 10lb

Don't let them ride a motorcycle or scooter especially on the road

Don't let them smoke and remind them why

Would like them to do an after-school club, Finn Stage Coach, Reef cubs

Would like driveway done

Never leave more than a week before making up – life is too short

Ruth good for parenting advice as she has two boys same age gap – if conflict between grandparent views

Find a woman to settle down with so the boys can
have a female influence and stability in their lives
Always kiss boys goodbye and good night
Grow a sunflower every now and again
Want them able to swim before boating on their own:
50m without mask and snorkel
Would like dining room table so you can have family
meals once a week at least
Would like school photos bought every year
Take the boys to see an international rugby match
Need to set up certificate boxes for swimming badges,
school achievements etc
Please teach them to respect women and not double
date
Would be good if they settled down sooner rather
than later so you get to see grandchildren
Would love them to find one of those fairy
mushrooms, the red ones with the white bits on
Would like you to take them for walks along Mummy's
favourite beach where she used to go as a child
Take the boys to Switzerland for New Year and visit
the special place where Daddy proposed to Mummy
Please use the money for a playroom for the boys as
Ken would probably let you have a bit of his land to
play on and call Mum's Place or Priddy Pools
Would like drawings (any ones from school etc),
pictures of boys and clothes with me [in box with
her ashes], Christmas cards, birthday cards
Would like to go on top of the wardrobe, with the
cuddly toys [in the box], to be with boys a bit longer

Mummy loved how sparkly Reef and Finn's eyes were in Lapland
Mummy loved Reef cuddles at night
Liked satellite spotting and watching for shooting stars
Loved guinea pigs and butterflies, Walnut Whips, strawberry cheesecake
Try not to let them go into the Forces
Move down south if rest of family thinking of doing so
Like wild flowers – red campion, cuckoo spit, daisies, primroses and flowers in wedding arrangement
Would like them to have a playroom and climbing wall
Mummy liked walks along the beach and Mendips, rock-pooling and walks in the woods and finding creatures of all kinds
Mummy liked phrase 'Infinity Elves'
Find four-leaf clovers at usual sites
Take lots of photos especially in your teens
Make scrapbook of your adventures
Pictures of us in boys' room
Kiss goodbye even if leaving for a short time
School photos in last book
Keep a record of achievements
Always help them if they ask
Finn's cuddles were always very special
Go and see Northern Lights
Mummy loved moths, snakes and slowworms, orange Club biscuits, jam and jelly, lemon curd
Mummy loved ivory roses, ivy, gypsophila
See Skippy and Rachel down under

Take boys to Lundy
Help All Saints School and try to get Reef extra help
Keep in touch with Maria and Lynne, Disabled Team
Go to Egypt and snorkel in the Red Sea
Blue Hole, Belize, when the boys are good enough divers
Buy a boat with seats so Reef and Finn can sit and watch the sea in it
In the summer, take the boys to Llantwit Major, the
beach in South Wales where Mummy spent holidays as a child
Celebrate birthdays big time
Sort out fish tank, pebble chess set, netball centre

When I had finished it I added to the top the words: 'Mum's List.'

Chapter 3

'Would like to go on top of the wardrobe, with the cuddly toys, to be with boys a bit longer'

Kate's dad had agreed to help me sort out our finances. *'Joint bank accounts into your name – Dad to help with finances'* was high up on the list.

I had rolled my eyes when Kate wrote that down.

'You know it makes sense,' she smiled encouragingly.

She was right. Martin was the perfect man for the job. We are like chalk and cheese: Martin meticulously well organized and risk-averse, me paperwork-phobic and happier to fly by the seat of my pants.

Kate and I never had everything in perfect order because she was more like me; too busy living to spend time micro-managing life. She was much more organized than me, though. While I would keep piles of old mail 'just in case', then lose important documents under all the junk, she could lay her hands on anything at a moment's notice.

Now, more than a week after her death, I felt very strongly that I wanted to put Kate's house in order. There was so much extra paperwork to deal with now, and I could envisage it turning from a chore to a nightmare, then descending into utter chaos. Kate wouldn't have liked that, and in any case there were many items on her list that would cost money. I needed to find out exactly where I stood financially so I could plan what to do next.

I was advised to visit the DSS to begin with, and Martin came with me. I was very grateful to him because as we walked in I felt sick and anxious. I was going to talk about unthinkable things like a widower's pension, and if Martin hadn't been by my side I think I might have just sat down and had a good cry, or turned on my heels and fled. We were introduced to a kindly older lady who explained to us that she specialized in bereavement legalities, and that it was her last day before she retired.

'How lucky is that?' I smiled, feeling relieved we had someone so experienced to help us.

'Meant to be,' she said, leaning across the table to hand me some forms and leaflets.

As she did so a silver four-leaf clover, dangling on her necklace, swung forward and glinted right under my nose. My mouth fell open.

'Oh,' I think was all I managed to say.

Martin looked at me and politely explained to the lady that Kate loved finding four-leaf clovers, and was very good at finding them. I could barely hear him. My focus was on Kate, the fuzzy vision of Kate in my mind's eye.

'Look what I found!' she said triumphantly, thrusting her hand out to me.

She had three freshly picked four-leaf clovers in her palm and her eyes were twinkling like sapphires.

'Isn't that amazing?' she grinned.

'Not really, you're so good at finding them,' I laughed. 'I don't know how you do it!'

'I haven't found any for ages, though, Singe,' she said softly, and it was true.

Kate used to find loads of them when she was a child, caravanning at Llantwit Major. Scampering off after a picnic, she told me how she would search for hours, scouring the grass, picking up bugs and chasing butterflies as she did so. She always covered the lucky clovers with Sellotape to flatten and preserve them and she kept them in a special little pot.

When she was older she found plenty more on walks in the country, and by the riverbank behind our house. She left them in their Sellotape parcels all over the place – in her handbag, the car, her dressing-table drawer – sprinkling luck all around her world, or at least trying to. It had been a good few years since I remembered her finding one, and it was amazing that she had found three, one after the other, while she was walking the dog by the river.

It happened on the day her grandmother died, and it was just after Kate's cancer treatment had ended in the autumn of 2009. She regarded the three clovers as a positive sign, and I was heartened to see that even on the day she was mourning the gran she loved so much, and when she was still weak from her drug treatment, she managed to be so positive and optimistic. It was endearing, and inspiring.

I tried to pull my focus back to the advice I was hearing, and I told myself the silver clover necklace was a positive sign. That's how Kate would have seen it, and that's why she wanted me to take Reef and Finn hunting for four-leaf clovers. *'Would love the boys to find their own four-leaf clovers,'* she wrote on the list, adding later, just to make extra sure: *'Find four-leaf clovers at usual sites.'*

Of course I would. I wasn't bitter. The clovers didn't bring Kate the luck she deserved, but they gave her hope, and that was important. I would make sure the boys grew up with hope in their hearts too.

It turned out there was good news on the financial front. After visiting the DSS, Martin and I went to the banks, where we discovered Kate had squirrelled money away in a total of twenty-seven accounts and investment funds. I run my own adventure activity company, Training Saints, and if I'd had a good month with the business or a dividend had been paid from the shares Kate got from the insurance company she worked for, she stashed some savings away. We both agreed that you couldn't take it with you, and we always spent as much as we could get away with. These were savings to be spent on holidays and having as much fun as possible with the boys.

I also learned that, thanks to Kate's sensible investments and insurance policies, the mortgage would be paid off and I'd get a lump sum on top of my widower's pension. This was a massive weight off my mind, and I felt as if I'd left several bags of stress behind when I left the High Street that day. I wouldn't have to work flat out to do all the things Kate wanted me to with Reef and Finn. The money would buy me more time with the boys and, as Kate knew all too well, you couldn't put a price on that.

As I drove home, my mind started flitting back and forth, thinking over Mum's List then darting into the future, where I envisaged ticking so many things off the list. We could extend the house to accommodate a dining table and create a playroom, complete with the secret passage the boys wanted. I could arrange to have Reef and Finn christened, make a good job of creating their memory boxes and even begin planning some of the bigger trips. Maybe we could start with snorkelling in the Red Sea? Kate and I had booked and cancelled that trip three times when she was ill, always hoping she'd be well enough to travel, but being disappointed time and time again.

'Your daughter was amazing,' I said to Martin when all this good news sank in.

He was very relieved about our financial situation, always having worried that we were frittering our money away on extravagant trips and adventures, concerned that we never saved for a 'rainy day'. Well, when the rain clouds burst open in spectacular style over our lives Kate was well prepared after all – and she'd had plenty of fun in the sunshine too.

Unexpectedly, Martin put his arm around my shoulder and gave me a squeeze.

'Thank you for giving her such a good life,' he said. There was a momentary pause, before he cleared his throat and added: 'You showed her the world, and thank God you did.'

I felt my face colour and my eyes fill with tears. It was such a generous thing to say. I had whisked his daughter away from him before he was ready to wave her off into the big wide world. I had worried him sick and caused him untold grief during Kate's youth. Even in recent years Martin and I had had our issues, never really seeing the world the same way despite him and Christine being the most dedicated and devoted parents, in-laws and grand-parents you could wish for.

'Thank you,' I said. 'That means such a lot. It's a massive thing to say. Thank you.'

I thought about that word 'grief'. The so-called grief I caused Kate's parents back then seemed so trivial compared to the real grief we were all experiencing now. Intense teenage passion matched by deep parental angst is small fry compared to this, I thought. Death shakes the ground beneath your feet, making you see the world from different angles. I was only just beginning to grieve.

I was very proud that Kate and I had always lived life to the full, and that she dearly wanted me to keep on living that way, teaching our sons to do the same. Having her dad's blessing was incredibly moving. It was like having a green light switched on before my eyes, allowing me to really get cracking on working my way though Mum's List.

I called a builder friend of mine that same night, buzzing with anticipation.

'I know exactly what I want,' I told him. 'Come round and see what you think.'

Kate and I had discussed extending the house many times. It was on our own 'to-do' list, but we had no idea when we'd be able to afford it. Reef was on the way when we bought the house. I'd only just set up my business and I was still developing the activity and training courses like power boating and snorkelling that I now run for various companies, schools and colleges. With Kate taking maternity leave from her office job as an insurance underwriter, money was a bit tight.

The previous owner of the house had had about a dozen dogs, so we had our work cut out just to get the place habitable. I think people thought we were mad to take on a property that needed so much work, but we could both see beyond the chewed window frames and dog hairs and were prepared to put in the work to build our dream home. With three garages to store our huge stock of sports and sailing equipment and jet-skis, not to mention space in the yard to keep a boat as well as to eventually extend, we knew we'd hit the jackpot.

'The only real problem is there's no space for a dining table as it is,' Kate said when we moved in. 'I want us to be able to sit round the table and eat family meals together.'

This was before Reef was born, even before we'd bought him a high chair. I teased her something rotten, because from the moment she fell pregnant Kate turned into a proper little earth mother.

'What happened to the old Kate?' I laughed. 'What happened to "let's dial a pizza" Kate? What happened to "let's curl up on the sofa with a TV dinner" Kate?'

I'd known Kate nearly twenty years before she became a mum, and it was fascinating and very endearing to see her maternal side burst into life and spread like wildfire. We discussed knocking down the conservatory that linked the garages on either side of the back of the house, replacing it with a wrap-around two-storey extension. That would create enough room for a big kitchen and dining area. On top of that we wanted to install a downstairs wet room, which would come in really handy when we came in damp and bedraggled from jet-skiing or diving. Upstairs, Kate and I agreed we would create lots more bedroom space.

'You know I want at least two children,' Kate said, stroking her blossoming tummy. 'But ideally, three. We'll have to take that into account when we get round to doing the extension.'

'Steady on! The first one isn't even here yet!' I chuckled.

I couldn't believe Kate was already thinking about the next child when she was still pregnant with the first, but that was Kate all over – an enthusiast if ever I knew one.

Now I relayed all of these plans to the builder, but instead of building several bedrooms as Kate and I had discussed, I decided to create one large room for the boys to share, which could be split down the middle with a dividing wall when they were older.

Kate and I had dreamed about having a little girl one day. We had already chosen a name: Coral, but when it became clear we weren't going to have any more children, we named our little terrier Coral instead.

'At least we've got our Coral,' we both laughed. 'She's pretty, even if she isn't quite the daughter we imagined!'

I told the builder I wanted to make sure there was enough room in the garden for the boys to play, as Kate had instructed, and I thought about how we could add on a secret passage that could take them into another play area in the loft. The dining area, I insisted, had to be big enough to have a proper big wooden dining table with at least six chairs so we could enjoy family dinners as Kate wanted, and we discussed installing a giant fish tank that could divide the dining area from the sitting room. Finally, with Reef registered disabled, having a downstairs bathroom was a priority rather than a luxury, and the ground-floor wet room was an absolute must.

The boys got very excited when they heard about the plans.

'Will it be ready soon, Daddy?' Finn asked. 'How many sleeps until we have a big, huge, massive bedroom?'

'Will we get new duvet covers?' asked Reef. 'Please can mine be Ben 10?'

'Boys, it will take a little while,' I said. 'It's a big job, and we also have Mummy's funeral to organize first.'

'Is Nanny helping you?' Reef asked.

'Do we have the day off school?' Finn asked.

'Yes to both,' I smiled. 'We'll make sure we make it a lovely day when we can remember Mummy and say goodbye.'

I had placed a death announcement in the local papers, and I read it now. Seeing it in black and white newsprint made it seem real and final, and it sent a shiver through my core.

GREENE Kate. A lovely wife and awesome Mum. You will always be with us on our adventures through life. We will so much miss our best friend and soul mate. Acres and acres. Your loving husband Singe and Infinity Elves, Reef and Finn.

Kate had called the boys elves in Lapland, and she tagged on the word 'infinity' because that's what she sometimes did when she told me she loved me. 'Infinity acres and acres,' she said. I couldn't top that, so I always replied: 'infinity acres and acres' back. Now the boys had the fitting nickname 'Infinity Elves'.

The next day, Christine accompanied me to the funeral parlour to pick out a coffin. I didn't want to put Kate in a hard wooden box, and when the funeral director showed us a beautiful seagrass casket Christine and I immediately agreed: 'That's Katie . . . we'll have that one.' It was woven like a picnic basket, and Kate loved picnics. Even the word 'seagrass' appealed to me. My star sign is Pisces and Kate's is Aries. I imagined the fish of Pisces and the ram of Aries joining sea and grass together.

Kate and I hadn't discussed her funeral in great detail. It was just too morbid, and she told me she trusted me to know what she would have wanted. One of the few instructions she gave was on the list: *'Would like drawings (any ones from school etc), pictures of boys and clothes with me, Christmas cards, birthday cards.'*

I didn't really want to see Kate in the funeral parlour. I wanted to remember her screaming her head off as she did a bungee jump, not lying cold and silent, but I felt I had to pay my respects and, besides, I had to deliver the items she wanted placed around her body.

I think I sort of brainwashed myself when the moment came. I could barely look at her, and what I saw wasn't my Kate, not really. I can barely remember her image, as I just didn't allow myself to take in what I was seeing. It was a replica Kate. A copy of my Kate. A dead Kate I didn't recognize, because I couldn't see the sparkle in her eyes.

The funeral was arranged for Tuesday 2 February at Worle Crematorium. As the day approached all I could think about was Reef and Finn. They had to be there, of course, but I was concerned about how they would cope. I decided the best policy was to just let them take it in their stride and keep a close eye on them. I allowed them to listen when I made arrangements, so they knew a bit about what to expect, and I told them they would look 'wicked' in smart new clothes.

'Can we have Blue Man at Mummy's funeral?' Reef asked after hearing me discuss music with the vicar.

''Course we can! She'd have loved that. What a great idea!'

Finn clapped his little hands excitedly. We had seen the Blue Man group perform at Universal Studios in America just a few months earlier, and Kate and the boys were enthralled by their theatrical comedy show. The performers were dressed like aliens with blue hands and faces, and I don't think I've ever seen the boys sit still for such a long time, eyes glued on the stage. Kate laughed so hard her sides hurt. It was brilliant to see. I wanted to remember her laughing, not silent and still.

On the day of the funeral the crematorium was absolutely heaving with people. Everywhere I looked there were literally hundreds of friends and relatives including lifeguards and paramedics, parents from school, police officer pals, leisure centre colleagues, old neighbours and many faces I hadn't seen for years.

The car park filled up in minutes, and the roads outside were blocked with cars. Someone told me the local buses had been diverted, which Kate would have really enjoyed. It felt like everybody Kate had come into contact with had turned up to say goodbye, and if they weren't there in person they'd sent messages from all over the planet. I wasn't at all surprised. Kate was such a lovely, popular person. You couldn't not like Kate; in fact you couldn't help but love her.

I looked around the packed pews and felt incredibly privileged to be her husband. I could feel emotion rising up my throat, and when the music started I lost control. First up was 'Can't Help Falling in Love' by Lick the Tins, and I burst into tears. We played that song at our wedding after first hearing a version of it in a Heath Ledger film we watched together called *10 Things I Hate About You*. Our wedding day was amazing. I had cried tears of joy as Kate walked up the aisle, resplendent in her ivory wedding gown. The line about 'take my whole life too' just cracked me up. Kate was my whole life then, and she still was now.

'Shush!' Reef said, giving me a steely glare that hoiked me firmly back into the present. 'Oh, for *goodness'* sake, Daddy, stop crying.'

That shut me up for a bit. Reef sounded like a bossy teacher giving me a proper telling-off. Kate would have cracked up laughing at that. Others in the congregation laughed when Abba's 'Does Your Mother Know?' rang out. It was my cheeky reference to our teenage romance, when Kate was always sneaking out to meet me. It was part of the soundtrack of our lives and was one of Kate's all-time favourite songs. I could just see her blasting it out of her car stereo, even when she was a mother herself.

Nobody but me and the boys had much of a clue what the instrumental Blue Man music was all about, but it took me right back to their stage show with Kate giggling her head off non-stop. It was probably the last time I saw her laughing uncontrollably, and it was one of the unexpected highlights of our American trip. How could that have possibly been less than three months earlier?

I looked at Kate's seagrass casket in disbelief. Then I cried again, just as I'd cried when I saw Kate stand beside me at the altar on our wedding day. She looked so beautiful, and now I had a too-vivid image of her in the casket. I knew exactly how she looked and what was inside, having helped pack the coffin before the lid finally went on.

Kate was dressed in her favourite black suit, which I had picked out of the wardrobe for her. I thought she would want to be smart. She was wearing dangly earrings and a dolphin necklace to remind her of Florida, and a pair of gloves she had asked for, to keep her hands warm. In her hand was a crystal. She liked the idea a crystal might bring comfort, if not healing. She didn't really believe in alternative therapies, but she was prepared to give anything a try that might extend her life. Kate wanted something the boys had worn to be placed in with her, and I had rolled up some of their T-shirts and little socks that still carried their scent. I added one of Finn's tiny baby-grows and placed all the clothes neatly and gently around her, while Christine added one of Kate's tiny silver christening bracelets.

I had also made sure Kate had half a dozen of the boys' pictures, some notes from Reef and Finn signed 'Infinity Elves', several happy family photographs plus the Christmas and birthday cards she had requested on her list. I put my own message in there too, which ended with: 'You'll never be forgotten, acres and acres.' Finally, I placed five shells all around Kate's body. They came from five of our favourite dive sites, representing the world we shared and treasured: Australia, the Caribbean, Llantwit, Torquay and the Maldives.

I can't say it was comforting to know she had everything she wanted around her. It was just very, very sad. I had done my best, but it didn't make things any better. It was just another step in a terrible process, something that unfortunately had to be done. There were lots of tears as the service progressed, especially when Christine took Reef and Finn up to the front to place snowdrops on Kate's coffin. Where she found the flowers I don't know, but I'm glad she did. As funerals go it wasn't too sombre, which came as a surprise and a relief.

Afterwards we had a gathering at a venue called Plantations in the middle of the moors at Kingston Seymour. It's a special place used by Reef's disabled team, and they very kindly let us use their facilities for the afternoon. It was perfect, not only because it is so private but because it is in such a lovely setting, surrounded by nature. Kate would have been outside hunting for bugs and four-leaf clovers given half the chance, because that's what she often did on our visits there.

Guests brought games and Harry Potter DVDs as gifts for the boys, and we had more Blue Man soundtracks playing, which kept them entertained. My uncle had edited together a video and a load of old photos, which were played on a loop on a large screen. I had no idea how he'd managed to pull so much together so quickly, and it took my breath away.

I saw snapshots of Kate's life and my life with her. I loved her so much, at every stage in her life. She never changed, and even when she was near the end of her life, suffering and in pain, she still had the mischievous glint in her eye I'd first seen in the teenage Kate.

The boys didn't really cry, they just got a bit upset when they saw others getting emotional. I was very glad when the day was over. We'd given Kate a wonderful send-off, but now I was looking forward to a more private kind of grief, one that Kate had instigated when she wrote on her list: '*Would like to go on top of the wardrobe, with the cuddly toys, to be with boys a bit longer.*'

I remembered being a bit taken aback, to say the least, when Kate explained this wish. I simply couldn't comprehend having my wife, the warm, tactile, sweet-smelling Kate, reduced to cold, black ashes and sitting in a box on top of a wardrobe – and not any old wardrobe, the wardrobe in the boys' bedroom. I was very wary, but Kate had it all worked out. She knew that, after she was cremated, there would be a gap before the interment, when we would finally bury her box of ashes. Kate had thought this through deeply, and she had decided that she didn't want to be left sitting on a shelf in a lonely undertaker's storeroom when she could be at home with us.

'The boys don't need to know,' she said. 'But if you could pop me up there, between the cuddly toys, I could be with them for a bit longer.'

My heart bled when she said that. She was so clear about her fate it had become almost mundane to talk about it. She sounded as if she was asking me to hang out the washing or feed the fish. I felt uncomfortable about it, though there was no way I was going to argue with her.

Now Kate's request seemed much less weird, and when I collected her from the crematorium the next day I told my brother quite matter-of-factly on the phone: 'I've just picked Kate up.'

'OK, Singe,' Matt said warily. 'I was just phoning to make sure you're OK – er, are you sure you're OK?'

'Yes,' I said. 'I'm fine, mate.'

Kate was in a beautiful basket that matched her coffin. It looked exactly like a little picnic basket, which was just what I wanted. It was very pretty, very Kate. I'd be able to hide her amongst the teddies in that without any problem at all.

Once we were safely home I carried Kate upstairs, telling her the boys were still at school and we had the house to ourselves for a while. I sat her on the carpet while I made a little space in between Finn's favourite lion, Reef's giraffe he had in hospital and a collection of cuddly Disney characters, teddies, floppy dogs and a fluffy guinea pig.

'There you go!' I said as I lifted her carefully into place and arranged the toys around her. 'That comfy enough for you, Kate?'

If anyone had heard me they'd have thought I'd lost it, but it didn't seem right not to talk to her. I wanted to talk to her, and I surprised myself by feeling quite comfortable doing so. I realized that Kate being on the wardrobe was not only going to fulfil her wish, it was going to help me grieve. She would get her wish to be with the boys for a bit longer, and I could be with her for a bit longer too. I just knew she'd thought of that already.

That night, after I tucked the boys in and kissed them both twice, I glanced up at the wardrobe before saying 'goodnight, sleep tight'. Two little voices came back: 'Night-night, Daddy.' I felt Kate's presence in the room so strongly I half expected to hear her voice too. I wanted to tell the boys Mummy was watching over them, that she wasn't quite gone yet, but I knew it could confuse them or even frighten them, and it was not the right thing to do at all. Besides, I didn't even know if that was true, or just silly wishful thinking on my part.

Kate and I shared Christian values and morals and chose

a Church school for the boys because we firmly believe in its ethos, but we weren't regular churchgoers. If there was a God I found it very hard to understand why we'd been put through so much. Having said that, Kate's presence felt so powerful it was almost tangible that night. There was a soft warmth in the air, and pushing the door open into the boys' room to wish them goodnight had felt like walking into a big cuddle. I liked it, and the boys floated off to sleep soundly, looking like a pair of very happy bunnies.

I trawled the Internet that evening, looking to buy memory boxes, and was delighted to come across some fantastic pirate chests on eBay. I ordered two the same size and one big one from a company in Germany, thinking it would be comforting to make a start on creating the memory boxes while Kate was still in the house. I knew the boys would love them too.

The interment of Kate's casket wasn't for a good few weeks. I'd chosen 31 March, as it was our wedding anniversary. We loved that date because we worked out that, if you typed it into your mobile phone, it made a heart shape from the numbers. It occurred to me that it would be fitting to get the boys christened on that date too, so we could celebrate their lives and Kate's on the same day as our wedding anniversary. Marriage in 1996, death in 2010. Who could ever have imagined those events would happen within such a short space of time?

This year was too soon for the christening, and it wouldn't be appropriate, let alone practical, to hold it on the day of the interment. But I decided next year was perfect, and on 31 March 2011 I would tick that one off the list: *'Christen boys – Noel.'* That way we would create a new, happy memory for that date. I told Kate my idea and I knew she would have approved.

'It's a shame we didn't christen the boys sooner,' I said. 'You'd have loved it. At least it's something to look forward to, a date to cherish.'

I knew Noel would be only too happy to help. He is the vicar in the church attached to All Saints School, where Reef was a pupil and Finn soon would be. Noel has also got two little boys and is a school governor, and he and Kate got on well.

Privately, I ran through the occasions in my mind again and again. Marriage, interment and the christening of our children. It wasn't the right order at all. I picked up my mobile to type in the date, wanting to see the heart shape and remember how Kate and I would text it to each other, anniversary or not. Before I did so the phone rang, my Transvision Vamp ring-tone, startling me.

'Have you remembered about tomorrow night?'

It was Rachael, a good old mate of mine and Kate's. She and her husband Stuart had talked me into going to a local barn dance. I vaguely remembered agreeing to go, under duress. I love Rachael and Stuart, mainly because they are a bit wacky like me and Kate. Rachael always takes the mickey out of me and makes me giggle, and Stuart is a great laugh too. He's also a skilled carpenter, and I'd already asked him if he'd work on our extension. I wanted as many mates involved as possible, as that's the way Kate would have done things.

'It'll do you good to have a night out,' Rachael was saying. 'Can't have you moping around on your own, no, no, no!'

She knew all about Kate's wishes, and she clearly wasn't going to waste any time getting me out and about and meeting new people, even though it was only a couple of weeks after Kate's death.

'I haven't booked a babysitter,' I said, feeling strangely jittery about the dance and scrabbling around for an excuse not to go.

'Surely Kate's parents will have the boys? They're always brilliant like that. Or what about Kirsty, your babysitter?'

'OK, I can see you've got this all sussed,' I chuckled. 'What do I have to wear to a barn dance? I don't want to look like a fat cowboy on my first night out as a single bloke!'

Rachael cracked up laughing.

'Pick you up at seven tomorrow,' she said. 'Stuart and I will walk there with you.'

I went over to my side of the wardrobe and started picking through my shirts. I felt odd, like a teenager again, fretting about what I was letting myself in for and who I might meet. Thinking about it, I realized I hadn't been single since I was about thirteen years old – over thirty years. I didn't want to be single and forty-four, yet I was nowhere near ready for the dating scene, let alone another relationship.

Going out as a single man was a whole new challenge, an alien pursuit, but one I knew I was going to have to get used to. I worried about the dance on and off all the next day, but with hindsight I really needn't have. When we arrived at the venue Stuart bought me a Woods Rum and Coke even though I rarely drink, which helped me let my hair down a bit. I had a couple of dances and a few giggles with some mums from school, and it turned out to be a thoroughly enjoyable evening.

Rachael and Stuart walked me home at midnight. It was a cold, frosty night, and my deep breaths made the air fog in front of me. It was actually a relief to be out of the house, I realized. I had missed not having Kate to dance with and chat to, but I'd enjoyed getting out and breathing some fresh air, away from the memories piled up at home. I was an adult for the evening; just a single male, swapping jokes and socializing with friends. The pressures of being a single dad and a grieving widower were left behind for the first time in weeks, and I was glad I'd made the effort.

Unexpectedly, a car sped round the corner, and its headlights illuminated a couple walking along the pavement on the other side of the street. Their heads and bodies were pushed up so closely together they looked like one huge person. I felt a pang of jealousy that seemed to come from nowhere, puncturing my mellow mood and flooding me with feelings of self-pity.

Why couldn't that be me and Kate? Why was I on the other side of the road, on my own, with just the cold night air wrapped around my shoulders? I looked up at the sky, wondering if Kate was looking down on me. The sky was clear, and the stars were shining brightly. The sight of them cheered me up, reminding me of the nights Kate and I had had midnight picnics in the Mendip Hills when we first dated.

'Don't worry, I won't get old and bitter,' I told Kate silently when I got home. 'Don't worry if you see me get cross and upset. It won't last for ever, I promise.'

The next morning I left the boys watching Saturday-morning TV while I showered. *Scooby Doo* was on, which the boys love. As I stepped out of the bathroom I heard the most amazing peals of laughter ringing up the stairs. Both Reef and Finn were absolutely chuckling their heads off, and their giggles were rocking the whole house. I went downstairs in my towel, curious to see what could possibly be so funny on *Scooby Doo*, only to find them watching an old Norman Wisdom film they'd flicked on by chance. The pair of them literally had tears streaming down their faces and were pointing at the screen, doubled up with laughter.

'Look, Daddy, that silly man is being chased by a policeman!' Finn managed to spit out.

'He's like the blue men,' Reef said, his voice breaking into giggles. 'Mummy would have laughed really hard at this.'

She certainly would. The slapstick humour was right up her street, but, much more than that, she would have given anything to hear her boys laugh like that again. That was a bit of a moment for me. I remembered feeling sorry for myself when I saw that couple knitted tightly together on the pavement the previous night and I gave myself a little ticking-off. I had so much to be grateful for; I mustn't let myself get down. I had to keep smiling like Reef and Finn, because what was the alternative? There wasn't one, at least not one Kate would have approved of.

I'd baulked when she'd told me she wanted me to find someone else. It seemed an impossible task. Kate was irreplaceable, I told her that straight. She was my soul mate and I wasn't sure you ever got the chance to have two soul mates in one lifetime. But Kate insisted. I watched as she selflessly said and wrote the words: *'Find a woman to settle down with so the boys can have a female influence and stability in their lives.'*

Remembering the look on her face as she read the words out loud was painful. She was trying to smile at me, willing me to be happy, but was unable to stop the tears spilling from her eyes. Now, for the first time, I fully understood why she had insisted on putting this on her list. As a wife she was being selfless and thoughtful and incredibly generous. I already got that. It was her final, ultimate act of love for me. But I could see the richer meaning in her words too. I could see something Kate's maternal instinct had alerted her to long before: with the boys being so very young, my happiness had a direct impact on theirs. Having a miserable single dad as their only parent was no good for the boys at all. I had to look for happiness and stay positive, and she knew me well enough to realize that I'd struggle to do that on my own.

I received another invitation that week, this time for my brother's girlfriend's eighteenth birthday party, which she was holding in a nightclub in Weston-super-Mare. It was on 12 February, just ten days after Kate's funeral, and I think friends and family were surprised but delighted when I agreed to go. It helped that I'd already been to the barn dance, and I was less wary this time, knowing I'd be surrounded by family.

It was still a bit of an ordeal getting ready on my own and driving to the club all by myself. I turned the music up loud in the car on the way there, trying to fill the empty space next to me. When I finally arrived and walked into the party my head was banging with tunes, and I think I must have been on auto-pilot. I hadn't wanted to think about being there without Kate, I just wanted to get through the evening and maybe even manage to have another night off from full-time grief. My mind had other ideas, though, and my subconscious was playing tricks on me.

'What d'you want to drink?' Matt asked.

I will remember my brother asking that question for ever, and I will never forget turning round and asking Kate what she fancied to drink. I was convinced she was there, standing beside me at the bar in the nightclub. I could see her outline against the backdrop of disco lights and dry ice, I was sure of it. It was so good to see her again, or at least to see a vision of Kate, the vision I projected into the empty space beside me.

My brother was shocked by my mistake, of course, but it certainly didn't spoil the evening. I quickly reassured him I was fine and I moved on, mingling easily around the party. I smiled and chatted and I coped with other people's awkward reactions when they saw me and didn't know what to say or do. I'd lost my wife, not my personality, I thought, as I broke the ice and showed them I was the same old Singe, up for a laugh and a chat.

I knew some people were amazed to see me at a party so soon after losing Kate, and I think those who knew I had accepted the invitation half expected me to be sitting in the corner moping and crying. Driving home, I felt quite pleased with how the evening had gone, and I told Kate as much when I got in that night, tiptoeing into the boys' bedroom and whispering in the dark to the collection of strangely shaped shadows on the top of the wardrobe.

I told her how my brother had been shocked when he realized what I'd done, thinking she was beside me. I explained how I'd thought she was on my arm at the bar as usual, and when the penny dropped how I wasn't upset, but realized I had quietly enjoyed seeing her. I also told her how, later in the evening, memories flooded back when I saw the teenagers on the dance floor. They reminded me of our early days together, when we melted into each other on our midnight picnics at Priddy. Finally, I told Kate that I would take the boys to the play area at Priddy Pools, where we'd hunt for bugs and reptiles and toads and lie in the little grassy bowls pitted into the landscape, because that's what Mummy liked to do.

'I will also do my best to find a new woman, one day,' I said, not quite believing what I was saying. 'I'm not promising anything, though, and it won't be for a long time yet.'

Chapter 4

'Mummy loved how sparkly Reef and Finn's eyes were in Lapland'

A couple of weeks after Kate's funeral we returned to Plantations in Kingston Seymour for a family fun day, organized by the North Somerset Disabled Team. *'Keep in touch with Maria and Lynne, Disabled Team,'* Kate had asked, and I fully intended to.

Maria and Lynne are a great team, and Kate had got on with them brilliantly. When she was very poorly, they sometimes took the boys to school, taking the pressure off so I could go to work early or take Kate to a hospital appointment. They both had a great sense of humour that always shone out, regardless of how sick or disabled the children in their care were.

'Hello, Singe, hello, Reef, hello, Finn!' Maria boomed cheerfully as we arrived.

The boys' eyes were on stalks, taking in the huge bouncy castle, brightly dressed magician and rainbow-coloured ice cream stand. Maria scooped the boys in her cuddly arms, smothering them with love and affection. Lynne spotted us too and started running over, waving and smiling. There was always banter between the pair of them, with Maria teasing Lynne that she was far too thin from all the yoga she did and Lynne having a crack back about Maria's love of cakes and chocolates. Today was no exception.

'I haven't finished my cuddle yet!' Maria warned Lynne as she approached.

Winking at the boys, she added, 'And they like mine better than yours as there's more of me to go round!'

Lynne rolled her eyes, and I instantly relaxed. I had been a little bit concerned about coming today, wondering how I would cope alone. It was a place Kate and I always loved visiting, because it was a relaxing retreat, far away from the draining, depressing world of children's cancer wards. You could have a coffee and chat to other parents, and when Reef was undergoing treatment it was a godsend, as he could play outdoors without running the risk of infection he might in a public play area.

'How's Kate doing?' one of the other dads asked.

The question took me by surprise because I thought it was so obvious she had passed away. Kate and I did everything together, and to me the fact she wasn't by my side as usual said it all.

'I'm afraid we lost Kate, a few weeks ago,' I said.

He looked mortified. Most of the other parents had a child with a disability. This wasn't a retreat for sick parents and widowers, and I could see he was struggling to take in what I'd said.

'I'm so sorry,' he said.

'So are we,' I replied, trying to give him a reassuring smile. 'Thanks for asking after her, you weren't to know.'

I sat down on the end of a bench, feeling like half a person. Kate and I were a perfect team, a couple who made up a whole, just as Maria and Lynne are a perfect couple of work mates. Now I had to be a whole all by myself, and it felt weird.

The boys had a brilliant day, their eyes shining as they feasted on all the treats laid on for them. I remembered their eyes shining like that before, and so did Kate. *'Mummy loved how sparkly Reef and Finn's eyes were in Lapland,'* she wrote. I loved how sparkly their eyes were in Lapland too, and I loved how sparkly their eyes were today. How lucky I was to still be able to look into their eyes. That's what I told myself as I sat beside an empty space that day.

Kate insisted we took the boys to Lapland in December 2009, even though she was still very weak from more than a year of cancer treatment.

'Kate, are you sure about this trip?' I asked. 'I know we've planned it and looked forward to it for ages, but there's always next year.'

Kate had finished all her chemo and radiotherapy, as well as a drug trial she went through, and we'd had our wonderful holiday to Disney World in Florida just a month earlier. We were so glad our lives didn't revolve around hospital appointments any more, but even so Kate wasn't fully back to normal, not by a long stretch. The disease and all the drugs she'd been given had left her tired and frail. Her back was hurting, and she had developed a nasty, irritating cough. It was clear she had a lot of recovering still to do.

As with most cancer patients, it would be five years before Kate could declare herself technically in remission or even hope to hear those magic words: 'all clear'. Even Reef hadn't quite got there yet, and he was several years ahead of Kate. All we did know was that Kate's treatment was over, it appeared to have been successful and Kate was hoping to be strong enough soon to have the breast reconstruction she longed for.

'I always wanted a boob job and now I'm going to have one on the NHS,' Kate giggled.

I heard her say that to friends many times. I loved hearing her say it because it was a positive move forward, closing another door on breast cancer.

'No, Singe, I don't want to put off going to Lapland,' Kate said firmly. 'Imagine how much the boys will love it. They're the perfect ages to see Father Christmas in the North Pole. It will just be so magical. We have to do it now before it's too late.'

I took that to mean before the boys got too old. In theory, Kate was right. Reef was five and a half and Finn was very nearly four, so they were the absolutely ideal ages.

'The thing is, Kate, you can't put the boys first all the time,' I said. 'Of course, it's the perfect time for them, but they'll still enjoy it next year, and you will too, because you'll be stronger.'

She shook her head, and I could see a steely glint in her eye.

'We're going,' she said firmly. 'Nothing you can say will talk me out of it. We won't regret it. And anyway, since when have you been the one trying to talk yourself out of a holiday?'

I laughed. 'There's a first time for everything,' I said.

'And this Christmas will be the first time the boys go to Lapland,' Kate replied.

I didn't argue any more, and we booked the holiday for the day the boys broke up from school, returning on

Christmas Eve. Kate was beside herself with excitement, clapping her hands with glee like a little girl when the tickets arrived. Reef and Finn jumped up and down, squealing and cheering when we broke the good news, and the whole of December turned into an excited countdown, with the boys constantly asking: 'How many sleeps until Lapland?'

Kate absolutely loved the build-up and threw herself wholeheartedly into the preparations, even though she looked really wiped out at the end of each day.

'Are you absolutely sure you're up to this?' I asked her several times.

'Singe, stop asking me!' she protested. 'I'll be fine.'

Kate had done such a good job psyching the boys up for the trip that I'd got caught up in the magic too. I imagined that when we stepped off the plane we'd be in a perfect Christmas fantasyland, like Disney World but with snow. In fact, I was in for a shock, because I hadn't banked on how very cold and dark it would be. When we arrived it was early afternoon, but the sky was already black, and it felt colder than anywhere I'd ever been before. The freezing air caught in my throat, and every exposed bit of skin stung with cold.

'I didn't expect this,' I said to Kate, bracing myself against the bitter wind. 'Are you all right? Have we got enough warm stuff?'

'Plenty,' Kate smiled, pulling on a big fur hat and wrapping up Reef and Finn in anoraks, hats, scarves and gloves.

Kate looked glamorous and beautiful. Her hair had grown back since the chemo, but it was short and wispy, and much darker than it was before. With her new hair hidden under the hat, Kate looked more like her old self.

I wouldn't have been surprised if her shiny blonde hair hadn't reappeared when she took off the hat, because at a glance it looked just like my old Kate had returned.

We took Reef and Finn sledging down the side of the hotel on the first night. Both boys flung themselves fearlessly down the slope, careering at breakneck speed through the freezing air. Finn, in typical style, wanted to go faster and further than anyone else.

'Wonder who he gets that off?' Kate teased me. 'He's an absolute nutter!'

'You can talk,' I teased back. 'I think he's got quite a few of his daredevil mum's genes too!'

At that very moment Finn launched himself even more flamboyantly than before, headfirst in skeleton-bob style. He took off like a rocket. 'You nutter, Finn!' Kate shouted. Then, in unison, we both screamed 'Finn, NO!' as we saw he was heading straight for a barbecue stand that was positioned near the hotel's picnic area.

'Singe!' Kate yelled, turning to me in panic. 'Quick, stop him!'

I started to slip and slide down the slope, but it was no good. Finn was belting down at lightning speed, and I had no chance of catching him. There was a sickening crashing sound, and everything went silent. It was very dark in the distance, and we couldn't make out what had happened. A second later, out of the darkness, we were incredibly relieved to hear Finn cry for help.

Skidding towards the barbecue, I was amazed to see Finn and the sledge stuck fast underneath the stand. His feet were sticking out of one side and his head was poking out of the other. He had soot on his yellow hat and had scared the living daylights out of himself, but he appeared to be miraculously unharmed.

'Help, Daddy!' he said. 'Pull me out quick!'

It took me a good few minutes to work him free, and once he was back on his feet he started to giggle. Kate stared at him in amazement and then absolutely cracked up laughing too. She had tears streaming down her face she laughed so hard, mainly from relief, I have to say.

'What did I tell you?' she gasped. 'A nutter like his daddy!'

'Oi, don't say that,' I laughed, picking up a snowball and chucking it at her.

When she eventually stopped laughing Kate started to cough. The cold air was catching in her throat too, and we decided to call it a night. I could tell she was making a huge effort for the boys, and I think she could tell I was making an effort to be supportive and have a laugh like normal.

It wasn't easy, I can tell you. I wanted to wrap Kate up in cotton wool and keep her warm and safe, not see her exposed to the elements, struggling on and pretending she was back to normal. I knew there was no stopping her, though. Kate was determined she was going to tick off everything we dreamed of doing in Lapland, and there was no point in arguing with her.

Over the next few days the boys visited Father Christmas in his twinkly grotto in the North Pole, and we took reindeer rides together. The boys' innocence was heartbreaking. They told Santa they wanted remote-controlled cars and a Blue Man DVD. As Santa launched into his line about wishes coming true for 'good boys', Finn whispered under his breath 'and Mummy to not be poorly any more'. Santa patted his head kindly and looked slightly lost for words.

Kate was very moved and gave the boys a big cuddle. She was so happy, even when she had to finally admit she was worn out and we needed to borrow a wheelchair from the hotel to get around. She soon swapped it for a snow-mobile, and I will never forget seeing her riding merrily up to the hotel, wrapped in a blanket with Reef and Finn tucked in cosily on either side. The boys were cackling with glee, and Kate had a smile as wide as Santa's belt stretched across her face.

'Thank you,' she whispered to me one night. 'Lapland is a dream come true.'

'You made it happen,' I told her.

'Singe, can you do something for me?' she asked suddenly. 'There's a chance we could see the Northern Lights from here, I've looked it up on my phone. Can you go outside and have a look for me? I'd love to see them, it's good luck, you know.'

I wrapped up warm and crunched out into the snow, but I could see immediately that there was no sign of the Northern Lights. I'd seen them many years earlier, on Skye in Scotland, just before I met Kate, and had been amazed by them. Here, the sky was pitch black, with barely a visible star in the sky.

'No luck tonight,' I told her sadly, returning to find her already tucked up in bed, just like the boys.

She drifted off to sleep while I stayed awake, worrying about her breathing. It sounded laboured, and I was afraid she'd overdone it. She sent me out every night after that to look for the Northern Lights, but was disappointed each time.

'There'll be other chances,' I told her. 'If we don't see them here we could go to Skye sometime.'

After a week I was looking forward to getting home for Christmas, so we could batten down the hatches and keep Kate wrapped up snugly at home.

'How are you getting on with the memory boxes?' Maria asked, her friendly voice returning me to the bench at Plantations and rescuing me from the icy memory of what happened next, after Lapland.

'Funny you should mention memories,' I said, smiling as I tried to retain the image of Kate in the snowmobile in my mind.

Maria gave me a lovely warm smile. I explained about the pirate chests I'd ordered from Germany, and she talked to me about arranging some professional help, to have newspaper cuttings preserved and photographs laminated and so on.

'I expect there's a lot of sorting out to do in the meantime,' she said intuitively.

I watched the boys bouncing on the inflatable castle. They looked like they didn't have a care in the world. Their memories of Kate could only stretch back two, maybe three years at the most. They'd remember Lapland and Disney World, and I was pretty sure Reef would remember something of his time in hospital with his mum at his bedside. Both boys would hopefully remember catching crabs with Kate on the beach last summer, as we'd made quite a fuss about that and had a wonderful framed photo to jog their memory. A copy of that would definitely take pride of place in their pirate chests.

But what else? There were so many birthdays and Christmases to think about, so many highs Kate would want them to remember.

There were low points too, of course, and it occurred to me that I had to be careful not to glorify the past. Life wasn't one big celebration, and Kate was a person who appreciated the simple things in life as much as the big, exciting things.

Mum's List reminded me of that. *'Mummy loved moths, snakes and slowworms, orange Club biscuits, jam and jelly, lemon curd.' 'Loved guinea pigs and butterflies, Walnut Whips, strawberry cheesecake.'*

I had to take the lead from Kate and include reminders of ordinary, everyday life, even though in our world we always tried to make each day special and extraordinary.

That night, the boys fell asleep the minute their heads hit the pillows. It had been a great day, and I felt motivated to work on the memory boxes. I told Kate what I was going to do after I kissed the boys goodnight.

'Keep an eye on the boys, will you?' I whispered up to her on the wardrobe. 'I've got a big job on my hands.'

We had countless piles of photo albums and packets of photos stacked up in cupboards around the house. I knew some were hastily thrown together while others were lovingly labelled by Kate and interspersed with mementos like bungee-jump tickets or a receipt from a café at the Great Barrier Reef. I'd been daunted by the prospect of going through them at first, but now I felt ready, and I padded quietly round the house, gathering them up.

I also collected together old newspaper and magazine

cuttings we'd kept in folders and envelopes that had gathered dust over the years, and I reopened the boxes of love letters, wondering whether to add one or two to the boys' memory boxes, along with some wedding pictures. Finally I sat on the wooden floor at the foot of my bed, surrounded by so many souvenirs of my life with Kate.

I took the lid off an old document box first and saw images of our past that sprang to life vividly in my mind. There was Katie Johnson, aged seventeen, posing in a swimsuit and holding up a beach ball at the old Lido in Clifton. 'Beach Babe' the caption in the local paper said, and it wasn't wrong. She was a total blonde bombshell. I remembered other lads checking her out in her black swimsuit, and feeling glad I was on duty as a lifeguard that day, keeping a close eye on my Katie. The paper was yellowing now, but I could still see Kate clearly. I remembered her like that as if the photograph was taken yesterday.

Next, I found some modelling shots that showed the pair of us looking ridiculously young. Someone at Kate's college was training to be a photographer and asked her to sit for him. She did a fabulous job and looked dazzling as she posed in a pretty garden, smiling so cheerfully her cheeks bulged like peaches.

'Come on, Singe, help me out,' she called, holding out her hand to me. I went and sat beside her.

'Beauty and the beast, is it?' I joked, smiling for the camera.

In contrast to the 'Beach Babe' picture, the modelling shots felt like they'd been taken several lifetimes ago. Memories are unpredictable things, I thought. You never know how they are going to affect you. Next, I saw a faded photo of Katie sitting on a plane, and I was there, sitting next to her again. We were on a flight about to take off for Austria, where we were going skiing. How strange, I thought. Our very first holiday together was in the snow, and our very last holiday, to Lapland, was in the snow too. The photo captured Kate as she was about to take her first ever flight, and in the picture I could still see the excitement radiating from her face as we prepared for take-off.

It turned out to be a horrendous flight, the worst I had ever been on. Kate felt so lucky to be on it, because her parents didn't want us to go on holiday together. She had even forged her dad's signature to get a passport, but was soon found out when he opened a letter from Customs after she filled in the form incorrectly. Inevitably, there were fireworks and tears, apologies and ultimatums, before Kate's parents finally gave her permission to go.

'Is this normal?' Kate asked, grabbing my hand.

It was a night flight, and we had terrible turbulence as we lurched through one thunderstorm after another. Passengers were screaming as they were bounced about in their seats. Bags and ski boots were tumbling out of the overhead lockers, and the air hostesses were being thrown about like matchsticks.

'Er, it can get a bit choppy in the sky sometimes,' I blagged. 'Don't worry, Katie, keep holding my hand and you'll be fine. Not long to go now.'

By the time we started the descent I must admit I felt a bit frightened myself. You could feel the plane being pushed around by the wind before it suddenly dropped like a stone from the sky. We landed with an enormous bounce, half on the runway and half on grassland. Kate held my hand so tight I had nail marks in my skin. Later, I found out we'd had a 500 mph tail wind and 50 mph cross winds – a very precarious combination.

'It wasn't really normal, was it, Singe?' Kate asked accusingly when we were safely inside the terminal.

'Er, not quite,' I smiled guiltily. 'I've never experienced such a bad flight in my life before. It'll be worth it, though. I can't wait to teach you to ski, you'll be a natural.'

She whacked me on the back playfully.

'Just as well you're worth it,' she said.

Katie wasn't afraid of anything, not really. As I anticipated, she picked up skiing incredibly quickly and loved it. I couldn't believe I was with someone who was not only gorgeous-looking, but shared my appetite for sport and adventure. Just like me, Kate wanted to pack as much as possible into every single day, and she wanted every moment to be as exciting as possible.

I put the Austria pictures down and picked up a heavy, expensive-looking photo album. There was a wedding picture on the first page showing Kate and me emerging from the church, smiling under a shower of confetti. Nobody thought we were the marrying type, and it took us years and years to get round to tying the knot after our engagement, because we always had another holiday booked, another memory to make.

We were married for almost fourteen years of our twenty-two years together, and I had no regrets about not doing it sooner. It didn't really matter whether we were married or not. Katie and I did everything together, before and after she became my wife. We were as besotted with each other on our wedding day as we were as love-struck youngsters, and we stayed that way until death parted us.

We took photos wherever we went and I'm so glad we did. I knew the boys would love looking back at these one day, and I felt close to Kate as I let my mind slip back in time over and over again.

I found a picture of Kate snorkelling that made me laugh out loud. In it she's nose to nose with an irate clownfish, which is puffing and blowing angrily at her. Kate is laughing her head off. The picture says so much about Kate. She always had this very funny personality, always finding something to laugh at. She knew clownfish get quite upset if you hover over their anemone. They swim out and can come within an inch of your face, and when they see their own reflection in your mask they go absolutely mad and give you a right old telling off.

That day Kate tormented lots of these little fish. She folded herself up into a seated position to get her buoyancy just perfect before cruising over loads of anemones. One tiny little clownfish was so furious with her it bit her hair and gave it a pull. Kate found it absolutely hilarious. The interaction between Kate and creatures of all kinds was amazing, and I enjoyed watching her in action as much as I loved diving and snorkelling myself.

Tucked inside another photo album I found an itinerary Kate had typed up, detailing where we went and what we did on a month-long holiday to Australia, New Zealand and Fiji in 1998.

Tuesday 3rd November: Drove into Cairns to book next boat trip and accommodation. Placed bet on the Melbourne Cup, chose Champagne who came in 2nd! Went to Crystal Cascades, saw butterflies and snakes then had a McDonald's for dinner. Went to Wild World, met an aborigine from Yeovil and a koala named Hamilton. Went to Port Douglas for tea.

Every day was action-packed. I couldn't help grinning when I read it. We were both in heaven together on that trip. We'd flown via Europe and Dubai to reach Australia, and after visiting New Zealand and Fiji we flew home after a stopover in America, so we could say we had circumnavigated the world. I read on, enjoying the memories.

'Wednesday 4th November: Did 4 dives today, all very good. Smoothed a Potato Cod and rescued Singe.

'I don't remember needing rescuing, Kate,' I said wryly, twisting my head in the direction of the wardrobe in the boys' room. I really didn't, and I wished I could ask Kate to remind me of the story.

Saturday 21st November: Got early plane to Auckland then on to Fiji. Saw the Sky Tower. Had helicopter ride to island, went snorkelling. Great stars and chased ghost crabs. Shark feed and night dive.

'We have to walk all the way around this island,' I said to Kate.

We were on Matamanoa Island in Fiji, very close to where Tom Hanks filmed the film *Castaway*. It was absolutely idyllic, but Kate looked at me with a horrified expression on her face.

'Singe, we've been told to avoid the far side of the island,' she complained.

She was right. We'd been warned there were dangerously jagged rocks and coral forming the coast on the opposite side of the island to where we were staying, but I couldn't resist the challenge of circumnavigating Matamanoa too.

'I know it's a bit jagged in parts,' I conceded. 'But it's only a few old rocks and bits of coral. We can do it.' Kate looked doubtful and a bit cross. 'Remember our saying? "If you're not living on the edge you're a waste of space."'

She sighed and shrugged and reluctantly nodded.

'I can't argue with that. Come on, then.'

'That's my Kate!'

I took her hand, and she gave me a smile. I felt her dainty little fingers tighten around mine. There was no way I would put Kate in danger, never in a million years. She was safe with me, and I would always look after her and protect her from harm.

It was a breathtaking walk. The sand was white beneath our feet, the sky was turquoise and silver, and the hot sun felt like it was shining just for me and Kate. We were the only people in the world, that's how it felt.

'I love you, Singe,' Kate said, 'Even if you are a total nutter sometimes.'

We were picking our way across the ragged bit of the coast now, and waves had started to rise up behind us. Kate didn't like it when they smashed on the rocks, growling and threatening to bite our heels like angry dogs. She shrieked every time and clung on to me for dear life.

'You're doing really well,' I said. 'Keep going!'

She did, but I was gutted when I realized that Kate was so worried she had started to cry a bit. That hadn't been the plan at all.

'Come on, keep going,' I encouraged. 'I'm not letting go of you. Hold me tight and keep walking.'

Gamely, Kate tackled the last craggy rock that finally led us back to where we'd started a couple of hours earlier.

'I need a medal for that,' she said, puffing with relief as she jumped down to the dry, flat sand of the beach.

'You certainly do. We'll find something to remember it.'

As I spoke a wave swept up the beach, leaving a perfect, shiny Nautilus shell at Kate's feet. I couldn't believe the timing, and I grabbed my camera and got a photo of her picking it up.

'There's your medal,' I laughed. 'For Kate, always a winner!'

I remembered the look of delight and satisfaction on Kate's face. In true style her fear was quickly forgotten, and finding the Nautilus shell became her abiding memory of Fiji.

I felt overwhelmed by my memories. They were all so happy, yet now that made them seem so tragic too. The reason we took so many photos and videos was so that we could enjoy the memories again together when we were old and grey, and too old to travel any more.

Now I couldn't revisit any of those places with Kate, either physically or mentally. They were just a part of our history, consigned to memory boxes. Our journey together was over, and I was gutted it had ended way too soon. I had to 'do a Kate', though. I had to hold on to the happy memories. We had the most wonderful life together, and nothing could change that.

My eyes fell on a picture of our clever old cairn terrier, Frazzle, who died a few years before Kate. He was very much my dog, and every morning he never failed to jump up on my side of the bed, completely ignoring Kate. When Reef was born we placed his crib on Kate's side of the bed, and when Frazzle came in the next morning he looked around cautiously before ignoring me and padding round to have a good look and a sniff at newborn Reef. Then Frazzle jumped up on Kate and licked her approvingly.

'I swear Frazzle's smiling,' Kate laughed. 'Look at his face!'

It was a lovely moment; a good omen, we thought. We were a happy little family, firmly bonded together by love, and even the dog was content.

Next, I opened a faded yellow packet of photographs, complete with negatives, and saw me and Kate in a restaurant in Minorca with her parents. For a starter Kate and I ordered the most expensive thing on the menu – giant prawns in garlic. We got horribly ill afterwards, and Kate's mum and dad, who'd played it safe with the minestrone soup, couldn't help taking the mickey out of us. I remembered Kate wore a T-shirt I'd bought with 'front' and 'back' printed on, my cheeky reference to the fact she was quite flat-chested.

'You can't have everything,' I said when she sulked about it. 'You've got the blonde hair and the blue eyes and the stunning figure – don't be greedy now!'

'I'll have a boob job one day,' she always said. 'I'd *love* to have a boob job.'

'You're perfect as you are,' I always replied and I meant it.

Thank God we didn't have a crystal ball.

In another album I saw the pair of us riding camels in a Bedouin encampment in Israel. We're at the front of the trek, as usual. Kate and I always made sure we got the best seats in the house, whatever we did. She looks so young, still in her teens I guessed. Once we'd been on that first trip to Austria nothing could stop us and we packed in as many holidays as we could possibly afford.

Once we won a £500 holiday voucher after entering a close-up picture of a puffer fish wearing Ray-Bans into a photography competition. We immediately agreed to put the money towards a trip to Antigua. I closed my eyes and thought about sailing round that beautiful island in the Caribbean. We'd gone on a boat trip, and Kate, not being used to drinking much, got very drunk on the free rum on board.

'Come and dance!' she called out to whoever was listening, and the owner of the boat joined her for a few high-energy rumbas and mambos. He thought Kate was fantastic and had such a whale of a time dancing with her he let me sail his £1 million catamaran, the *Kokomo Cat*, three-quarters of the way round Antigua, much to the annoyance of some German tourists whom he'd refused to give a turn to. That was a typical Kate moment. Good things happened when you were with Kate; at least they did back then.

We learned that Antigua has 365 beaches, one for every day of the year. I lost count of how many we walked along hand in hand, eating mangos, pineapples and coconuts we picked up from where they had fallen on the ground.

'Wouldn't it be amazing to spend a whole year here, a day on each beach?' Kate said.

We both thought about that for a minute and then shared a knowing look.

'Naah,' I laughed. 'Too many other places to see!'

'I agree,' Kate smiled. 'Where to next?'

Africa was the next album I picked out. Kate loved animals of all types, and I can see her now, hand-feeding bits of banana to a bush baby one minute, wrapping a giant python round her neck at our hotel in Kenya the next. I watched in admiration as she expertly stroked its scales while others shrieked and recoiled in horror. She wrote on Mum's List that she loved snakes, and how true that was.

We visited the Tsavo East and Tsavo West game reserves. Bumping along in a safari jeep, eating dust and baking in the heat, we saw zebras, giraffes, elephants, buffalo, black rhino and lions. One night we watched in awe as a herd of about fifty elephants, led by a gigantic matriarch, came silently to the watering hole outside our lodge. Despite their huge size, they didn't make a sound as the adults performed a well-practised routine of peeling off two by two, creating a safe passageway for the baby elephants to walk through and take a drink. It was breathtaking.

Another night we got a knock on our bedroom door at 1 a.m. The hotel had put fresh meat as bait on a platform that was visible from our window, and we had asked them to let us know if there was any action.

'There are two leopards outside,' the night porter whispered. 'Try to be very quiet, and stay inside. One of our waiters was killed last year.'

I was half asleep but very excited, and in my rush to get

dressed I accidentally put both legs down one leg of my trousers, which sent me crashing into the window. Kate gasped, then fell about laughing when she saw what I'd done. 'You could have ended up as bait yourself,' she said. I hope you haven't scared them off!'

We peered outside together and were absolutely thrilled to see two magnificent leopards on the prowl. We stared at them in wonderment, completely absorbed by their majesty and stealth. It was a male and a female, and after they had cautiously polished off the meat and licked their lips, they slunk into the distance, where we saw them mate.

'We'll have to come back and see their cubs,' Kate whispered.

We were older now, Kate in her late twenties, me in my thirties. We also talked about going to America and we both agreed it was on our 'must do' list.

'We should wait until we have children and go to Florida and Disney World,' Kate said.

I agreed wholeheartedly. I knew Kate's biological clock had started to tick. There was very little she said or did that I didn't agree with, and that seemed like a plan. We always wanted children together one day, and if and when we were lucky enough to have kids it was taken for granted we'd continue to travel and live life to the full. Our children would dive, jet-ski and bungee-jump their way round the world, just like we did. That's what we both hoped for.

We always had a boat parked on the drive or out in the back yard. The last one we had together, *Singe 1*, was a bright-yellow 4.8 metre rib craft that we'd fitted with a 90 hp engine to change it from a ski boat into something supersonic. We had it for about ten years and took it out at every opportunity, towing it to our favourite spots in Torquay, Lyme Regis and down on the Bristol Channel, complete with windsurfing and scuba-diving kit, or our silver jet-ski.

In the early days we didn't have much money and often broke down in our old Skoda or Cavalier, having to call the RAC to help get us home. It was always worth the hassle. We both adored being out at sea. Kate and I even slept on a waterbed for more than fifteen years, and we joked that we spent more time on the water than anyone else we knew. When the boys came along we took them with us, teaching them to steer the boat almost before they could walk.

Singe 1 was old now, and Kate had told me to use some of the money from her estate to buy a shiny new boat. Always thinking of the boys' safety, she instructed me to buy one with seats. *'Buy a boat with seats so Reef and Finn can sit and watch the sea in it.'*

'Please be careful, Singe,' she said, dwelling on this wish for quite some time as she wrote the words on her list. 'Diddy is a daredevil, like you,' she added, giving me a knowing look, one that was filled with a mixture of pride and worry. 'Be careful, that's all I ask.' Diddy is a pet name we gave to Finn after he was born prematurely and was a tiny little speck. 'And Reef has to be so careful with his balance, because of his leg. I don't want them riding on the tubes. Please buy a really good boat and make sure they have comfortable seats so they can hold on in safety.'

She closed her eyes for a moment, and I imagined she was picturing the three of us whizzing through the sea in a beautiful new boat. She looked calm and peaceful, I thought, but when she opened her eyes they were wet.

‘I promise,’ I said. ‘I will take good care of the boys, and I’ll teach them to love the water, like Mummy.’

We cried in each other’s arms, Kate dragging on the oxygen pipe as she broke down.

I cried again now as I closed the photo albums one by one, slowly bringing myself back to the present, back to sitting on the floor at the foot of my bed.

On 22 March it was Kate’s birthday. She would have been thirty-nine years old, and I was not looking forward to the day at all. Since her death I’d already had to navigate Valentine’s Day and Mother’s Day.

Valentine’s Day was dreadful. I think it was the first time since I was about ten that I hadn’t received a card. Kate and I always had a meal out. I bought her flowers, we drank champagne, and then she always let me take advantage of her, very willingly I might add. This year I had just tried to ignore it. The date was blank in my diary, and I told myself it didn’t mean a thing to me, and it didn’t matter. I remembered how, when the boys were in bed on Valentine’s night, I put the kettle on to make a cup of tea and flicked through the TV channels to find something to escape into. In quick succession I saw three images of couples smooching and kissing; one on a real-life documentary, one in a soap opera and another in a soppy film. I switched the TV off and went back to the kitchen, where I looked at the steam evaporating on the tiles and started to cry. I watched the droplets trickle down the wall for a while before remembering I was making a cup of tea. Then I couldn’t find any teabags, so I sat on the floor and bawled my eyes out instead.

On Mother's Day I tried to focus on all of my 'mothers' – my mum, my stepmum and Kate's mum. I bought them each a card and made a point of talking to them, and Martin and Christine took Reef and Finn up to Kate's grave to lay a rose each. The teachers at school were brilliant, making sure the boys still got to make cards, addressing them to 'Nanny' instead of 'Mummy'. Like Valentine's Day, I was glad when it was over. Reef and Finn didn't have a mummy any more, and the day only served to remind me of that.

Kate's birthday was different, though. She had expressly told me to *'Celebrate birthdays big time,'* and I decided to include hers in that plan, whether that's what she meant or not. I'd been shopping for boats for a couple of weeks already and was thrilled to discover the one I had finally chosen would be ready for collection on Kate's birthday, which fell on a Monday. As luck would have it, that was the day funds from Kate's estate would be released too, and I would be able to pay the mortgage off as well as buy the boat.

'I can't tell you how perfect the timing is,' I told Mark, the boss at Ribcraft in Yeovil, when he phoned to tell me the boat was ready. He had known Kate personally as she'd done her advanced powerboat training course with his staff. She'd made quite an impression as the only female on the course along with a group of fishermen, senior lifeguards and advanced sailing instructors, including me.

I remember that training course well. It was blowing a hoolie the night we went out of Weymouth Harbour, with six-foot-high waves crashing on the deck of our fishing boat. Kate lapped it up, but some of the other candidates were unhappy about the conditions, and we had to go back to shore. The next night the sea was flat, calm and crystal clear. 'I love it like this too,' Kate said. 'It feels like we're on a proper adventure!' I knew exactly what she meant. There was something exciting and almost primeval about being out on the still sea after dark, a black curtain of sky pulled overhead.

All the staff at Ribcraft had been gutted to hear about Kate's death and couldn't do enough for me when I went looking for a new boat. The one I chose was a rib – a rigid inflatable boat. It had been made for a boat show, and the moment I saw it I knew it had to be ours. Kate would have loved it. It had matt black tubes and the hull was vibrant shiny yellow, which were the type of colours we'd always had on our boats. 'It'll look like a wasp on steroids when we get it on the water,' I joked. 'The boys will be thrilled to bits. I've got to have it!'

I ordered all the extras, such as an A-frame and a towing point to teach Reef and Finn to water-ski, and it had a 100 hp Suzuki engine which would purr beautifully and go like the wind. As a tribute to Kate I was given a hefty discount, and I was very touched. The boys came with me to collect the rib after school.

'What's the new boat like, Daddy?' Reef asked excitedly.

'It's cool,' I said.

'How is it cool?' Finn asked.

'Wait and see,' I said.

I turned the music up in the car, and Reef took control of the iPod, blasting out hits by Rihanna, his favourite singer. Just as we approached Ribcraft Reef switched the music to 'The Boys Are Back in Town' by Thin Lizzy. We were all on a high, and my heart was beating fast as we pulled up outside the showroom.

'We've arrived!' Finn squealed.

I felt a real buzz through my veins. It was a familiar feeling, but one I hadn't felt in ages. I realized it was the first time since Kate's death that I'd felt anything like my old self; anything like happy and normal, let alone excited.

Finn spotted it first, pointing to the shiny black and yellow craft parked up outside the shop.

'Can we have one like that, Daddy?' he said, giggling.

'I'd *love* a boat like that,' Reef said. 'Can we get one like that?'

I let their words hang in the wind for a moment, just to build up the drama.

'That one?' I said, stopping to examine it.

'Yes!' they both shouted. 'Please, Daddy!'

'Yes, OK, we can!' I replied with glee, savouring the moment.

Both boys stared at me in amazement and let out a whoop of delight.

'Reeeeally?' Reef said in disbelief, 'Can we really?'

I put my arms around both boys.

'Yes we can . . . because *that* is our boat, boys!' I announced triumphantly.

I watched as they climbed all over it like a couple of excited ants, cheering and laughing, their eyes shining brightly. I told them she was named *4 Saints*. The boys both have St John as their middle name, so that made three saints including me. As Kate was now kind of on a cloud, I reckoned she was a saint of sorts too. The name seemed just right, especially with my company being called 'Training Saints'.

The boys sat themselves down in the two seats on the

back of the boat, and I asked them to listen carefully for a moment.

'Mummy wanted us to have this boat,' I told them. 'It is Mummy's birthday today, and I think it would be nice if we always called this day "Mum's Day". What do you think?'

'Yes!' Reef said eagerly.

'Yessss, Daddy,' Finn said. 'I like that. Can we go zooming fast in the boat now? How fast can we go?'

One of the salesmen came out to greet us. 'Everything all right, Singe?' he asked.

'You could say that,' I beamed, nodding towards Reef and Finn. 'The boys are in heaven!'

I lifted my eyes to the sky, wondering if Kate was in heaven too, and wondering if she really might be on a cloud, looking down on us.

'Thanks, Kate,' I said when I had a private moment later, just in case she was.

Kate would have loved to have seen the boys' eyes sparkling, just as they did in Lapland. She had made this happen, and I was so grateful I wanted to cry. I would make sure the boys packed in hours and hours of fun on this boat, and I would remember this fantastic gift every year on Kate's birthday.

That weekend we took *4 Saints* out around Bristol docks. The boys were so excited they wanted Coral to join us on our maiden voyage, so I dressed her in a dog-sized life jacket, and the four of us set off. I felt incredibly emotional when we hit the water, like I was setting out on a new journey, a new life without Kate.

'Can't we go any faster?' Finn nagged.

'Faster, faster!' Reef demanded.

'Boys, don't you remember what I said about us having to run the boat in? We have to do about twenty hours of going slow before we can go fast or we'll damage the new engine.'

They were both cross and annoyed and started moaning: 'It's boring!' I rolled my eyes and had one of those moments when I wanted to share a knowing glance with Kate like we used to. Instead I just looked up to the sky. She'd have laughed her head off at the boys' complaining, I just knew it.

Chapter 5

'Mummy liked catching crabs'

'It's your last day on the wardrobe,' I said to Kate. 'The boys are out with Nanny and Gramps, so I thought I'd tell you what I've got planned.' I was whispering, even though I was alone in the house. 'I decided to have your interment on 31 March, our wedding anniversary. I thought that way I'd always have happy memories of that date, as well as sad ones, and when I christen the boys on the same date next year, we'll have even more good memories.'

I tried to smile up at her, but my lips felt frozen in my face. If I moved them I knew the floodgates would open, releasing a waterfall of tears. I sat down on Reef's bed and tried to get a grip of myself. Beside me on his bedside shelf was a picture of Kate and the boys with Father Christmas in Lapland. It had been taken just three months before. Kate's cheeks were pink, and she was smiling proudly, arms placed protectively around the boys, who were dressed in matching blue anoraks. She looked so happy, so well.

I had already placed a few special photos and souvenirs and pictures the boys had made in the basket with her. I hadn't been sure whether she wanted them in her coffin at the funeral or in this basket with her ashes, but I guessed both. I didn't have any experience of cremations and interments; Kate's death had given me a crash course, and I was learning as I went along.

'I've designed you a headstone,' I stuttered.

I remembered her words very clearly. 'Make it special, Singe. You'll know what to do.'

'I've made it personal like you wanted, Kate . . .'

Saying her name out loud set me off, and I barely got the words out before the tears came tumbling down my cheeks, leaving big wet splodges on Reef's blue striped duvet.

My dad is a mason and had arranged the carving of Kate's headstone. I had chosen a piece of black granite and sketched the design I wanted: a spray of flowers including four-leaf clovers, one big daisy, two little daisies in bud and one wilted daisy. I signed it from Singe and the 'Infinity Elves' and added the inscription 'acres and acres'.

I explained all this to Kate through my tears and told her she would be buried in her basket next to her grandparents' grave, as we'd discussed. After the huge funeral, I wanted the interment to be a very small, private affair with just me and the boys and Kate's parents present. Noel, the vicar from the church attached to the boys' school, would carry out the ceremony, as Kate had wished.

I dreaded the finality of the interment and I told Kate as much. I had got used to having her on the wardrobe, and the thought of having her buried in a hole in the ground several miles from home upset me no end.

'We'll come and visit you lots,' I said. 'You won't be alone.'

That night I read the boys a stack of bedtime stories, knowing it would be Kate's last chance to hear them.

'Can we have one more?' Reef asked when we'd already got though at least half a dozen books.

'Oh, go on then!' I said, to squeals of incredulous delight from both boys. 'But after this it's lights out. We have another big day for Mummy tomorrow.'

'Do we get to miss school again?' Reef asked.

'Yes, you do,'

'Yipeeeeeeee!' Finn said.

I wished I could bottle some of that innocence and take a dose myself. I felt sick at the thought of carrying Kate to her final resting place tomorrow and I wondered how much more of this I could take. I felt tired out with grief and I wanted the pain of missing Kate to stop, yet at the same time I didn't want to let her go. I wanted to keep showing her how much I missed her and I wanted to do her memory justice every step of the way.

I slept badly. Spraying Kate's perfume on my pillow didn't help. I hugged the pillow like a little boy, lost and alone. Remembering happy times made me miss her more. Thinking of her slipping away from me, being buried in the ground, completely cracked me up, and willing her back was like the cruellest kind of self-torture, because I knew it was never going to happen. Trying not to think about her at all was another type of hell, one I didn't want either.

The next morning was like a hideous Groundhog Day. Opening my eyes, I had the same thought I had every morning. I remembered Kate was dead and then I looked at her side of the bed just to double-check. Its emptiness confirmed what I felt. I'd lost her. It wasn't a nightmare, and I was wide-awake, acknowledging the loss yet again.

This day I got a double dose of the Groundhog treatment, as the boys and I prepared for part two of Kate's funeral. I was dreading it. This really was the end. I would never touch Kate again, and the last fragments of her body would leave our house for the very last time.

The boys were quiet and thoughtful over breakfast. They knew the drill after Kate's cremation, which was upsetting in itself.

'Reef, look after your brother today,' I instructed.

'We'll be all right,' he said.

'Are we going to school after?' Finn asked.

I think he'd just realized that missing a day off school wasn't necessarily a treat.

'No, not today. We're just saying goodbye to Mummy again today.'

'Oh, OK then,' he shrugged sadly.

When the moment finally came in the churchyard of St Andrew's Church in Clevedon, it wasn't half as bad as I feared it would be. Kate's grandparents are buried in cliff-top plots overlooking the Bristol Channel. Behind the church's boundary hedge is a path running along the cliffs, forming the stunning Poet's Walk, which is famous for inspiring great writers like Tennyson, Thackeray and Coleridge. I couldn't have wished for a more perfect spot.

We put Kate in above her grandparents, placing her closest to the boundary. Reef pointed to a gap in the hedge, through which you could see the Channel. 'Mummy can keep an eye on us when we are on the boat,' he said.

Kate's little basket was sealed in the ground with her gravestone, which was laid flat over the top of her. It took a little while to complete the job, as the hole in the ground wasn't quit big enough for the basket to fit, and more earth had to be dug out. Trust Kate, I thought, creating a little drama right up until the end, showing the world she wasn't going willingly. The poets who'd walked this path would have had a field day with that idea, I reckoned.

I surrounded Kate's gravestone with a pretty white border of shells we'd gathered on our travels, and a robin sang cheerfully as Noel performed a simple ceremony. I felt very thankful Kate had been buried in such a beautiful spot. It was a great comfort to know that, whenever we were out in the boat, she could watch over us and we could look up to her, through the gap in the hedge. I scattered wildflower seeds around Kate's grave too, which I knew she would love.

When the ceremony was over I felt unexpectedly happy. I can't think of a better word to describe the feeling. I felt Kate was at peace and I was so relieved and reassured by that. I think the boys felt it too, as they each gave Kate's gravestone a poignant little smile and a wave before we left. It was more than two months since her death, and it suddenly felt right she had finally left the wardrobe, and right that we had to walk away now, without her.

'Can we come and see Mummy ever again?' Finn asked thoughtfully.

'Of course we can! We can come up here whenever we want, and we can wave up to her when we're out on the boat too.'

'Good,' he smiled, looking at his feet shyly. 'Mummy was kind and nice.'

'Yes, she was. She loved you boys very much indeed.'

As we slowly walked away Finn suddenly spun round to look at the grave again.

'Bye bye, Mummy,' he said, giving another little wave before turning to me and saying breezily: 'I love you, Daddy.'

It was usually Reef who hit a nerve, but Finn did it in spectacular style that day.

'I love you too,' I said, my voice wobbling.

'Are you crying, Daddy?' Finn asked.

'Yes, you little monkey. You set me off a treat!' I spluttered, trying to lighten the mood.

'Sorry.'

'Don't be sorry. Sometimes it's good to cry.'

I realized Reef was really quiet. He's always been the more thoughtful of the two boys, and I figured perhaps he was finding things a little tougher as he was that bit older. Kate's grave is very close to that of a young boy we knew who had died of cancer, but I wasn't sure if Reef remembered him or had even seen the grave. I didn't mention it because I didn't want to make Reef any glummer, and we all drove away in silence.

'Daddy, what will happen if my cancer comes back?' Reef asked.

It was a couple of weeks after Kate's interment when he landed that question on me, and I was immediately transported back to the graveyard, remembering how quiet and thoughtful he was that day. It should have been obvious really, I thought. I ought to have worked out what was playing on his little mind that day, on top of everything else.

Now we were in the car on the way to the hospital for his routine MRI scan. Doctors were pleased with Reef's progress, and his cancer was showing no signs of returning, but he still needed regular scans and check-ups and would be tested throughout his childhood, just to be on the safe side. I was not looking forward to the appointment. It was the first big one without Kate, and I wondered how Reef would cope without his mum's hand to hold.

Kate was phenomenal when Reef was ill. Even when she was heavily pregnant with Finn she was with Reef every step of the way, always ready with a soothing word, a cuddle or a packet of crayons produced at just the right moment to make him feel better. She put her own feelings to one side time and time again, even when it meant pinching Reef's arm to make him cry before an MRI scan, so he'd inhale the anaesthetic to knock him out and make him lie still in the machine. It broke her heart time and time again, but she did it for him because he was too afraid to go in the body scanner when he was awake.

What would Kate say to Reef now? How would she answer that awful question that was hanging in the air between us: 'What if my cancer comes back?'

'Please teach them to say what they mean.'

I turned the music off in the car.

'We'll cross that bridge if we ever come to it,' I said to Reef.

'What do you mean?' he asked earnestly.

'I mean, I don't know, Reef. I can't see into the future.'

'Will I die like Mummy? Mummy's lump made her die. Will my lump make me die?'

'Reef, nobody knows what's in the future. What we do know is that the doctors took away your lump and made you better, and you're doing really, really well.'

Reef said nothing, and I hoped I'd been as truthful and tactful as Kate would have wanted me to be.

'Another thing we know is that, when Mummy died, she left us a list of special things she wanted us to do,' I said slightly clumsily. I had a sing-song tone to my voice which sounded fake to my ears, but I carried on regardless, hoping Reef didn't spot it. 'One of those things is to go caravanning – so that's what we're doing later this week! First we have to see the doctor and have your scan, just to check you over, make sure you're fit and well.'

'Can we fly kites on holiday?'

'Yes, we can,' I said, letting out a sigh of relief.

I wished I could turn the car around, go down to the beach and fly a kite right now, but instead I drove on to the Bristol Royal Infirmary. How many times had I driven this route with Kate, both for Reef's treatment and for hers? How much longer would cancer go on interfering with our lives? I suddenly felt ashamed of the thought. I had so much to be grateful for, compared to Kate. She would have given anything to hold Reef's hand today.

I remembered seeing Kate holding Reef for the very first time, clasping his tiny little hand in hers when he was newborn. A look of incredible love filled her face, like a maternal light had been switched on. She looked radiant and fulfilled, and it was a look that became wonderfully familiar.

'Singe, isn't he beautiful?' she cooed. 'I can't believe he's ours.'

I could scarcely believe it either. We had first tried for a baby four or five years earlier, a couple of years after we married, but Kate suffered a miscarriage. It was absolutely awful, something I would rather forget. She was scared and she cried when she had to go into hospital because it reminded her of being a child, having operations to have her tonsils and adenoids removed. I wanted to protect her, like she was a little girl all over again.

If I'm honest, I was in no rush to try again for a baby after that experience, but when Kate didn't get pregnant month after month she began to worry.

'Singe, what if that was our only chance to have a baby? What if I can't get pregnant again?' she fretted.

'I just know we'll have kids together one day,' I always soothed. 'It will happen, we just have to be patient. Don't worry.'

Kate couldn't help but worry. I found it quite difficult to get my head around her reaction, because she was certainly not what you might describe as the 'maternal type' back then, far from it. First and foremost Kate was an action girl and an adrenaline junkie. Even though I was very sad and sorry about the miscarriage, it didn't make me panic. I knew Kate would make a brilliant mum one day, when the time was right.

'We've got plenty of time before we need to worry,' I reasoned. 'And we've got plenty of things we want to do together in the meantime. Perhaps it's just not the right time yet. Let nature take its course.'

Kate wasn't at all convinced by my words. The miscarriage had made her anxious, and she felt she was somehow letting the side down, not providing me with children, or her parents with grandchildren. We went for tests, and Kate was diagnosed with the fairly common condition of polycystic ovaries, which we learned makes it more difficult to get pregnant, but by no means make it impossible.

Kate was only just into her thirties by this point, and we had years and years stretching ahead of us, or so we thought. The diagnosis reassured her, up to a point. We both agreed not to obsess about pregnancy every month, but to use the extra time to tick a few more things off our 'to-do' list before we settled into parenthood.

A year went by, and we went on holiday to Tobago. Looking back, I can't believe how simple life was in those days. Apart from the miscarriage, nothing bad ever happened to us. We sailed through life, seizing opportunities, always planning the next big adventure. Kate wasn't pregnant, so we went on holiday. Life was that straightforward, though I must admit she was getting steadily more broody, month by month.

During that holiday, I remember sitting on a pontoon together, soaking up the sun after a dive in the Caribbean Sea. We'd just swapped smiley glances after we heard a dad making his little boy giggle like mad.

'What an amazing giggle,' Kate said. 'I wonder what our children's giggles will sound like?'

'Have you heard yourself?' I teased. 'You were talking about booking up to dive the Blue Hole yesterday.'

'Blue Hole, Belize, when the boys are good enough divers.' The Blue Hole – one of the most astounding dive sites on the planet – was on my and Kate's wish list long before it was on Mum's List. We'd started looking into flights and hotels, hoping to make it our latest big 'hurrah' as 'DINKYs' – the acronym for a couple with 'Dual Income No Kids Yet'.

'We can do both,' she grinned. 'Kids won't change us. I want to do *everything* with you.'

The ringing of the children's laughter mixed with Kate's romantic words was incredibly alluring. Kate was looking very sexy in a skimpy black bikini. The sun was warming our bodies as we watched the dive boat disappear, and I kissed her passionately. I wanted to father Kate's children, and I felt so blessed that such an awesome woman wanted my babies, our babies. We made a pact to seek more medical help when we got home, and also to book the holiday to Belize and the Blue Hole.

Without hesitation our doctor prescribed the fertility drug Clomid to boost Kate's chances of conceiving, but he warned it could still take years to get pregnant because of the polycystic ovaries. We discussed the possibility of IVF if the fertility drug failed, and Kate and I both agreed we should look into starting treatment once we returned from the Blue Hole.

Kate wanted to upgrade her scuba-diving qualifications before such a major dive holiday, and we decided to book a trip to Tenerife so she could do an intensive scuba instructor's course in the sunshine. In the meantime, Kate was very keen we should keep 'practising' for a baby. I could be wearing rubber gloves, up to my armpits in washing up, or packing up life jackets in the garage when she'd pounce without warning.

'No time like the present,' she would purr, eyes glinting saucily, already pulling at my clothing.

Making love with Kate was always amazing, and making babies was absolutely mind-blowing.

'This won't take long, with all this practising,' I joked, but still Kate didn't fall pregnant.

We went to Tenerife in November 2003. I remember two events very clearly during that holiday. England won the Rugby World Cup, and Kate uttered the life-changing words: 'I'm late. I think I'm pregnant.'

'Shut up!' I replied, stunned. 'Don't be stupid!'

She was only halfway through her scuba course, and this wasn't what I expected to hear at all. I think I'd conditioned myself to believe the baby would arrive as ordered, after the Blue Hole and before we had to go down the road of IVF.

Kate's instinct was true, of course. She was actually pregnant, and when the test confirmed it once we returned home we both cried buckets.

'Are you crying because we can't do the Blue Hole right now or because you're going to be a daddy?' Kate mocked.

'The Blue Hole will still be there when the baby is old enough to come with us,' I said. 'I thought you said kids wouldn't change our lifestyle. Does that answer your question?'

'Yes, we'll all go together,' she beamed. 'You, me, and our children.'

'Steady on, how many are we having?'

'I'd like three,' she said.

'Three?!' I spluttered.

'Yes, three,' she said, rolling her eyes and planting a kiss on my lips that made my heart melt. 'You know I've always wanted three!'

'Let's have the first one, and take it from there,' I smiled.

We chose the name Coral for a girl and Reef if we had a boy, derived from Tenerife as well as from the coral reefs we loved to explore.

A few months on I videoed one of Kate's baby scans at the hospital, even though you're not meant to, and there was no mistaking we had a little boy on the way.

'Hello, Reef,' Kate waved ecstatically at the ultrasound screen.

I can remember our excitement, the sheer thrill of having our baby growing inside Kate, and seeing his outline on the screen. It gave me the biggest adrenaline rush of my life, and that's saying something.

Now here I was, taking Reef for an MRI scan without his mummy. Our tiny little miracle had grown into a lively five-year-old boy, against so many odds.

Reef turned the music back on in the car as I drove on to the hospital, and I was surprised when he selected OPM's 'Brighter Side'. I'd forgotten the track was even on my iPod, but Reef found it that day as we headed into Bristol.

'Listen to this,' he said. 'It reminds me of Mummy.'

He whacked up the volume, and the words hit me like an avalanche. I bit my lip to stop the tears falling, but it was no use. I'd heard the song countless times before, but now every line sounded like it was written for Kate. I imagined her as the song said, a beautiful soul in a brighter place, yet still always a part of us, as the moon is always a part of the sea. Just as the lyrics said, every moment she lived was a blessing to us. Now she had flown away we had to carry on without her, but everything was going to be all right.

'Does it remind you of Mummy too?' Reef asked innocently, catching my eye in the rear-view mirror.

‘Yes, Reef,’ I said in a cracked voice, failing to hide my emotions. ‘Sorry, Reef, you really got me there,’ I added, sniffing and wiping my eyes. ‘That really does remind me of Mummy.’

‘Are you all right, Daddy?’

‘Yes, Reef. Are you?’

‘Everything’s gonna be all right,’ he nodded, mimicking the song and smiling.

Kate’s mum met me at the hospital.

‘Thought you might be glad of some help,’ Christine said kindly.

‘I’m always glad of help with little Mike Tyson here,’ I joked, reminiscing about the time Reef got so fed up with the anaesthetist he clocked him one right under the chin.

Now Reef was five I hoped he might be able to manage going in the scanner without a fight, and without being unconscious. To my relief he agreed to give it a go.

‘Do I get a present afterwards?’ he asked cheekily.

‘Yes,’ Christine and I replied in unison.

The scanner makes a horrible drumming and clicking sound, and I put some headphones on Reef so he could listen to music instead. I also managed to stand in a position where I could hold his hand and he could see me while the machine did its work. He had to stay still for more than twenty minutes, which was a heck of a big ask, but he did it.

‘Well done, you did amazingly well, Reef,’ I told him afterwards.

‘Can I have the remote-controlled car, the one with lasers on?’

‘Yes you can,’ I agreed.

‘You have to get one for Finn too so we can do battles.

If I knock out three of his lights he's OUT!' he told me, clearly reciting something he'd heard on an advert.

After the scan Reef had to go through the usual routine of giving blood samples and being weighed, prodded and poked by doctors and nurses.

'Everything looks as it should be,' a doctor said eventually. 'We should get the MRI results back in three to four days' time.'

The waiting was torturous, despite the doctor's positive attitude, and I couldn't concentrate on anything else. The following evening I sat alone on the sofa, watching the boys do battle with their laser cars. They were completely enthralled, which was just as well, as the cars Reef chose had set me back about £70, which was a lot more than I had bargained for, the cheeky monkey.

I thought back to when Reef was a baby, and Kate sat with him in the same spot on this sofa, worrying about his high temperature.

'It's not normal, Singe,' she fretted. 'He's got a temperature of thirty-nine degrees.'

Reef was nine months old and had recently had his MMR jab, which we were warned could cause a fever and make him unsettled. Up until this point he had been a lively bundle of trouble, already able to walk, which was incredibly early. Now, though, he was as white as a ghost and floppy in the evenings, and he was so hot you could feel the heat radiating through his baby-grow. We gave him Calpol at first, and when that didn't work we took him back to the doctor, again and again. Eventually, when Reef showed no improvement, and days stretched into weeks, it was suggested he could have reactive arthritis, a possible side effect of the MMR jab. It was explained to us that this can cause temporary pain and swelling in the joints, which would hopefully disappear without treatment. Kate was horrified; we both were.

'So we just have to wait and see?' Kate said, incredulous that giving her baby a routine immunization might have had such a devastating effect. 'Singe, this is a nightmare.'

I remember Kate's words clearly, because we really had walked into a nightmare, although we had absolutely no idea just how hideous that nightmare was. Now, five years on, I was still worrying and waiting, and I was doing it on my own. It was incredibly tough, despite the fact Reef was doing so well, and the worst of the nightmare was over.

The phone rang in the living room, making me jump.

'How did you get on at the hospital?' Ruth asked.

'No news yet, we've got clinic on Thursday.'

'What? You have to wait two more days for the results?'

''Fraid so, you know how it is.'

'How was Reef?'

'Awesome! We didn't have to gas him.'

'That's great, Singe, well done you! Let me know as soon as you know?'

I promised I would, and I was very grateful for Ruth's call. She made me focus on what an achievement it had been to get Reef though the MRI not only without his mum, but without the anaesthetic. He'd done brilliantly, and deep down I had a good feeling about the results. Still, as Finn would say, I had two more sleeps to get through before I knew for certain, and they weren't peaceful.

I felt exhausted when I finally walked into the clinic on

the Thursday, and I could scarcely believe my ears when the doctor delivered the news.

'The scan is all clear,' he told me with a smile.

I have to say, I felt more relieved than jubilant. Perhaps I was just too tired to do celebratory cartwheels down the corridor, or perhaps my self-preservation instinct had kicked in. We thought Kate's cancer had gone, but then it came back. I'd learned not to get carried away with cancer results, because you never really know what's around the corner. The words 'all clear' were undoubtedly encouraging, but we were only four years on from the start of Reef's treatment. He was not officially in remission, and I knew all too well that receiving an 'all clear' after the all-important five-year check would be far more significant. I also felt lonely, I realized, not having Kate with me to share this good news.

'It's a great result,' I told Ruth later.

'Singe! You must be so delighted,' she replied.

'Yes, it's absolutely brilliant news,' I said, though I was not feeling 100 per cent brilliant in myself. I was delighted with Reef's news, of course, but I missed Kate so much. I wanted her to scoop our little boy in her arms and kiss him and tell him how brave he was. I wanted her to see how we were moving further away from the nightmare that had started more than five years earlier, but I couldn't. Kate wasn't even on the wardrobe now. I was well and truly on my own, and she had missed out on this heartening step forward.

The next day we were going on our Easter holiday. I'd agreed to take the boys caravanning to Ruda Holiday Park in Croyde Bay, Devon, with about twenty-odd members of Kate's side of the family. Kate loved that sort of holiday, because it's what she did as a child, and it brought back happy memories.

I hate caravanning. I never could see the point of sleeping in a box in a field when you could go home to your own comfortable bed. To me holidays are all about spoiling yourself and being waited on hand and foot. Caravanning reminded me of work; I'd organized countless camping trips for Duke of Edinburgh Award students and always enjoyed them, but roughing it was not something I wanted to do in my leisure time.

I remembered the last time I went caravanning with Kate's extended family. It was Easter 2008, and we were completely worn out after nursing Reef through his chemo and radiotherapy treatment for practically three years. Finn was an extremely boisterous two-year-old by then. I remember feeling absolutely shattered as we packed up the car with a ridiculous amount of stuff. It was bad enough packing for a camping trip at the best of times, but with two very young children we needed everything from a travel cot, bottles and nappies for Finn to wipes, toys and a mind-boggling collection of medicines for Reef. Both boys began playing up the minute I started the engine, kicking the back of our seats, wailing and asking for drinks.

'I don't know why I ever agreed to this,' I snapped at Kate. 'I must be completely insane!'

Kate looked upset and tried to calm me down.

'We'll enjoy it once we're there,' she soothed. 'The break will do us all good. I do appreciate the effort you're making, Singe.'

'OK, but this is the very last time I'm doing this!' I huffed.

The boys eventually fell asleep, and Kate and I ignored each other. After a while the frosty silence was replaced with the extremely noisy sound of the engine straining up Telegraph Hill, less than halfway into our journey. I'd burned out about three clutches on that steep hill, and I suddenly recognized the warning sounds. Moments later we clunked to an abrupt halt, and smoke started billowing from the engine.

'I don't believe it!' I bellowed. 'That's all we need! We've broken down!'

Both boys woke up and stared crying. We had to call the RAC, and by the time the rescue vehicle arrived I think I had more steam coming out of my ears than the car did from its bonnet.

'You just don't want to spend any time with my family,' Kate accused hotly. 'You've been difficult about this whole trip right from the start!'

'I wish I'd never agreed to this in the first place,' I retorted. 'I go along with it and all I get is a load of earache and criticism. I don't know why I bother.'

We continued to row the whole way there and were still absolutely furious with each other when we arrived at the campsite. It was obvious to everyone what foul tempers we were in. Kate was embarrassed in front of her family, and I was not in the mood to make an effort and keep the peace, so the atmosphere was tense and visibly hostile.

'There is no way I'm sleeping in a caravan after the day I've had,' I shouted as soon as the car was unpacked.

'Good!' Kate replied.

'That's it, I'm going home!' I retorted.

'Told you!' Kate spat. 'You just don't want to spend time with my family!'

'I hate caravanning, Kate, not your family! Give me a break!'

I'd been there all of twenty minutes, and I drove the two-hour journey home alone, feeling absolutely livid. Kate phoned me later that night, when we'd both calmed down.

'You probably did the right thing,' she said generously. 'I think caravanning is one thing we have to agree to disagree on.'

'I'm sorry, Kate. I miss you. Kiss the boys for me. Acres and acres.'

'Acres and acres.'

We never went to bed on a row. *'Never leave more than a week before making up – life is too short.'*

When Kate put that on her list I promised I would always remember that phone call and teach the boys to kiss and make up as quickly as possible.

Now I packed up the car ready for just me and the boys. The next morning an excited Finn raced into the kitchen at the crack of dawn wearing sunglasses and a cap and with a rucksack already on his back, bulging with books and toys.

'Can we go now, Daddy? Can we?' he asked excitedly.

'We certainly can, as soon as you've eaten up your breakfast,' I smiled, ruffling his hair.

Reef appeared, looking bright-eyed and bushy-tailed.

'I can't wait to see Nanny,' he said.

'That's nice,' I said.

'She's got me a new game for my DS for doing the scan.'

My heart went out to him. It wasn't out of the ordinary for Reef to talk about scans. He knew more than a child his age ever should about hospitals and cancer, and I vowed in that moment to do my level best to make this holiday as much fun as possible.

'Come on, happy campers!' I said, and the three of us climbed into the Freelander with a spring in our step.

Despite our argument, Kate remained a devotee of family caravan holidays and *'Go caravanning with cousins or let boys go for long weekends'* was right up there at the top of Mum's List. She had thoughtfully given me a get-out clause, knowing her parents would always take the boys caravanning with them if I didn't want to go. It was too soon after her death for that, I thought. I wanted to be with Reef and Finn as much as possible, even if it did mean sleeping in a box in a field.

The car was rammed from floor to ceiling with kites, snorkelling equipment and buckets and spades, and we played loud music and told each other silly jokes all the way down to Ruda.

'What do you call a man with a spade in his head?' I said.

'Don't know! Tell us, Daddy!' said Finn.

'Doug!' I said.

'Da-ddddy, that's soooo silly!' Reef chuckled. 'Tell us another one!'

The sun was shining when we arrived at the campsite, and the holiday park seemed quieter than I remembered it. I soon realized why; the ash cloud from the Icelandic volcano eruption had grounded flights, so the sky above was unusually silent and still. I explained this to the boys, and Reef thought for a moment before saying, 'Mummy won't be able to send us any kisses.' It had become something of a hobby for the boys to spot white kisses in the sky, ever since the day Kate died and they saw the two planes leaving a perfect cross above us. Even so, I didn't see that comment coming.

'It won't be for long,' I said, feeling choked and completely taken aback at how Reef had managed to get me once again, out of the blue.

The boys and I soon got into a routine of me cooking bacon and eggs for breakfast and the kids invading Nanny and Grandad's caravan and playing with various cousins, aunts and uncles before we flew kites together or headed to the pool or the beach.

Kate's family were brilliant. We had about eight caravans between us, and there was always a familiar face around. Everyone offered practical help and support, and I was rarely alone, but I still felt incredibly lonely without Kate.

'Mummy took us down there,' Finn said, pointing to some rock pools on the beach one morning.

'Mummy was very good at catching crabs,' Reef said.

'I know,' I said. 'Do you remember that day when we all went rock-pooling at Llantwit Major and Mummy picked up that really big crab?'

Both boys nodded. They were only little when we did that, I thought. It was well over a year ago, and perhaps they remembered the fantastic photograph we took that day more than the day itself, as we had it framed and displayed at home.

'We *have* to take the boys to Llantwit,' Kate said. 'I can't wait to teach them how to crab.'

It was spring 2009 when the four of us went there. Kate was flying through her chemo and was already talking about when her treatment would be over, and how she couldn't wait to have her long-awaited reconstruction.

'I'm not going to put my life on hold,' she said so many times, and she was true to her word. If Kate wanted to do something, there was no time like the present. She told the boys all about her childhood trips to Llantwit on our journey there that spring.

'Me and my cousins and your Uncle Ben would walk down the path from the caravan park to the beach,' she said. 'It was a long path and would take us about half a day, but it was always worth the walk. When we got to the beach we went rock-pooling for hours and hours, catching lots of crabs and shrimps.'

I chipped in. 'Mummy is too modest to tell you she was the champion crab-catcher,' I told the boys conspiratorially. 'Just you wait 'til you see her in action – she's awesome!'

Kate laughed.

'I had my own rock,' she went on. 'And I'd sit on it for hours and hours, catching crabs. I hope we can find it.'

For old times' sake, we decided to park up at the campsite and follow Kate's well-trodden path down to the beach. We took the buggy for Reef, worrying it would be too far for him to walk. Much to my amusement, we'd only been walking for about ten minutes when we reached the beach, and I teased Kate mercilessly.

'A half-day trek, you said! It's a hop, skip and a jump!'

She was amazed. 'Honestly, it felt like a major hike back

then,' she laughed. 'Isn't it funny what time and age does to you?'

It was very easy to find Kate's old rock, as the patch of beach the path took us to didn't have that many rocks to choose from, which was another surprise. From Kate's starry-eyed description anyone would have expected a vast, rambling landscape filled with rock pools galore as far as the eye could see. Kate was very excited when she sat on the old rock and crouched down over the pool of cloudy water, and Reef and Finn were as captive an audience as anyone could wish for.

I loved her so much. She had no hair but was wearing a wig, and she had a 'Picc line' tube dangling from her arm, which led up her arm and across her chest to a large vein just above her heart, to deliver chemo and other drugs. When she had the alarmingly long piece of tubing inserted under local anaesthetic, just thinking about it made me cringe and cower. Kate shrugged and just got on with it, accepting that with the amount of drugs she needed, it was the most efficient method of receiving them, and there was no point in worrying about it.

'Wait for it, wait for it . . .' she cautioned, before expertly scooping up a wonderful specimen of a crab.

The boys shrieked with glee.

'Daddy, look what Mummy's caught!' said Reef.

Before he knew it she'd scooped up another crab, which she gave to him to hold, carefully showing him how to handle it.

'I told you she was a champion,' I said, smiling at Kate as I got the three of them to pose for a photograph.

I absolutely love that photo. Kate was in her element,

and she looked so well and happy, her eyes glowing with love for her little boys as she shared their fun. Nobody could have guessed she had cancer, and I felt that day was a great landmark in her recovery. We had an ice cream, and Kate said: 'We must do this again next year.' To anybody watching we were just a normal family on a day trip to the beach; a happily married couple with two cute little boys wearing matching grins and T-shirts.

Soon we really would be normal again. Soon Kate's treatment would be over, and soon we would be lying on the beach, just as we did when Reef's treatment had ended the year before, saying; 'We made it!' At least, that's what I hoped and prayed and fully expected would happen.

I managed to give the boys a good holiday at Ruda, but it wasn't easy by any stretch. After our falling-out in 2008, Kate had done the trip on her own with the boys in 2009. Now it was my turn to be on my own, and I had a constant feeling that I was walking in Kate's footsteps. '*Would like you to take them for walks along Mummy's favourite beach where she used to go as a child,*' Kate said. She had several favourite beaches as well as the one at Llantwit Major, and Croyde Bay near the caravan park was one of them.

I took the boys there and felt bereft. I had some bubble gum in my pocket, and this felt like one of those moments when we should all have a piece.

'Why are you sad, Daddy?' Finn asked, when he saw my face flush with emotion as I dished out the gum.

'It's special to come to one of Mummy's favourite places,' I explained.

He nodded and scampered off along the shore to find crabs with his brother.

'This is how you do it,' I heard Reef saying to Finn, who had begun splashing around like a maniac in a rock pool, no doubt frightening off every crab on the coast.

'You've got to be gentle and quiiiii-et!' Reef shouted as they both grabbed at the water.

'Come on, boys, let's try another pool, how about that one over there? Can I have a try this time?'

I could just hear Kate saying that, but the words came from my mouth. For an uncomfortable moment I felt I was trying to actually *be* Kate, and I didn't like it. Even her family expected me to be like Kate and do exactly what she did or might have done; at least, that's how I felt.

They knew Kate as the perfect daughter, the devoted mother, the caring, fun-loving sister, cousin, niece or auntie. She was all of those things, but I knew a Kate nobody else did. She was my blonde, passionate, gorgeous wife and lover. Nobody else knew that side of Kate, and nor should they. That was our private life, but on that holiday it made me feel slightly disconnected from the rest of the family. I could join in when they occasionally shared an old family story about Kate, but they didn't know the half of my life with Kate and all the wonderful memories we had. Only I and Kate knew; and now I had nobody to share them with.

'Come back, Kate, all is forgiven,' somebody said one day when I spilt sun cream on Reef's T-shirt. The words were meant as a light-hearted tribute to Kate, praising her skills as a mum, but they shocked me. I knew it was just a way of remembering Kate, of referring to her without really talking about her. I could see that, but I didn't like it.

I would have been much happier to have a heart to heart, to sit down and really reminisce about Kate, than to hear obtuse references about what a great mother she was.

I bit my tongue and rather begrudgingly accepted I had to fit in with lots of other people, all of who loved and missed Kate in their own different ways. The last day was the worst. We visited a dinosaur park, where we quite literally retraced Kate's footsteps. It felt like the boys spent the entire day saying: 'Mummy did this' and 'Mummy did that' as they worked their way around the attractions, and it was draining.

I could clearly envisage Kate explaining all about meat-eaters and plant-eaters, calling the boys over to look at the dinosaur eggs and fossils and laughing her head off when the giant model velociraptor shook its head and roared angrily, making visitors jump out of their skin.

There was a bit of light relief at one point, when Reef was so desperate for the loo he had to nip behind a bush. Hilariously, he waited until the model T-rex was looking the other way and whispered conspiratorially: 'Hope he doesn't turn round now or we're all in BIG trouble!' It was a funny moment, and I laughed. It reminded me of a similar occasion, during Reef's treatment, when he had made Kate laugh on a caravan holiday to Wales, as he tiptoed into a wood and spent ages picking out a suitable bush, where nobody would see him.

I realized so much of the pleasure of family days out came from seeing Kate's reaction to the boys. Normally on days out like that we'd hold hands, walking just behind the boys so we could keep an eye on them and enjoy seeing their reactions. Now I felt lonely, smiling away to myself.

In the restaurant the boys and I sat at what turned out to be the exact table Kate had sat at with them the previous April, practically a year to the day in fact.

'Mummy had a HUGE strawberry ice cream!' Reef remembered when he looked at the menu card.

'Mummy catched a butterfly,' Finn said later. 'Can you catch one, Daddy?'

'No,' I said instinctively. 'Mummy was really good at catching butterflies, much better than me. I can't do everything as well as Mummy did, you know.'

There was a slightly awkward silence and both boys studied my face.

'That's OK, Daddy,' Reef said eventually. 'You are still cool, you know.'

'Gimme five,' I said, grinning as I raised my hands. Both boys gave me a 'high five', and we climbed in the car.

I felt relieved as we drove home. I'd not only survived the holiday, I'd learned from it. I didn't have to be a clone of Kate to keep the boys happy. In fact, it wouldn't be right if I tried to copy Kate. She was their mum, and she was a hard act to follow. It was right to keep her memory alive, but it was also right to let the boys know things were different now.

Chapter 6

'Mummy liked walks along the beach and Mendips, rock-pooling and walks in the woods and finding creatures of all kinds'

'How long before I start big school, Daddy?' Finn asked one morning.

He was still at the lovely little Montessori nursery Kate had first chosen for Reef in Clevedon, but he was desperate to join his big brother at All Saints School.

'Well, it's nearly June, and you start in September,' I said. Finn looked a bit blank. 'It's lots and lots and lots of sleeps – about a hundred,' I explained. 'There are about eight more weeks left before the summer holidays, and then about six weeks off, and then you start big school.'

Finn's face fell. 'That's aaages and aaaages,' he complained. 'Why can't I go now!'

He raced off up to the spare room before I could answer, and I heard him batter his toy drum kit for all it was worth. It had been given to him as a gift from a neighbour, who had heard about Kate's wish for him to learn drums, and he absolutely loved it.

'Be quiet, Finn,' Reef shouted from their bedroom. 'Why are you always so LOUD!'

Reef was reading a book, and I realized how quickly both boys were growing up. It didn't seem five minutes since they were crawling around in nappies and now, to my delight, I suddenly saw them as two little men who were developing their own amazing characters at a rate of knots. I thought about Kate's list. I'd done so many things already, but I wondered now if I was ticking things off quickly enough. Even some of the simple things hadn't been arranged, like recorder or guitar lessons for Reef and drum and keyboard classes for Finn. When Kate was alive I always wanted to be the perfect husband, because Kate was such a perfect wife. Now she was gone I still wanted to be her perfect husband, but was I managing it? Reef and Finn would soon both be at school, and before I knew it they would need me less and less. What if I actually didn't complete the list before the boys grew up? I couldn't live with myself if I let Kate down.

I went upstairs and picked up the copy of Mum's List from my bedside table. It was the first time I'd really studied it in months, and I scanned it quickly at first, before savouring the words. I looked across to Kate's side of the bed.

'Always help them if they ask,' she said.

'Of course I will,' I said, feeling slightly puzzled. I thought what an obvious thing that was to ask me to do. She knew I would always help them, even without them having to ask, and certainly without the need for it to be spelt out on the list. Now, though, I saw a deeper meaning. The boys would *always* need me. I would still be their dad when they were grown up and had children of their own. I realized lots of other things on the list would always stay with us too, no matter how much time passed.

I looked at the little things Kate had detailed that she liked and disliked. *'Loved guinea pigs and butterflies, Walnut*

Whips, strawberry cheesecake.' 'Did not like windy weather.' 'Like wild flowers – red campion, cuckoo spit, daisies, primroses and flowers in wedding arrangement.' 'Mummy loved moths, snakes and slow-worms, orange Club biscuits, jam and jelly, lemon curd.' 'Did not like tomatoes unless in sauce or soup.' 'Mummy loved ivory roses, ivy, gypsophila.'

I stared at the words and they became images, projected on to my brain like video clips, showing Kate cuddling our guinea pigs in the back garden, then peeling the wrapper off an orange Club biscuit and picking up a knife to spread lemon curd on her toast. I saw Kate getting all narked up on the beach as she tried to pack up the jet-ski and the wind blew her hair in her face. She hated the wind, she really did. In the next clip I saw her holding her wedding bouquet, which was packed with the prettiest ivory roses and gypsophila I'd ever seen, and Kate gave a broad, contented smile as she leaned forward and breathed the sweet perfume of the flowers.

When she wrote those things I saw them as touching, personal details of her life, but I didn't view them with the same importance as the instructions and requests she included. Now I saw them in a different light. They were incredibly important reminders of Kate that might otherwise have been lost and forgotten in time. They were things I could tell the boys any time I wanted, poignant reminders of Kate that would stay with us throughout our lifetimes.

I gazed at Mum's List for a long time. For the first time, I noticed how Kate had written it in the past tense when she was talking about herself. She knew there was no 'if' about it when I asked, 'What if you leave me?' 'If' was not a word she used. She knew before I did that it was a question of *when* she would leave me, not *if*.

I took a deep breath, thinking how strong and brave she was. I had a lifetime to care for Reef and Finn, and there was no need to rush through anything on the list. Kate would not want her list to be dashed off as quickly as possible, and that thought was comforting and liberating.

Another item caught my attention: *'Mummy liked walks along the beach and Mendips, rock-pooling and walks in the woods and finding creatures of all kinds.'* Priddy was always our favourite spot in the Mendips. It has natural springs, and if you know where to look you can find a huge variety of leeches, toads, frogs, lizards, snakes and newts.

'We don't need a rug, the grass is like a rug!' Kate giggled the first time I took her there, when we were courting.

'Do you know why it's so smooth?' I asked her.

'No, tell me.'

'There are millions of rabbits round here and they've nibbled the grass down so it always looks newly mown.'

She was delighted with that fact.

'Where's the best place to look for slowworms?' she asked. 'I really love slowworms.'

Kate was special. I loved that earthy side to her, and it never left her. Years later I ran courses taking groups out on mountain bikes in Priddy. Kate helped me develop interesting routes, always ensuring we avoided areas of precious fauna, to protect the natural habitat. In more recent years we spoilt ourselves from time to time with special picnics there. I'd make saucisson sandwiches with our favourite crusty tiger bread and butter, and we'd take the bottle of champagne from the glove compartment in the car and chill it amongst the reeds in the spring until it was ice-cold.

'Who's driving?' Kate asked the last time.

'Me,' I replied.

'Just one glass for you then, Singe.'

'It's a deal, but you know what that means?' I replied.

Kate giggled. It meant she could get tipsy, and I got to take her to bed.

'Deal,' she said, leaning over to kiss me as passionately as we did decades earlier, when we lay on a blanket having midnight picnics.

We both loved teaching the boys to explore at Priddy Pools, the perfect spot for kids.

'Why are we hunting here, there's nothing to see!' Reef said one time.

'Come with me,' Kate said, taking his hand. 'Let's lift up this stone and see, shall we?'

Reef's little face lit up when he saw the collection of bugs his mummy unearthed.

'Now you can't say there's nothing to see, can you? Shall we look for snakes next? Some of them are poisonous here, but most aren't. I'll tell you how to spot the difference . . .'

Both boys loved Priddy, but, with everything we'd been through recently, I think a whole year had passed without us going there for a picnic. I'd certainly not taken the boys since Kate's death.

'Boys, shall we go and have a picnic at Priddy?' I called up the stairs. Finn's drumming stopped immediately.

'Yeeeeessssss!' they both shouted down.

'Can Kirsty come?' Reef added.

Kirsty is our babysitter, and she's also a brilliant mate.

She'd been a fantastic help over the past few months, and the boys adored her. She's only in her twenties and is always a breath of fresh air to have around. Kate adored her too.

'I'll ring her,' I said without hesitation, dialling Kirsty's number.

'Singe, I'd love to come!' Kirsty said moments later. 'Thanks for inviting me. It'll be great fun. Tell the boys I can't wait.'

I loved doing things on the spur of the moment. It's how Kate and I came to have some of our most memorable picnics, and this one proved to be another great success. I think Kirsty being there helped no end. Not only was it great for me to have some adult company, but it meant the trip was not a rerun of picnics Kate and I had done together. Kirsty didn't hunt for slowworms or snakes or four-leaf clovers, and we didn't eat saucisson on tiger bread. It was just a fun day out, provoked by memories but not ruled by them. The boys ran around in the fresh air, I set them challenges to hunt for bugs, and we all just chilled out in the sunshine.

At one point Kirsty took both boys by the hand and went for a stroll to the spring. I lay back on the rabbit-nibbled grass and closed my eyes. I could feel the warmth of the sun on my eyelids, and I actually felt relaxed for the first time in ages. There were no hospital visits to plan, no funeral details to finalize and no legal or financial documents to fill in.

As we drove home I thought about the bottle of champagne in my glove compartment. Kate and I always replaced it straight away whenever we drank a bottle at Priddy, so there was always one waiting for us to share next time. I liked having it there. It was a reminder of how we lived our lives together, how we always looked forward with optimism, ready and waiting to enjoy the next celebration. We kept a bottle there throughout Reef's treatment. We drank it when his chemo was over, and we did the same when Kate's treatment ended.

I realized the next bottle, the one in the glove compartment today, had been to toast to Kate's brilliant recovery. That's what I fully expected and imagined, without a shadow of a doubt. Now I had no idea when I would open that bottle, or even who I might share it with, but it absolutely never occurred to me to get rid of it. Kate would have wanted me to keep it there, and I was very pleased to realize *I* wanted to keep it there too.

My day with Kirsty and the boys had been such fun, and for the very first time since losing Kate I could actually envisage a day when I might have another woman in my life. I didn't know who she might be, and I still could not imagine finding another soul mate, but I knew I didn't want to be on my own. I couldn't be on my own. I missed the closeness of being in a relationship, feeling another heartbeat next to mine. It wasn't just a wish or a desire, it was a physical need.

'Kate set the bar extremely high,' I had repeated to many close friends over the past few months. It was my stock answer whenever anyone alluded to me finding another partner. Ruth and a few of the mums from school did more than allude, of course. In recent weeks some good old friends had started to tell me straight they were going to find me another woman, and some had even started to send me photos on my phone of single friends who were 'available'. I laughed them off at first.

'Let's have a look at them,' Ruth demanded, when I told

her about a couple I'd received recently. We were catching up on gossip as we waited to buy cinema tickets. Ruth had been a star like that, dragging me out to the pictures or for a meal out whenever she could. She knew what it was like to be a single parent. She had done a fantastic job of raising her two teenage boys since her divorce, and I admired her so much. We were already very close when Kate was alive. Now she felt like my sister; nagging me, bossing me but most of all looking out for me every step of the way.

I showed her two pictures of attractive women, accompanied by excited little notes in text messages on my phone. 'What d'you think, Singe . . . per-fect or what?!!' one said. Another, accompanied by a funny picture of a fair-haired lady pulling a silly face, said: 'Lovely lady for you . . . mad as a hatter like you!'

Ruth studied the pictures and read the texts.

'You should just meet them for a drink, have a night out and see what happens,' she said. 'It'll be good company for you, even if nothing comes of it.'

'You're right, as usual,' I said reluctantly, giving her a big bear hug. 'What would I do without you?'

Thanks to Ruth and the 'mums' army' that had set itself up to rescue me from singledom, I was slowly starting to come round to the idea that, even if I couldn't find another Kate, I could still have fun trying.

It was the week after the Priddy picnic when I finally agreed to have a drink with a newly divorced friend of a friend. Kirsty came over to babysit, and as I tucked the boys up in bed, Reef managed to floor me yet again, this time with his most spectacular blow yet.

'When are we going to get a new mummy?' he asked very seriously, looking me straight in the eye.

'I don't know,' I replied slowly, keeping my face deadpan as I didn't know what else to do at first.

Finn looked at me expectantly, raising his eyebrows as if to prompt an answer.

'OK, you cheeky pair,' I stuttered slightly nervously, trying to lighten the atmosphere. 'I'm doing my best, is that good enough for you?'

They both nodded and smiled.

'OK, Daddy. You better be quick, though!' Reef said, pulling the duvet over his head and dissolving into giggles.

Finn joined in with the laughter, and I couldn't help laughing too. I went out with quite a spring in my step, feeling I now not only had Kate's blessing to see other women, but the boys' too.

As it turned out, when I met my 'date' for the evening, it didn't feel like a date at all. We chatted very amiably about our children, their schools, our jobs and plans for the summer and beyond. I told her I wanted to get even more involved with the boys' school, and we talked a bit about school governors.

'Kate wanted me to help out even more at All Saints,' I said without feeling awkward, and she mentioned her ex-husband several times.

We enjoyed each other's company, had a couple of laughs and said that, perhaps, we might meet up again some time. Driving home, I felt pleased I'd taken the plunge. She was an entertaining lady and we'd had a pleasant evening, even though I felt it didn't quite work in terms of us taking things further. I think the feeling was mutual, and that was absolutely fine.

'Well?' Ruth quizzed me the next day on the phone. 'How did it go with the date?'

'Fine,' I said, meaning it.

'Just "fine"?' Ruth pressed.

'Yes,' I said. 'Fine is good enough for me. I enjoyed myself. Forty-something dating is not quite the same as teenage dating, though, is it?'

Ruth laughed. 'I think you've hit the nail on the head there, Singe. Glad you're giving it a whirl, though. Kate would be pleased.'

If she'd been standing beside me I would have given Ruth a great big cuddle. She always says the right thing, and says it how it is, and I loved her for it that day.

'Ruth, you are fan-bloody-tastic,' I said.

Over the next few weeks I made a decision to put myself forward as Chair of Governors at All Saints. It was a way of being more involved in the boys' education, as Kate wished, and it's something I felt she might have done herself if she were here. Even when she was going through chemo she was always volunteering to run stalls, help out on sports day and organize fundraisers. I wanted to do enough for both of us and more, and the fact I didn't have to work full-time any more meant I would have more hours to devote to the school.

I was already a school governor and had already organized a few 'wow' activities for the kids, as I called them. I'd done bushcraft and forest survival courses and I'd arranged an 'animal encounters' day, where the kids got to handle scorpions, spiders and bearded dragon lizards brought in by a local expert. I loved it. At one point we let loads of crickets loose all over the floor, which made the kids shriek and jump, and then we let the lizards loose to gobble up the insects. It was fantastic fun, and was also very useful to the school's growing reputation for innovative teaching.

I started thinking about what else I had to offer the school, over and above the usual governor duties. Thanks to my boating contacts, I'd been asked several times to accompany *The Matthew* around Bristol Harbour. It's a fabulous replica of an old Tudor merchant ship, and I thought how brilliant it would be to get the kids from school on board. I was fired up with excitement and couldn't wait to tell the boys my idea, but I knew I had to pull it off first.

I was thinking all this through when Reef ran upstairs into my home office, breathless. What he said took my breath away too.

'Mummy's fish and mummy's prawns are dying,' he announced, tears springing from his eyes.

My enthusiastic mood evaporated instantly, and I thundered down the stairs with a horrible sinking feeling in my stomach. The massive four-foot-long fish tank in our lounge had been a gift for Kate. I brought it home for her two weeks after her diagnosis, knowing her treatment would prevent her from diving, and knowing how much she would miss the sea.

'Singe, it is just amazing, the best thing ever,' she beamed, her eyes devouring the tropical fish, coral and prawns I'd stocked it with. 'You couldn't have got me anything better. I love you, I love you!'

'Are you talking to me or the fish?' I joked.

'Both!' she said. 'Look! Look at that one. Can you see it, hiding behind the hermit crab?'

Kate had a knack of spotting interesting little stunts the fish pulled, and was forever calling me over to come and see. Sometimes it took me ages to work out what I was meant to be looking at.

'See the coral, well, as it pulses watch that tree worm behind it . . .'

Kate's eyes would dance from fish to fish as she tracked their movements excitedly, like a child glued to colourful cartoons. When her treatment stole her energy she often sat in front of the fish tank for hours and hours, munching Coco Pops when she had no appetite for anything else.

Now I looked at the tank in absolute horror. Every fish was swimming upside down, and the shrimps looked pitifully lifeless.

'Has the fish tank died, Daddy?' Finn asked sadly.

'I don't know,' I said. My throat was tight; I was so upset.

Finn started crying, and Reef repeated pitifully: 'Mummy's fish and mummy's prawns are dying.'

I thought back guiltily over the past few weeks. We had a huge leather coral that had quadrupled in size. I had bought more water for the tank from a local garden centre and bunged that in, but the tank was overdue a clean. The PH balance must have been wrong, and it was all my fault. I'd neglected it.

'I'm so sorry,' I said, looking at Reef and Finn and seeing, envisaging, Kate standing between them. 'We'll rescue as many as we can.'

'Mummy would be sad,' Finn said, and Reef started to cry too.

I couldn't bear to see the boys so upset, especially at something dying, something belonging to Kate that was dying. It was hideous.

'Do you know what Mummy wants us to do?' I said.

'Clean the tank?' Reef replied in true logical style.

'Yes, she would want that,' I said. 'And I will do that and save as many of Mummy's fish and prawns as possible. But she has also asked me to take you to a real coral reef, so you can go scuba diving and see tropical fish up close in the sea, like she used to.'

'Is it like a holiday?' Finn asked.

'Yes, Finn, it is a holiday. I've decided I'm going to take you to the Red Sea in Egypt. Mummy asked me to do that.'

'When can we go?' Reef said, brightening up. I noticed he was holding Finn's hand now, something he had started to do instinctively, whenever Finn got upset.

I was thinking on my feet now, but I desperately wanted to cheer the boys up and this felt like exactly the way to do it.

'How about Christmas?' I said.

Their eyes widened. 'Won't it be cold at Christmas?' Finn said.

'Not in Egypt. Lapland was cold because it's near the North Pole, but Egypt is a lovely hot country with beaches and warm sea to dive in.' Kate and I had actually taken the boys to Sharm El Sheik when they were very small, but they were far too young to remember.

As I discussed the holiday I felt a little tremor tingle through my heart. It was part excitement, part relief. I couldn't face another freezing-cold Christmas, that's for sure. I didn't want to be anywhere near snow, as it would remind me too much of last year, of Kate's poor lungs having to cope with the icy-cold air in Lapland. I also couldn't face Christmas at home. We were already halfway through the year, and my grieving wasn't going to end any time soon. Christmas would be here before we knew it, and it would be too painful to be at home without Kate.

Getting away, doing something fun in the sun with the boys, that seemed the perfect answer. The idea of going to Egypt had been floating round in my head for ages, because of course it was on Kate's list, but I hadn't had a chance to give it a great deal of thought. Now it was going to happen, and it felt right.

'You have to keep doing well with your swimming lessons,' I told both boys. 'You have to be good swimmers to snorkel in the Red Sea. Deal?'

'Deal,' Reef said.

Finn nodded obediently, eyes as wide as dinner plates.

It would be a challenge and a huge responsibility taking them on holiday on my own, especially a snorkelling holiday, but it was one I was definitely up for. I thought again how Kate and I had tried to do the trip three times but had had to cancel because of her treatment. I was so lucky to have a fourth chance, and I was going to make it a holiday to remember.

'We'd better get plenty of boating practice in too,' I said. 'We'll take the boat out round the harbour tomorrow. That OK, shipmates?'

The boys nodded. Kate and I lost ourselves when we were on the sea, and I wanted the boys to experience that same sense of freedom. I didn't want them stuck in the house with the dying fish tank. They needed to be outdoors, blowing the clouds away.

'Don't worry, I'll sort the fish tank out first,' I reassured them. 'We'll see what we can rescue.'

It turned out the tank had suffered what is known as a 'coral crash', which sent the PH through the roof, killing all of the invertebrates and coral and most of the fish. We were all absolutely gutted, but I did manage to stabilize the water, and the few fish that did survive pacified the boys a bit. The tank looked trashed, though, and it would have to be thoroughly cleaned and revamped or, better still, replaced with a new one once the extension was done.

The next morning I got the boys up and out early. The fish tank dominates the living room and can't be avoided, so I thought it was best to lay on some entertainment out at sea to distract them. I loved seeing them kitted out in their lifejackets, squealing with delight as we bombed along the water, and now the boat was fully run in I could push it to its limits.

'Go faster, Daddy! Go faster!' they said, even when I was close to breaking the speed limit and it felt like we were doing 100 mph along the Bristol Channel. Kate would have absolutely loved to see them like that, the wind in their hair and eyes shimmering like the sea. Finn was giggling like mad the whole time, and she absolutely loved his giggles.

As we sailed I thought about Kate's grave and felt heartened to think she was just up on the cliff top, not too far away from us, perhaps even looking down on us through the gap in the hedgerow.

I also thought about one of my favourite memories of Kate on the water. She was pregnant with Reef at the time, so it must have been around the spring of 2004. We'd taken our old boat out from a local sailing club in Portishead. The weather was lovely but didn't stay that way for long as clouds started to form overhead and the wind picked up. As we got further down the Bristol Channel, we were being pushed around as the sea was getting choppier by the minute.

'Lifeboat training,' I said, nodding over to a large rib with eight big hairy blokes on board, which was also being blown about.

Kate complained about the wind in her face, though she wasn't in the least bit afraid of the blowy conditions. 'Good practice for the lifeboat men,' was all she commented.

'I reckon we should get back,' I said a few minutes later.

'Why?'

'Because you're five months pregnant and the weather's turned!'

'OK, you're right, spoilsport!' Kate reluctantly agreed.

We headed back and watched as the lifeboat crew followed us in and attempted to secure their craft to its cradle. They failed spectacularly, and Kate and I watched in amusement as a series of giant waves smashed into the side of the boat, throwing three of the strapping blokes unceremoniously overboard. The rest of them jumped ship as they were very close to the slipway, and they scrambled ashore looking embarrassed and a bit shaken up.

'Want some help?' I shouted.

'Yes please, Singe!' came the grateful reply from one of the crew I recognized.

'You OK to drive our boat in while I help them?' I said to Kate.

Kate nodded, and I climbed overboard, leaving her in charge of *Singe 1*. She always rose to a challenge, and 'did a Kate', as I used to say. This was no exception, and she 'did a Kate' with considerable style that day, steering our boat beautifully and coming in at a perfect angle before sitting it expertly on the trailer.

'Well done, Kate,' I shouted before glancing over to the eight astonished men who were now standing on the slipway. They were all gaping open-mouthed, absolutely gobsmacked that this petite blonde had brought her boat in single-handed, and done it with such finesse in such choppy conditions, while they had collectively failed.

'Bloody hell, it's a blonde bird!' I heard one say as I brought their rib safely in too.

My heart swelled, and Kate looked absolutely brilliant as she slid over the side of *Singe 1* and skipped up the slipway.

'And I'm pregnant!' she said, flashing a feisty smile at the men.

We laughed our heads off remembering that story so many times, and I told the boys a shortened version of it that day.

'Mummy was really brave and fearless,' I said. 'She'd be very proud of you two little sailors, you're doing really well.'

Reef and Finn were delighted with themselves. I could see it in their little faces each time they learned something new on the boat, which gave me a great deal of pleasure.

'Tell us the jet-ski story, Daddy!' Reef said. 'I like that story about Mummy!'

I don't think Finn remembered it, and I took great delight in retelling another of my favourite Kate stories.

'Well, as you probably remember, Mummy was a very, very good jet-skier,' I said. The boys both nodded. 'One day we took the jet-ski down to the beach at Clevedon. I watched Mummy go out first, and she looked really cool. She was wearing a big silver helmet that matched the silver flashes down the side of her jet-ski. Mummy loved to go really fast, just like you two, and she could do tricks like jumping the waves.'

'Tell Finn about the old people, Daddy!' Reef said, eyes shining.

'I'm just coming to that bit. Anyway, it was the middle of the afternoon, and lots of grannies were out for a stroll from one of the old folks' homes on the prom. I heard one of the old ladies say: "Oooh, look at that boy racer, Gladys," and do you know who they were talking about?'

'Mummy!' Finn squealed.

'That's right. Then it was my turn to go out, and I waved at Mummy to come back in. She headed to the shore as if she was going to give me my go, but then changed her mind. She shouted "Naaah" really cheekily as she shook her head and giggled. At the same time she turned the jet-ski sharply, like doing a handbrake turn in a car, which absolutely soaked me with a gigantic gush of sea water, and nearly knocked me off my feet. The old people were going "Oooh" and "Ah", and one of them said, "Just look how fast he's going! I think he's a bit dangerous!" I couldn't wait for Mummy to finally come in, and when she did, and pulled off her helmet, I thought some of the old ladies were going to faint! "It's a girl!" they said, pointing at Mummy with her long, blonde hair tumbling down the back of her wetsuit. Mummy skipped up the beach, flicking out her hair and giggling. I don't think the old people had ever had such a big shock!'

The boys beamed, just as Kate had beamed that day. They had inherited her sense of fun and adventure, and it was my job, my pleasure, to keep that alive.

Luckily, I had another little adventure already lined up for the boys, as I'd agreed to take them caravanning with my parents in just a few weeks' time. That night, I explained to Reef and Finn we would be staying with Grampy and Nanny P., my dad Bob and stepmum Pauline, at a caravan park near Bridport in Dorset, on the World Heritage Coast. It's pretty stunning, and we'd been before, but I don't think they remembered it.

'The view is amazing, and our caravan will be near the cliff edge, so we have the best view on the site,' I told the boys enthusiastically.

I hadn't changed my tune about caravanning. I will never understand the attraction of sleeping in a flimsy van and having to cook and wash up just like you do at home, but with worse facilities. It's an adventure for the boys, though, and one that is relatively easy to deliver, so I'm prepared to do it for their sakes. I also think that, since losing their mum, it's very important they spent time with all of their grandparents, which is another reason for me to make the effort.

'What is there to do there, Daddy?' Reef asked.

'Swimming in the pool, days out on the beach with the boat, bit of shopping in Lyme Regis, fossil hunting on the beach . . . how does that grab you?'

Both boys cheered. 'I can't wait!' Reef said. 'Do I *have* to go shopping? How many sleeps?'

'Well, the quicker you get to bed tonight, the less sleeps it will be,' I said. 'It's time you two went upstairs and got in the bath.'

They scampered upstairs, and I followed them, running the bath while the boys got undressed. They were ready before the water was, and I took the opportunity to check over Reef's tummy. It was something I did every now and again, a habit I would probably never be able to break. I'd been told that the majority of cancers that return come back in the same place the original tumour was removed from – either that or it goes into the lymph nodes and explodes around the body, like Kate's did.

'Let's have a little look at that belly,' I said routinely, asking Reef to lie flat on the bath mat.

After the surgery to remove the tumour from his abdomen, Reef was left with what are known as 'shotty nodes' on his stomach and groin, which look like tiny lumps under the surface of the skin. I'd been told to keep an eye on them because if they grew in size it could be a warning sign that all was not well.

My heart cramped in my chest when I looked at Reef's stomach that night, and my nerves twanged so violently it felt like shards of glass were shattering in my veins. The nodes were very visibly enlarged. My mouth went dry, and I felt like I'd been winded, as if butterflies and knots had crowded into my body, pushing out my breath. 'It can't be, it can't be,' I thought, gulping in as much air as possible without scaring Reef.

'Is it OK, Daddy?' Reef asked brightly.

'How are you feeling?' I asked him, though I could barely speak.

Kate at seventeen. The girl with sun in her hair.

Kate with Barnaby the teddy, just before I came on the scene.

Kate's eighteenth birthday party – Kate in the middle, with that famous twinkle in her eye, and me standing behind her.

Gorgeous Kate, golden brown in Majorca.

Teenage sweethearts, on one of our first holidays together.

The obligatory holiday snaps. Here we are testing our strength in Cyprus.

Kate got the most out of life wherever she went. Here she is in Egypt on her 200th dive.

Skiing in Switzerland in 1995, where I proposed to Kate.

Me in a rented Porsche in the days before kids, when I drove like a maniac.

With Kate's mum, dad and brother Ben in Switzerland, and in Turkey.

Covered in confetti, outside Clifton College Chapel, the grinning groom and blushing bride.

On our honeymoon, arriving at the famous pontoon in the Maldives for the best holiday so far.

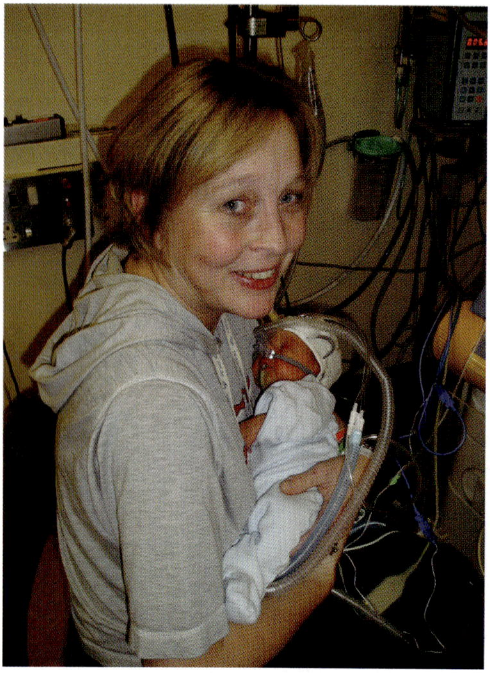

Fighting for his life – a tiny Finn born two months premature.

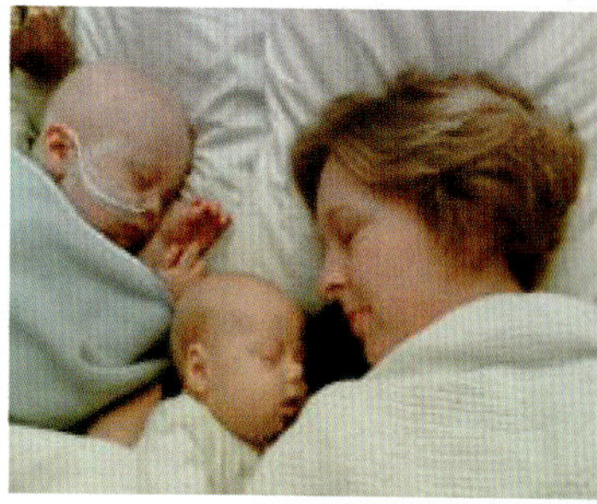

A rare moment of sleep after one of Reef's doses of radiotherapy.

(*left*) A whole lot of fun – the boys together.

The day I worried I'd never see – Finn and Reef's first day at school together. What a morning.

Reef's Make a Wish trip to Disney World in Florida. So many amazing memories were made on this holiday.

(*left*) Kate, halfway through her treatment, and the boys with the Tree of Life behind them. We had hoped that this would bring us good luck.

Kate's last summer with us was full of fun. Here she is leading the boys on a pony ride in the Mendips, and with Reef on the Weston Eye.

I still have every love letter Kate wrote to me, allowing me to travel back in time to when we first met.

Our boat *4 Saints* really helped lift our spirits in the months following Kate's death.

Our first Christmas without Kate was painful beyond words. The whole family spent it in Egypt, and it felt incredible to be able to cross one of her wishes off the list.

'Celebrate birthdays big time'. Reef's sixth birthday on board *The Matthew.*

Photo © Northcliffemedia

‘Good!’ he said, bursting into giggles as I touched his stomach. ‘You’re tickling me! Stop!’

‘OK, now jump in the bath then, quick as a flash and we might just have time for a story.’

I got straight on the phone to the consultant, Professor Mike Stevens. He’s the most fantastic guy, one of the top consultants in Europe for rare cancers like Reef’s. We’d got to know each other so well over the years I had a direct line to him, for which I was extremely grateful.

‘Bring him in tomorrow,’ he said after listening to my description of the lumps. ‘We’ll give him a thorough check-up. Try not to worry too much.’

I could barely sleep that night. The same two thoughts kept running through my head, as if on a loop. Reef was not expected to live, whereas Kate was expected to make a good recovery.

‘His chances of survival are so small,’ Kate sobbed. ‘What if we lose him?’

Reef beat the odds, and then it was Kate’s turn to beat her odds. They were much, much better than Reef’s – an eighty per cent chance of survival compared to his meagre six per cent on initial diagnosis. ‘You’ll make it,’ we all told Kate, convinced she would. We were all wrong. Reef survived, Kate died. Reef was not expected to live and he survived. Kate was expected to live and she died. I drifted in and out of sleep, thinking those same thoughts over and over again and wishing Kate was with me. I wanted to feel the warmth of her skin against mine.

‘Singe, what if we lose him?’

I could hear her saying it, and I could hear my reply.

‘We have to stay positive,’ I told her. ‘He has the most

fantastic mummy on his side. He'll make it, I'm sure he'll make it. We have to believe he will.'

Kate clung to me, and I was happy to be her rock. I had to be a rock still, and I had to stay positive even though my body felt compacted with dread and fear. Stay positive, I said. Go to sleep, I told myself. I tried to conjure up images of Reef when his treatment was over, telling myself he had slain his cancer like a little dragon-killer. He was victorious and he would always be a survivor.

I thought about Reef's fourth birthday party. Even though he was still having treatment and was not quite in remission, it was such an achievement for him to come this far. It was July 2008.

'Let's celebrate his birthday big time,' Kate said.

'Too right! What shall we do?'

We were like a couple of kids looking forward to Christmas morning. Reef's improving health was an incredible gift. We could scarcely believe he was turning four; it was a miracle he had reached this landmark.

We hired the Curzon cinema in Clevedon. It's one of the oldest cinemas in the world, and we invited more than 200 friends and family to a private showing of *Ice Age 3*.

'We'll party like there's no tomorrow!' I chuckled.

'Don't you mean like there are lots of tomorrows?' Kate pointed out.

'Actually, yes! Here's to the future, to celebrating lots and lots of birthdays.'

When I woke the next morning I immediately remembered Reef's lumps, and any positive thoughts I'd had the night before seemed to have completely deserted me. I felt frightened and alone. The house was quiet, and I couldn't stop one very persistent negative thought from banging on my skull. 'You looked on the bright side with Kate,' it said nastily. 'You were wrong.'

I saw Kate's outline appear in the doorframe. 'Singe, I've got a little lump,' she said, stepping into the bedroom from the shower. She was wearing a towel and was smoothing her hand protectively over her left breast. It was a hot day in August 2008, just a few weeks after Reef's birthday celebration at the cinema.

Poor Kate, I thought. I could hardly blame her being paranoid about her health after what had happened to Reef. Each time we gave him Calpol to calm his raging temperature Kate had worried we were missing something.

'What if there's something really wrong with him?' she kept asking. 'What if we're missing something?'

When she got no answers, she didn't give up, neither of us did. Reef had test after test, but still it took months and months to work out what had happened to our once-active child.

'We wasted nine months,' Kate sobbed when Reef's cancer was finally diagnosed. 'We treated cancer with Calpol,' she cried. 'If he'd been diagnosed sooner he might never have been disabled.'

The thought haunted Kate, and I had to keep telling her she had done her best, we both had. We followed our instincts and kept insisting Reef was tested and tested again and again, and the doctors had done their best too, even though months and months slipped by as Reef's condition worsened.

I could imagine what was racing through her head that

morning when she emerged from the bathroom, but I really didn't want her worrying unnecessarily. She'd suffered too much stress already.

'Kate, it'll be a cyst or something,' I said as she got me to feel the tiny little lump.

It didn't feel much bigger than the tip of a pencil.

'Make an appointment and have it looked at. I'll come with you if you like.'

I think Kate looked at me that morning and decided I'd had enough stress too.

'No,' she said bravely. 'I'm sure you're right. I'll book an appointment, just to be on the safe side, but there's no need for you to take time off work.'

Over the previous year Kate had decided to give blood. She wanted to give something back to the NHS for everything they had done for Reef; it was her way of saying thank you. Both Kate and Reef had a fairly rare blood type – O negative – so it was a very worthwhile thing to do. Kate gave blood successfully several times, but I remember she looked worn out when she came home from the latest session.

'You're amazing,' I told her. 'Most people wouldn't volunteer to go anywhere near a nurse or a syringe after all Reef's treatment.'

'Actually, they wouldn't let me give blood today,' she said, sounding fed up. 'Apparently I'm anaemic. They told me not to worry, just to take iron tablets. I'm probably a bit run down.'

The words came back to me when Kate went to have her lump checked out. I was teaching a life-guarding course at an Esporta leisure centre in Weston-super-Mare and was trying to stay positive. Kate would be fine, I reasoned. Just like with the anaemia, this would be absolutely nothing to worry about, and there would be a simple explanation.

Kate's appointment was at Weston General Hospital, just down the road, and all morning I expected a relieved phone call from her saying: 'You were right, Singe – it's a harmless cyst. Nothing to worry about!' My phone never rang, though. I still tried to be positive, imagining the clinic was simply running late, hoping she'd been left at the back of the queue as she was not an urgent case.

At lunchtime I'd just sat down with the lifeguards for a bite to eat when Kate walked in the door. She just about pulled on a smile for the group before saying quietly to me: 'Can I have a quick chat with you outside?' I knew something was wrong because it was so unlike Kate not to say 'hello' and be bubbly and chatty with people, even those she didn't know.

'Excuse me, guys, I've got to nip out for a minute,' I said, feeling the hairs on the back of my neck bristle uncomfortably.

Kate walked silently out to the car park with me pacing after her. When she stopped by her car her head was bowed and she looked apologetic.

'The scan wasn't good,' she said. 'I'm sorry, Singe, I have to go for a biopsy this afternoon.'

She left the words hanging in the air as she climbed in the car, as if to get away from them. I sat in beside her, and she grabbed me and held me really tight, as tight as she physically could. She started to cry, and for someone so little she squeezed me really hard, pushing the air out of my lungs.

'I'm here for you,' I stuttered. 'We'll get through it together.'

'I just can't believe what's happening,' she said. She was sobbing so hard I could feel her hot tears soaking through my shirt. 'How are we going to tell the boys?' she wailed. 'What are we going to tell them?'

She was absolutely distraught, and it was painful to see her like that.

'Kate, if it's breast cancer at least there's a good chance it'll be OK,' I said, trying to keep my head but feeling shocked by what I was saying. We both knew what I meant, that it couldn't possibly be any worse than Reef's cancer, and we looked at each other in horror.

I had not expected to be plunged back into the dark hole of hospitals we'd just escaped from, and I could scarcely believe I was now asking Kate what the procedure was for the appointment, just as I had so many times with Reef. How could one family be so unlucky as to have two cancers, I thought. Reef's cancer was so rare, and we had been reassured it was not genetic. Perhaps there was some mistake. Or perhaps Kate's tiny little lump had been caught so early it could be removed quickly and easily?

'There's no point in worrying too much until we get the results of the biopsy,' I told Kate. 'It might not even be cancer at all. Sit tight while I talk to the lifeguards, and we'll get straight back up to the hospital.'

Kate was extremely brave when the needle went in, clenching her teeth and holding my gaze with a steely, determined look that told me generously: 'You know I'm a fighter.' She was also incredibly brave when a specialist cancer nurse called us into a comfortable little side room some time later.

Even though Kate and I had tried to comfort and reassure each other as we sipped warm tea to calm our nerves, I think we both knew it was bad news even before we were invited to sit down in that cosy, pastel-coloured room. The atmosphere was choking, and the nurse had a kind but sympathetic look on her face, one we recognized from when we were given Reef's diagnosis.

'I'm very sorry, it's serious,' she said. 'I'm afraid there are two lumps, one smaller than the other. We are going to go for a full mastectomy.'

Kate didn't cry, she just stared at the floor solemnly. I felt myself falling to pieces from the inside out. My heart was pumping blood frantically around my body, and my brain was pulsing, fit to burst. I could feel goosebumps erupting down my spine, and veins bulging angrily under my collar. I was trembling with shock, and my tears ran into the sweat that was forming on my flushed-red face.

The cancer nurse looked a bit bemused, seeing me looking so much more visibly upset than Kate.

'It's not the worst news I've heard,' Kate said calmly, by way of explanation.

Now the nurse was looking completely confused, and as I held my head in my trembling hands I could hear Kate telling the nurse a bit about Reef, about how his cancer was so rare he was just one of eight in the world to be diagnosed with it.

'He was given a six per cent chance of survival, and he celebrated his fourth birthday last month,' Kate said courageously. 'We hired a whole cinema and had a big celebration.'

Then Kate broke down, and we both cried in each other's arms while the shocked nurse slipped out of the room, telling us to take our time and explaining she was going to get us some information leaflets that might be useful.

In the coming weeks we learned that Kate's cancer was what is known as 'triple negative', and she would need chemotherapy and radiotherapy after the mastectomy. We were also offered a trial of a new drug called Avastin that could improve her chances of survival, which were eventually estimated at an encouraging eighty per cent.

'I'll take the lot,' Kate said boldly. 'Bring it on. If Reef can beat cancer, so can I.'

I truly believed she would. There was no question in my mind, and I don't think there was a shadow of doubt in hers either, not for a very long time. We clung to each other in bed the night before her mastectomy.

'Will you still fancy me when I only have one boob?' she asked miserably, looking at me with big blue puppy-dog eyes.

'Are you kidding?' I laughed. 'I will never stop fancying you – and I might just fancy you a bit more when you have a boob job.'

She giggled and kissed me tenderly. 'What about chemo? What will it do to me? I'm going to look terrible.'

'Well, perhaps you could get a sexy, long blonde wig when your hair falls out,' I suggested playfully.

She thumped me on the chest and hugged me tight. 'I love you, Singe,' she said.

'I love you too,' I replied, kissing her hair. 'I wish you didn't have to go through all this, and I wish we could fast-forward to the end of all this treatment, but we can't. I suppose we've got through it once, and we'll just have to do it all over again.'

'And here we go again,' I thought, pulling up at Bristol General for Reef's appointment with Professor Stevens, the enlarged nodes weighing heavily on my mind. Thankfully, Reef seemed to have accepted it was just another routine check-up and didn't question why we were going back to the hospital not that long after his successful MRI scan.

'Are we going to the blue floor first?' he asked, knowing the drill.

'That's right,' I said as brightly as I could muster, pleased he seemed at ease.

We both knew the routine so well. After signing in we took an X-ray card, then headed to floor three to wait to be called in for the X-ray. Reef took it in his stride, sitting very still for the radiographer and remembering his pleases and thank-yous. My heart was overflowing with love for him. If I lost Reef too . . .

'Reef Greene for Professor Stevens,' the nurse called. I felt immediately calmer, seeing Reef in Professor Stevens' expert hands, but I was still worried sick. We ran though all the usual questions about Reef's recent health and discussed any temperatures, sickness, stomach trouble or falls he might have had.

'He fell over in the playground and got a nasty cut on his leg, but of course that's not unusual,' I reported. Reef was always covered in cuts and bruises as he refused to let his bad leg slow him down. He loses his balance more than most kids, and has had more than his fair share of tumbles as a result.

Professor Stevens examined the lumps on Reef's lower abdomen and admitted he was a little concerned and wanted to scan them. The colour drained from my face, but Professor Stevens was brilliant, explaining that an infection from the cut leg could have travelled up to the nodes, making them swell as they fought off any invading bugs.

I gave a quiet sigh of relief, but I wouldn't be convinced until I got the results of the scan the following week. It felt like déjà vu, waiting for yet more scan results and counting the days and hours until I received them and could, hopefully, resume normal life once more. I busied myself with preparations for our latest caravan trip.

We were all packed up and ready to go on the Monday morning when the phone rang. I'd been willing it to ring before we set off, and I held my breath as I listened to the message being passed on from Professor Stevens.

'Reef's lumps are nothing to worry about,' the gentle voice reassured me. 'As Professor Stevens had hoped, they are harmless "shotty nodes", most probably aggravated by Reef's recent fall.' The words were so soothing I felt as if they had actually pushed themselves out of the phone and physically rubbed the frown from my brow as they filtered through to my brain.

'Thank you so much,' I said, suddenly gulping in air to compensate for holding my breath. My pulse was racing, and I felt dizzy with relief. I could almost feel my fear bubbling away, being converted into a massive dose of happiness that percolated into every cell in my body.

I was ecstatic, and I had the biggest smile on my face all the way down to the caravan site.

'We're going to have such fun,' I told the boys with genuine gusto, and we did.

Kate had loved this site, because there were always loads of rabbits running round the caravan. She watched them with fascination as they chased each other and nibbled the grass and she drank in the views along the Jurassic Coast with wonder in her eyes. It was lovely to remember her like that, but once we'd settled into the holiday I was relieved to find that this trip wasn't dominated by memories of Kate, like the last caravan trip had been. I don't think the boys mentioned Mummy once, and perhaps that's because we were with my side of the family instead of hers, but it didn't seem wrong. Kate would never be forgotten, but life was moving on, and I had a good feeling about the future.

Chapter 7

'Celebrate birthdays big time'

'Am I having a birthday party, Daddy?' Reef asked.

'Dunno, haven't thought about it,' I said, unable to suppress a smile.

'Tell me what it is!' Reef squealed eagerly, knowing immediately I had a trick up my sleeve.

'Oh, I thought we'd take a boat out . . .'

'What boat? Our boat? That's booorring, we do that all the time!'

'Oh well, if boats are booorring, then . . .'

'Tell me, Daddy!' Reef begged, seeing my smirk and realizing I didn't mean our boat. He was jumping up and down now, unable to contain his excitement.

'Tell me, pleeeaaase!'

'I thought we'd take *The Matthew* out on the harbour, and invite your whole class. We can all dress up as pirates and fire a real cannon. How does that grab you?'

Reef was rolling round on the floor now, clutching his sides because he was laughing so much.

'Is that real? Is it true?'

I assured him that it most certainly was, and that it was exactly the sort of party he deserved for his very important sixth birthday. Ever since Reef got ill birthdays had taken on greater importance each year as they marked out another leap in his recovery, and there was no way I wasn't going to celebrate his birthday 'big time', as Kate wished.

Reef skipped out happily into the conservatory, suddenly intent on finding his plastic pirate's sword.

'Good luck, it could be buried deeper than a hidden treasure chest under all those toys you've got out there,' I called. 'And there's no X to mark the spot!'

Reef rolled his eyes. I thoroughly enjoyed listening to him telling Finn about his birthday party as he recruited him in the hunt for the sword, and I delighted in hearing Finn giggling with excitement too.

Six years. I had been a parent for almost six years, and for most of that time I'd lived on a knife's edge. Looking back, it was as if a black curtain was drawn across our old life when Reef got ill. It blocked out the sun, trapping us in a stifling, frightening, exhausting world of hospitals, operating theatres and chemotherapy suites. Then, just as the curtain started to lift and light chinked through, bloody big shutters fell when Kate was diagnosed too.

I thought about the nine long months when Reef was poorly but his cancer hadn't yet been diagnosed. As Reef's health started to deteriorate Kate found out she was pregnant with Finn. I remember being shocked.

'How did that happen?' I asked Kate, nonplussed. 'You told me you weren't back in a normal cycle after Reef. You told me you couldn't get pregnant!'

'I didn't see you complaining that night,' she winked.

It was true. Our sex life had taken a battering since Reef was born and we grappled with sleepless nights, but Kate had seduced me one memorable evening. It was the first time we'd had sex in many months, and I jokingly accused her of getting me drunk and dragging me upstairs to have her wicked way with me. Of course, it wasn't like that. I never needed dragging into bed with Kate, and we had our wicked way with each other, very willingly. Afterwards, Kate confessed she'd chosen that night as she had worked out that, if she did get pregnant, our next child could well be born on Valentine's Day. 'How can I argue with that, romantic fool that I am?' I conceded when the news sank in. I'm as soppy as they come, and Kate knew that all too well, the clever little minx.

However, as Kate got bigger, Reef got more ill, which clearly wasn't part of the plan at all. At first his high temperatures only came on at night, when he went floppy and alarmingly pale, but within weeks he became ill during the daytime too. Our little boy, who used to amaze and delight us by crawling through the cat-flap with the stealth of a fox, was practically immobile.

When doctors suggested his sickness was down to the reactive arthritis triggered by his MMR jab that they suspected, we prayed it would pass, and that Reef would grow out of it, without the need for treatment. It was frightening and almost impossible to accept that we had to wait and see, though there seemed no other explanation.

But Reef got steadily worse instead of better, and we began to spend more time at the hospital than at home as he underwent a battery of tests to work out why he was becoming increasingly lethargic and unresponsive. Kate went through an incredible amount of stress. Pregnant and pushing a sick child in a buggy, she struggled in and out of hospital again and again, instinctively knowing there was something seriously wrong with Reef and praying that doctors would come up with a diagnosis, and some effective treatment, soon.

I remember life becoming a blur of heart monitors, X-rays, tubes, injections and tears as the investigations intensified. Kate cried every day, and I barely slept. I did countless night shifts in hospital, drinking Red Bull to stay awake as I watched over Reef whenever he was too ill to come home. As the months wore on he seemed completely sapped of energy, and soon after his first birthday he became so weak he had to be fed through a tube.

'I can't take much more of this,' Kate cried so many times.

'You're doing amazingly well,' I said. 'Look around. There are other parents here splitting up and falling to pieces. You're so strong. You're magnificent. We'll get though this together.'

She nodded and returned the compliment. 'We are tight-knit,' she said, recalling a phrase she used often when we were courting. I hadn't heard her say it for years.

'Never to be split,' I said, delighted to remember the second half of the line.

The breakthrough finally came when, on Kate's insistence, we got a private consultant to look at Reef. Breakthrough is perhaps not the right word, as it was certainly not positive news.

'We have found a large lump in Reef's abdomen,' a voice said.

It could have been an alien talking, it sounded so extraordinary. Previous scans and X-rays had been carried out on Reef's knee and hips, but this was the first time his pelvic area had been scanned. Reef was seventeen months old by this time, and bedridden.

The lump wasn't just large, it was gigantic. As big as a grapefruit, it filled three-quarters of his abdomen and reached down to his groin. Kate and I clung to each other and wept for a very long time, and through our tears we asked the same hopeful question: 'How can it be treated?'

The discovery of the lump brought mixed, confused feelings. I can recall feeling some peculiar sort of relief to have finally found the source of Reef's illness after eight long months of uncertainty, but of course it was not good news by any stretch of the imagination. We now had another terrible, nagging worry hanging over us, one we could barely contemplate.

'Singe, what sort of a lump is it?' Kate sobbed, her eyes searching mine for some desperate shred of comfort. 'I'm so frightened. I'm terrified of losing him. I couldn't live if he died.'

'Please don't cry, Kate. You're seven months pregnant now. Please don't think like that. Stay positive, it's the best thing for Reef. He needs you to be strong.'

Kate just couldn't help crying. I held her as she sobbed silently in my arms, her head turned away from Reef. He had black rings around his sunken eyes, and was staring into space. His skin was snow-white, and his breathing was shallow. It was very difficult to conjure up words of encouragement for Kate. Neither of us mentioned the 'C' word, although it was shadowing us everywhere, a sinister, predatory elephant in the room, threatening to stampede and smash our world apart.

We had several days to wait for the test results on the

lump, and it was absolute agony. I sent Kate home to rest, and stayed in overnight with Reef, watching over him as he slept. He looked pitiful, he really did.

'Singe, I'm scared,' Kate sobbed down the phone.

'I know, so am I, but think about our new baby. Try to put your feet up, listen to some music, anything you can to take your mind off things. You have two months to go, and you need to look after yourself. I'm here for Reef. I'll stay all night and you can come in the daytime, when I'm at work. I love you, acres and acres.'

We went through two nights and three days like that before Reef was allowed home, test results pending. The weather was filthy, and the sky was heavy with snow clouds. It was the week between Christmas and New Year, and shops and houses were glittering with fairy lights and decorations. Kate and I had gone through the motions of exchanging presents and eating turkey with the family, but we didn't celebrate, not really. We'd expected Christmas to be extra magical once we were parents; instead it was absolute hell, wondering if Reef would live to see another one.

On 29 December Kate took Reef back into hospital for yet another examination. Her mum and dad drove her to the Bristol Royal Infirmary and back, as I had a job to do a few miles away in Nailsea.

When my phone rang I was expecting an update on Reef's condition.

'Singe, can you come home quick?' Kate said urgently. I'm in labour. It started on the way home from hospital.'

'You're having a giraffe,' I said. It was something I often said to make her laugh, when I meant 'you're having a laugh.' She didn't laugh this time though.

'No, a baby,' she said, deadpan.

'On my way,' I said.

'Be careful,' Kate warned. 'It's snowing.'

'I know – how cool is that?' I said enthusiastically, suddenly feeling giddy with anticipation. I was feeling nervously excited, a crazy mixture of emotions rushing in different directions round my body.

'*You* were born in a snowstorm!' I said to Kate. 'Isn't that amazing?'

I was awash with adrenaline and desperately wanted to be with Kate as quickly as humanly possible.

'Yes, Singe,' Kate said, pausing to let out a little groan. 'The snow is amazing, but I was hoping it would be rather more spring-like when this baby arrived!'

'I know, I know, I'm on my way, I'll drive carefully.'

As soon as she saw me turn the corner of our cul-de-sac, Kate started waddling out of the house, panting and clutching her stomach. 'Mum and Dad will stay with Reef,' she said. 'We need to get to Southmead Hospital as quickly as possible.'

I did a little mental calculation. The maternity unit at Southmead Hospital was north of Bristol, about twenty miles away, and would take a good half an hour in these conditions.

I put my foot down in our little Rover Metro as best as I could without skidding, and we dashed to the hospital with Kate squeezing my left leg the whole way there.

It was already dark, and it was a stressful journey through heavy, whirling snow. My adrenaline rush flattened, forming a pool of sickly fluid in the pit of my stomach. Kate was only seven months pregnant. Our baby was not meant to be born for another two months. What if Reef's diagnosis was really bad, and what if the baby really was to be born tonight?

I kept my thoughts to myself and looked at Kate's determined little face. Whatever happened, she would do a blinding job. I trusted her and I tried to tell myself that, in any case, the labour might very well stop once Kate was settled in hospital. She'd suffered so much stress worrying about Reef, and perhaps bed rest was all she needed.

Pulling in to the hospital, I abandoned the car by the entrance and I helped Kate get out and stagger to the maternity unit. I was shocked when she told the first midwife she saw: 'I want a C-Section, NOW!'

I actually laughed as I steered her hastily to a delivery room, no doubt more through nerves than anything. Kate had desperately wanted a natural birth with Reef but ended up needing an emergency Caesarean because he was getting distressed in the womb. I had a flashback of watching the surgeon mark Kate's belly before she made the cut. 'Can you go a bit lower, please?' I cheekily asked, knowing Kate wouldn't want the scar to be visible in a bikini. The surgeon recognized me from my work as a paramedic and did her best to give Kate the lowest possible cut, and she even let me help her lift Reef out into the world, which was just phenomenal.

'I thought you'd want to try for a natural birth this time round,' I blurted out.

'Shut it, Singe!' Kate said, managing a smirk in between painful grimaces.

Kate had told me in the car that her labour started almost as soon as her mum and dad had driven her out of the

Bristol Royal Infirmary car park following Reef's appointment. Her contractions became so intense so quickly Christine started to time them. As soon as they realized they were getting quicker and quicker, they phoned me and then Southmead Hospital, to let them know we were coming.

Our appointed midwife appeared moments later, to Kate's obvious relief.

'I want a C-Section,' Kate practically begged her.

'OK, my love, let's see, shall we? I'll just examine you.'

The midwife was very tall and willowy, and she cranked the bed up to its full height to carry out the examination, so she didn't have to stoop too low. There was a momentary pause, and then the midwife announced: 'You're far too late for a C-Section, my love – I can see the head!'

I looked at the midwife in absolute astonishment before giving Kate a quick kiss and taking a step towards the foot of the bed, not wanting to miss a thing. An unexpected 'bang' stopped me in my tracks. It sounded like a water balloon popping, and when I looked again at the midwife she was drenched from head to toe in all sorts of nasty-looking liquid. A shocked Kate, who was sucking on gas and air to help with the pain, just stared in disbelief for a moment. Next I saw her look at the midwife, who was wiping her face and hair with paper towels, and Kate then burst into peals of hysterical laughter, only pausing to drag on more gas and air.

'Singe, did that just happen?' Kate gasped. 'Did my waters explode all over the midwife?'

I nodded, and she cracked up laughing again, setting me off a bit too, even though, without the benefit of laughing gas, I was actually feeling quite embarrassed.

'I'm really, really sorry,' I said to the midwife. 'I don't know what else to say.'

Thankfully, Kate's giggling was as contagious as ever, and the midwife very gamely began to laugh herself.

'It's OK,' she said, 'Just give us a minute. I'll have to get you a replacement midwife while I get cleaned up.'

She went across the corridor to the nurses' station, and the roar of laughter we heard when her colleagues saw her standing there dripping wet set Kate off giggling again. Moments later a new midwife appeared. To my surprise, this one looked about three foot shorter than her colleague and could barely reach Kate on the elevated bed. There was a button on the side of the bed frame that she began to press quickly and repeatedly, but it lowered the bed in what felt like torturously slow steps. Each time it cranked down another notch Kate's labour seemed to crank up a pace. Then, just as the bed was almost at the desired height, Kate let out an ear-piercing scream. To everyone's amazement, our baby suddenly shot out at what looked like a hundred miles an hour.

I actually caught him before he hit the bed, and I looked at him in awe and fright. He was the tiniest little mite I'd ever seen, so small I was shocked to see that my wedding ring was bigger than his whole hand.

'Is he all right?' Kate asked anxiously, peering down.

The midwife and I were sorting him out together, cutting and clamping his cord. I was thrilled to have played a role in his birth too. With Reef, I also got to cut his cord after helping to lift him into the world. In fact, I had him cleaned up and put him in a nappy before the midwife had a chance. She wasn't very pleased and told me he was the only baby she hadn't put a nappy on in twenty-odd years of deliveries. Kate and I were too deliriously happy to let the ticking-off bother us. All we wanted to do was take turns cuddling Reef.

This birth was very different, and there was certainly no time for cuddles. As soon as Finn's cord was clamped he was dressed in a doll-sized nappy and rushed into an incubator, pumped with oxygen and put under ultraviolet lights.

'He's going to need a bit of help but he looks fine,' the midwife said. 'Congratulations!'

Finn weighed just 5lbs. As with Reef, we'd known he was a little boy and had chosen a name in advance.

'He's big for a premature baby,' I reassured Kate.

'He's diddy, though,' she said. 'I just want to cuddle him.'

'I know, but "Diddy" needs to go to NICU, the neonatal intensive care unit.'

'How long for? How long do I have to wait for a cuddle?'

'They don't know yet, Kate, but don't worry. He's in the best place. Cuddle me instead.'

I gave her a gentle hug as she smoothed her hands over her deflated belly.

'He should still be in here,' she said flatly. I couldn't argue. You didn't need to be a doctor to figure out Kate's premature labour had been brought on by extreme stress. Her face was etched with worry.

'What if it's bad news about Reef? What if Finn has complications? Anything can happen with prem babies, especially ones born this early. What if he . . . doesn't make it?'

I kissed Kate's forehead. My wife and my two little boys

were all lying in hospital, one way or another. The truth was both Reef and Finn's lives were hanging in the balance, and it was nigh-on impossible to keep coming up with positive things to say.

'Don't think like that,' was the best I could manage, even though it must have been written all over my face that I shared Kate's darkest fears.

'Found it!' Reef bellowed. 'Can I take it to my party?'

I'd been so lost in memories I'd forgotten where I was and what Reef was searching for. He charged at me from the conservatory, swishing his plastic sword, with Finn hot on his heels.

'We've been playing pirates for aaaages, Daddy. What have you been doing?'

'Thinking,' I said.

'About what?' Reef asked.

'Lots and lots of things – your birthday included.'

'Not fair, I haven't got a sword, Daddy,' Finn said crossly. 'Can I get one for the party? Can I, please?'

'I can do better than that,' I said, feeling a welcome surge of gratitude flow through my body, washing away the dark fears of the past. It was incredible we'd come this far, with both boys thriving. 'I'm going to get full pirate costumes for all three of us. It'll be the best pirate party EVER!'

I sat the boys down and told them all about the history of *The Matthew*.

'More than five hundred years ago a man called John Cabot set sail for Asia aboard the original *Matthew*. It was a Tudor merchant ship, and he wanted to trade with people in Asia. But do you know where he actually went?'

Both boys shook their heads.

'America!' He landed on the coast of Newfoundland – so he was actually the man who discovered America, not Christopher Columbus!'

'Oooh,' said Reef. 'Is it the zact same ship we go on?'

'No, it's the replica one in the docks. It's been built to look exactly like the original one and it's a really cool boat with big sails.'

We had lots more conversations like that over the next week or so as we waited for Reef's big day – 29 July – to come round. We also had great fun putting together our pirate costumes, complete with eye patches, bandannas and white shirts with billowing sleeves.

A local paper got wind of the party and wanted to run a story, as Kate and I had given a few interviews over the years about Reef's cancer, plus Kate's death had been widely reported. Talking to the reporter on the phone made me remember one particularly cheery headline about Reef's progress which I'd read when the memory boxes had arrived. 'Our Little Miracle,' the old newspaper clipping said. I wanted to read it again, and on the night before Reef's party I decided to dig it out so I could enjoy reading it once more. I remembered there was a happy photograph of me and Kate and both boys splashed across the page, and I remembered Kate giving a detailed account of Reef's illness to the journalist who wrote the story.

I had a rummage through the treasure chests and found the article on the top of a pile of faded newspaper cuttings I'd tucked into a brown envelope. My eyes fell immediately on Kate. The way the photograph was taken, there was a shadow over most of her face. It made her skin look greyer than it was, and she looked older than her years. The article was in the *Weston Mercury*, and it was dated 30 July 2008, the day after Reef's fourth birthday. I scanned the piece for Kate's words and, as I read them, I remembered her sitting on the sofa downstairs and saying them out loud to the reporter, bravely.

'We never thought we'd see this day. When we heard the prognosis there was no way we thought we'd get to this stage. He really has done remarkably well . . . It was surreal with one son in one hospital and one in another. At that time we had two children with minimal chances of survival . . . Reef has had sixty general anaesthetics, thirty lots of radiotherapy and forty different lots of chemotherapy, but he's coped remarkably well and he's always happy and smiley . . . He adapts so he can do things. He can't walk up the stairs very well and has trouble putting on his socks, but he adapts to everything. He's learning and improvising all the time; he's remarkable . . .'

That was tough, reading Kate's words, hearing Kate saying them in my head. Exactly two years had passed since then. It was no time at all, yet in that time Kate had fought for her life, and lost, while her 'little miracle' continued to make incredible progress.

I remembered Kate's reaction when we were finally given Reef's full diagnosis. It was four days after Finn's birth, and we were both in a terrible state. 'Diddy' was still in special care under ultraviolet lights and receiving oxygen to help him breathe. Nobody could promise us we'd be taking home a healthy baby any time soon, and Kate was distraught as she looked at Finn through his sterile glass bubble, denied the chance to hold her newborn boy. All she could do was give him a little stroke or a tickle through the portholes in the plastic cot, which broke her heart.

Leaving Finn alone at Southmead Hospital to travel across town to hear Reef's diagnosis felt surreal in the extreme. Kate and I tried our best to reason with each other that we couldn't possibly receive yet more bad news, but of course that was exactly what was waiting for us. When we arrived at the Bristol Royal Infirmary we were ushered into a private family room, and you didn't need to be a genius to work out we were about to hear something very serious. As well as a concerned-looking consultant and several nurses, including Reef's ward manager, Jamie, there was a CLIC Sargent nurse in attendance, who I knew was specially trained to deal with cancer in children.

Kate and I held hands as the consultant delivered the blow in a hushed but serious and authoritative voice. He said something like: 'I'm afraid we are going to be blunt and honest . . .' before delivering the first horrendous line: 'I'm very sorry to have to tell you that the lump, the tumour, in Reef's abdomen is cancerous, and it's malignant.'

The 'C' word that had stalked us and frightened us was no longer a shadowy threat, it was real. Cancer was attacking Reef and in so doing it was attacking me and Kate. The words struck me like a physical blow. I felt wounded and I wanted to be sick. Kate searched my face, and I watched hers crumble. 'Oh, Singe,' she sobbed. 'I can't believe it. I just can't believe it.' I held her tight, feeling her shake and sob as my own tears splashed down my cheeks and soaked into Kate's hair.

'Nor can I,' was all I could say. 'Nor can I.'

Through a haze of tears, we learned that Reef's was an

extremely rare form of cancer called rhabdoid soft tissue sarcoma. As the tumour had grown it had wrapped around the large femoral nerve in his leg, and the aggressive treatment he needed would be likely to damage the nerve further still. He was given a six per cent chance of survival, and we were warned he might never be able to walk again.

It wasn't meant to be like this. We should have been taking an excited Reef to meet his brand-new baby brother, yet even little Finn's life was in jeopardy, being so frail and premature. The situation was absolutely hideous. I felt battered and helpless, like I was in an icy sea with wave after frozen wave crashing over me, stealing my strength and my breath whichever way I tried to swim.

We were also told that Reef's cancer was so rare he was one of just eight cases in the world to be diagnosed, and we discovered that the oldest surviving victim of such a cancer had only lived until the age of sixteen. The consultant explained gently that Reef's tumour was so aggressive they feared it could kill him far sooner than that. They had never seen a case like his before, with the tumour positioned in the pelvic area, and they had not yet worked out how to treat him.

'How long has he got?' Kate asked bravely. She was shaking from head to foot.

In my mind I was dreading them saying five years, or even ten. He was a toddler, just eighteen months old, but surely he would live to be a teenager, even if he didn't make his sixteenth birthday?

'We are very sorry, but Reef may not survive for more than a few days,' the unbelievable reply came back.

'Days?' Kate said desperately. 'Days?' Her voice sounded

withered and confused. Every bit of colour drained from her face, and she looked like a shrunken, wounded version of herself. I wrapped my quivering arms around her, afraid she might shrivel up and sink to the ground. We clung together and stared at each other in utter disbelief, and then listened in horror as a discussion began about whether the doctors should wait until they knew more about Reef's tumour before starting a tailored regime of chemotherapy.

Despite feeling devastated and forlorn, Kate and I were in clear agreement on this point: Reef was so poorly he should be given some form of generic cancer treatment immediately. 'Start treating him now, please,' Kate begged. 'I don't want to waste any time at all. We don't have any time to waste.' I squeezed her hand and nodded my support. The doctors agreed, and they were amazing. They tried to calm the waters even though they had a very tough job on their hands, both in keeping our heads up and in treating Reef. Despite the dire prognosis we were not to give up hope, they told us.

Reef was given his first cancer drugs whilst also undergoing emergency bone scans, blood tests and cardiograms to work out his long-term chemotherapy plan. We gave our approval for Reef to be blasted with as much chemo and radiotherapy as his little body could take, which we were told would go on for about a year, should he be lucky enough to survive that long.

'The chances of getting this type of cancer are like winning the Lottery forty times on the trot,' I remember one doctor told us in the blurry aftermath of Reef's diagnosis. It was a surreal thing to hear, but then again everything felt surreal.

Kate broke down so many times I lost count. She should have been still in the last bloom of pregnancy, enjoying her well-earned maternity leave, not struggling to digest all this horrific news while Finn was fighting for his life too in his lonely little incubator across town. We both walked around like zombies, crying, shaking with fear, feeling sick with nerves, expecting a phone call or a tap on the shoulder from a doctor, delivering yet more bad news.

'I wish it was me who had cancer, not Reef,' Kate said when we were alone one night. I knew she meant every word.

'Don't say that, Kate,' I said, not wanting to let such a thought into my head for even a split second.

'It's true. I'd swap places with him in a flash. How can such a little boy take so much aggressive treatment?'

I had no answer.

'What if Finn takes a turn for the worse? The way our luck is going we could lose both of them.'

Every fibre of my body throbbed with pain and tension, and my heart ached with love for Kate. I couldn't answer her because I couldn't comprehend how our life had taken such a terrible twist in such a short pace of time. For the first time in my life I felt I had no control over our future. I'd never felt so vulnerable before. It seemed that our lives had been turned upside down in the blink of an eye.

How had this happened? Kate and I were always the lucky ones, the golden couple who travelled around the planet together, lapping up one adventure while already planning the next. You make your own luck; that's what I always said when friends told us they envied our exciting lifestyle. When Reef came along he was everything we'd dreamed of and more. I know every parent says it of their child, but Reef really was the most perfect, beautiful baby you could imagine. He was stunning-looking, with a bright, sunny personality to match his shock of blond hair, and we doted on him.

When Reef started to get ill I had every faith that our blue-eyed boy would shrug it off and come up smiling. I prayed that by the time Kate gave birth to our second child we'd be the perfect family of four, sailing through life on the crest of a wave together, never looking back, and saying: 'Thank God that's all over. How lucky are we to have two awesome little boys?' In our darkest days, as we travelled between the two hospitals visiting both our fragile sons, all I wanted was to see my wife happy again. To see her cuddling our two gorgeous little boys in the sunshine was a dream I willed would come true. I couldn't ask for more than that.

I got that wish, eventually, after Reef survived more than two years of relentless cancer treatment, which included major surgery to remove the tumour, countless blood and platelet transfusions, scores of scans and X-rays to check things like his kidneys and heart, plus intensive courses of antibiotics to compensate for his battered immune system, which left his little body wide open to a host of nasty infections that made him vomit and writhe in pain. All that, of course, was on top of his mega-doses of chemotherapy and radiotherapy, which also made him sick and dangerously weak – so poorly, in fact, that the treatment almost killed him on more than one occasion.

The newspaper cutting in my hand reminded me of how incredibly well Reef had done to survive. He was indeed our 'little miracle', and, of course, Finn had pulled through too, even if it was four long weeks before he finally emerged from his incubator and Kate could actually hold him and kiss him. Kate, healthy Kate, cuddled both of our little boys every single day after that, longing for normality but feeling grateful for what she had. She had to wait those two long years before she started to believe that Reef really was a medical marvel, and he was going to survive just like 'Diddy'.

Reef's fourth birthday was such a precious milestone, and of course reaching his fifth in July 2009 was an even greater landmark. Kate was almost a year into her own cancer treatment by then, but it didn't stop her celebrating with him and hoping for her own precious recovery.

Now, if Kate were watching, she would want to see me cuddling our two little boys in the sunshine just like she did, seizing the moment and living with hope in my heart.

'Make scrapbook of your adventures,' she wrote on her list.

'I will,' I said quietly as I packed the newspaper cutting away.

When I kissed the boys goodnight, I told them the local paper was coming to take our photograph on *The Matthew* during Reef's sixth birthday party.

'It'll be a great adventure, and we can keep a record of it for ever,' I told them cheerfully.

I was confident the party would be a rip-roaring success. By this time I'd already taken out several classes of older children from Reef's school on *The Matthew* for an activity day as I'd planned, which went down a storm.

The headmaster, Mr Webber, joined us for the school trip, as did the Lord Mayor of Bristol, who dressed up as a Tudor merchant. The highlight that day was when we sailed past a local pub in Pill, where lots of parents had gathered to wave at their children on board. The adults were sitting out in the sun drinking pints and glasses of wine when we came into view, and didn't have a clue what we had planned. All the children were in on the secret, though, and were fired up with excitement.

'Remember what I said?' I asked them. There were about fifty children, all nodding and giggling in anticipation.

'When we fire the cannons don't put your hands in your ears as it will make them pop. You need to all shout "have a care" just like the proper pirates did in the olden days. Are we ready, shipmates?'

The kids all cheered and made blood-curdling pirate roars as we fired two cannons in quick succession, letting the parents have an ear-splitting broadside. They hadn't suspected a thing, and it was hilarious to see them jump out of their skin as the wall of sound hit them. Several parents who had been sitting on the pub wall actually fell off, and I could see them spilling drinks and laughing and gasping in shock. It was as funny as you like, and I wanted Reef's birthday to be just as memorable.

I spent weeks and weeks before his party buying pirate-themed goodies as well as perfecting our pirate outfits. We invited Reef's entire class plus other friends, and all their parents came down to watch as I set sail with about fifty swashbuckling kids. I allowed parents who'd dressed up to come on board, but there were so many of us we also had two ribs alongside *The Matthew*, stuffed to the gunwales with mums and dads wearing eye patches, fake scars and spotted headscarves.

We floated around Bristol Harbour with the Jolly Roger

flag flying while the kids had loads of fun, climbing the rigging, exploring the ship from stem to stern and playing pirate games. They thoroughly enjoyed bashing the parrot piñatas, and the deck was awash with sweets shaped like skull and crossbones, gold chocolate coins and silver pirate rings, which the kids fell upon. We stopped off to collect chips to eat with the party food, and the adults tucked into a cream tea. The adventure culminated with a rousing chorus of 'Happy Birthday' from the whole crew as well as the guests, and Reef blew out the six candles on his chocolate skull-and-crossbones cake. His little face was a picture of happiness. He loved every moment and didn't want to get off the boat at the end of the day.

'Thank you, Daddy,' he beamed. 'I love you, Daddy.' I hugged him close. 'Happy birthday,' I said. 'I love you too.'

I was thrilled to bits.

'All I can say is "wow"!' said one of the mums from school. Another jokingly told me off for setting the bar so high. 'What on earth are the rest of us meant to do for kids' parties after this? How can you top this?' she laughed.

'D'you think Kate would have loved it?' I asked, already knowing the answer.

'You know she would!' came the emphatic reply. 'Well done!'

At bedtime that night Reef asked me if I would measure him on their bedroom doorframe, like Mummy used to do on birthdays.

'Can we do Mummy properly too?' he asked, looking at me with puppy dog eyes which meant I couldn't possibly refuse, even though both he and Finn were absolutely shattered and ready for their beds.

I recalled how, last year, Kate and the boys had messed about balancing books on each other's heads. There was a faint scribble Reef had made with a pencil, which I remembered was meant to mark Kate's height. It wasn't accurate at all, as he couldn't reach high enough up the frame, but she humoured him and left it there anyway.

'Need to measure me on door frame – Mummy was 5ft 1in,' was on the list, so we would do it properly now.

'Go and get a book and a pencil, and I'll find a tape measure,' I agreed.

Reef gave me a cheeky, victorious smile, which told me this was as much about putting off bedtime as it was about recording heights. Needless to say, Finn got in on the act too, and the pair of them milked the exercise for all it was worth as I measured them, then added a notch at five foot one, for Mummy. I'd have to watch that tactic, I thought. Finn was a bit young, but Reef was old enough to play my heart strings like a fiddle.

A couple of days later the *Bristol Evening Post* printed a story under the headline: 'Brave Reef enjoys a pirate's birthday in memory of mum.'

There was a fantastic picture of me and the boys dressed up to the nines in our pirate outfits on board *The Matthew*, and I was quoted as saying: 'We always celebrate birthdays big time . . . it is something Kate said she would have liked to have done with the boys.'

It was very satisfying to clip out the article and carry it up to the memory boxes, before placing it neatly in a scrapbook. I'd ticked off another item on Kate's list, one I vowed to tick off again and again.

I remembered what another mum had said to me on the

day of the party: 'Not many people could do what you're doing so soon . . .' she said sweetly, giving me a slightly pitiful smile as she trailed off from what I knew she was about to say: 'after losing Kate.' I just smiled at the time and shrugged.

'I love it,' I said, meaning it. 'I'm a big kid at heart, you know!'

Now I felt a pang of longing for Kate as I remembered that conversation. 'What choice do I have but to carry on and make my kids happy?' I thought. 'The alternative doesn't bear thinking about.'

Looking at the partied-out boys that night, I immediately gave myself a mental telling-off. I wasn't putting on a show or going through the motions here by any stretch. It was really tough bringing the boys up alone, but on the whole we were having fun, and lots of it. As long as we keep doing that, we're winning, I told myself.

I did, however, let another, less positive, thought into my head. It had been festering since the other mum's remark at the party about 'setting the bar so high' with such an extravagant celebration. I faced it now, asking myself frankly: 'Singe, are you spoiling the boys?' It felt the right time to answer, and I indulged in a candid conversation with myself, playing out both sides in my head. 'Yes, I do spoil the boys,' my soft, paternal side admitted without hesitation. 'But why not?' it argued. 'Reef and Finn have gone through an awful lot of crap, and I'm making up for them not having a mum. Where's the harm in that?' My harsher, more macho side wasn't entirely convinced. 'You don't want to bring up a couple of spoilt brats,' it accused. 'Kate would hate them to become a pair of namby-pambys.'

Happily, those reproachful words didn't cut any ice. It wasn't that I didn't want to hear them, it was because they didn't ring true at all. 'I might spoil the boys, but they are not spoilt brats,' I replied with confidence. 'They have to do lots of chores that other kids their age have their mums there to do for them. Reef and Finn help me make the beds and sort the laundry and load the dishwasher, because I can't do everything on my own. They've been forced to grow up fast in many ways, and as a result I think they earn their treats.' I was on a roll now, and I argued my case with ease. 'Besides, because of my line of business they were always going to experience lots of exciting activities,' I asserted. 'If Kate were still alive, they'd be having loads of amazing fun out on the water in any case, and they'd always have great birthday parties, because that's how we always lived our lives.'

I had a version of that conversation with Ruth a few days later, to thoroughly test out my argument. 'I don't want to change the way I do things, but am I right?' I asked her bluntly.

'Singe,' she replied. 'You tell everyone to live for each minute, and to make the most of each moment. And you know what? You're absolutely right,' she said. 'I'm glad you practise what you preach, you are showing the boys how to live.'

I told her I'd really enjoyed planning Reef's birthday party, and it had been great to have something so exciting to look forward to. I also said that now it was over, and the souvenir newspaper clipping was filed for posterity, I felt the urge to get the next adventure booked.

'Well, what are you waiting for?' she smiled.

'Thanks, Ruth,' I grinned. 'It's what I wanted to hear, but I know you would be the first to tell me if I was making a pig's ear of things.'

I thought about Egypt and I was very pleased I'd decided to make it a priority to take the boys there. After our previous trips, both as a couple and when the boys were very small, Kate was absolutely desperate to see Reef and Finn snorkelling in the Red Sea. It was one of her favourite places on the planet, and I will never forget one dive I did there with her.

We were forty feet down, feeding a kaleidoscope of fish, when a shoal of hammerhead sharks appeared from nowhere. I looked across at Kate, who looked tiny compared to these sixteen-foot beasts. Some were bigger than mini-buses. Her arms were flapping, and for a split second I thought she might be panicking, but then I realized what she was doing. Kate was in fact pulling out her video camera, and moments later she started swimming right up to the sharks, completely fearlessly. A silvertip shark appeared behind the hammerheads, and Kate captured him on film too.

Most other divers fled, but not Kate. For the size of her she was incredibly brave and had so much bottle it was unreal. She got some cracking footage, then laughed off the close encounter when we were back on dry land.

'What was I supposed to do?' Kate giggled. 'The sharks were in my reef – I wasn't shifting!'

She was exhilarated by the experience, and it was a pleasure to see. I know nobody deserves to get cancer, but why did it have to happen to such a brave and brilliant woman?

'You're a nightmare!' I said.

'Well, you're the one who taught me not to be afraid of sharks,' she giggled.

I knew exactly what she meant by that, and I enjoyed the next memory all over again, laughing out loud to myself. It happened during our honeymoon in the Maldives, and it's a story I will never tire of telling.

It was a beautiful, moonlit night, and we were all ready to go on an evening dive on a pretty house reef, attached to the island we were staying on.

'This is going to be absolutely mind-blowing,' I said to Kate. It was her first night dive, and I was very excited for her. 'Night diving is so much more exciting,' I said. 'We'll hopefully see angelfish, barracudas, clownfish, parrot fish, eagle rays . . . it'll be totally stunning down there.'

Kate peered cautiously over the edge of the jetty, which to be fair looked dark and mysterious, and pretty daunting.

'Will there be any sharks?' she asked nervously.

'Sharks?' I scoffed gently. 'No, the sharks are all sleeping at this time of night.'

'Are you sure, Singe?'

'Don't worry!' I said, seeing Kate's eyes flickering with worry. 'I'll be right beside you. Listen, some of the nocturnal fish change colour at night, and we might be lucky enough to see squid or octopus, as they're more active at night. It'll be amazing. You'll never forget your first night dive.'

Kate took a deep breath and agreed to go for it, pulling on her mask and then bracing herself to take a giant stride into the watery unknown. I had entered the water moments before and was floating five metres away from the end of the jetty. I signalled to Kate I was clear and that she could enter the water, but as I checked below I saw a small white tip reef shark cruising towards us. What happened next was absolutely unbelievable. Kate strode off the pontoon, and I watched in amazement as she managed to land completely astride the shark. The timing was incredible, and very funny indeed.

The startled shark fled like a scalded cat, and Kate surfaced in a flurry of bubbles and curses. I surfaced too and was absolutely killing myself laughing, but Kate was clearly not impressed, and it took me several minutes to stop her hitting me and demanding we abandon the dive.

'I thought you said sharks go to sleep at night,' she said. 'Did you plan that?'

'Like I could!' I laughed. 'He wasn't clockwork, you know!'

Nevertheless, I was forced to confess that lots of sharks are actually nocturnal and come out hunting for food at night.

'I hate you, Singe,' Kate said, narrowing her eyes.

'Do you really?' I asked.

'No!' she laughed. 'I suppose now you're my husband I have to love you for better or worse, and I'll have to write that moment off as one of the worst. My heart nearly jumped out of my wetsuit, and I dread to think what the poor shark thought!'

'Life's not about the number of breaths you take,' I said, borrowing a line I'd heard in a film to try to sweet-talk my way out of trouble. 'It's about the moments that take your breath away.'

Kate continued to huff and puff for a while before

agreeing to try again, and the dive proved to be every bit as stunning as I predicted. At one point we turned off our torches and played with the phosphorescent plankton in the water, watching it spark and glow like a million electric blue halogen bulbs. We only called it a night after I was stung by some fire coral, giving Kate the last laugh.

The boys would love Egypt now they were old enough to snorkel, and I decided to get it booked up that week and arrange for them to have their holiday vaccinations, so we could start looking forward to it. The issue of the jabs was a bit of a tricky one. When Reef was diagnosed with cancer we inevitably looked for a cause, desperate to know what could have possibly gone so wrong to have triggered such a rare and aggressive form of the disease.

When Kate was diagnosed too, we thought there had to be some sort of a genetic link, despite the fact there is no significant history of cancer on either side of the family. The doctors, however, concluded there was no link whatsoever between Reef's cancer and Kate's. We were told it was just another one of those alarming Lottery statistics, with the odds of both mother and son being struck down with two entirely unrelated, aggressive cancers being completely off the scale.

'It must have been the jabs,' Kate said, desperately fishing for answers, maternal guilt making her blame herself when Reef was diagnosed. 'I've had every inoculation under the sun because of all our foreign holidays. One of them must have affected me when I was pregnant, or even before I got pregnant. Or maybe it was a mixture of jabs that didn't agree with me?'

There was absolutely no medical evidence to back this

up, but jabs were the only possible culprit Kate could come up with as she tried to answer the unanswerable questions surrounding Reef's condition. Her own cancer fed her fears and suspicions, and when she came to write her list she wrote very clearly: *'Please don't go on off-the-beaten-track holidays as I strongly believe vaccinations in Reef and me triggered the cancer.'*

I discussed the dilemma with a few members of my family, who all immediately told me not to worry. 'Kate wanted you to take the boys to Egypt, it's on the list,' my dad said. 'And she tried to go with you, more than once. You don't need to worry.'

'Egypt isn't off the beaten track,' my brother added. 'The boys don't need any exotic inoculations, just routine ones. Kate would not have wanted you to take them there otherwise.' It was what I wanted to hear, and I knew they were right.

'By the way, can we come with you?' both my brother and my dad asked a few weeks later.

'What? Really?'

I was quite surprised they wanted to join me, but then again I guess I would be away for Christmas, and that was family time.

'Most definitely,' my dad said, adding that my stepmum was fully in favour of coming too.

'It'll be great,' my brother added, telling me his girlfriend also wanted to join us.

When I told Kate's parents about the plans, they also wanted to come.

'Well, I'm going anyway and if you want to come, then come,' I said to everyone who expressed an interest, and by the time we booked the trip we were a party of thirteen.

My brother Matt, his girlfriend Olivia, my little sister Lucinda, my dad and stepmum and their best friends, known to me as Uncle Norman and Auntie Chris, would come with us for the full fortnight, and Christine and Martin, along with Kate's brother Ben, would join us for the second week.

I was quite surprised they were all up for it, and I didn't quite believe it until everything was booked and paid for some time later. I guess nobody wanted me to be on my own for Christmas, but the thought had never really crossed my mind. I never thought I would be on my own because I actually wouldn't be: I'd have Reef and Finn to keep me company the whole time.

Nevertheless, once I'd got my head round the idea of a big family Christmas holiday, I decided it would be fun, and no doubt more fun than if it were just the three of us. The date was set for 17 December, a year on from when Kate and the boys and I flew to Lapland, and I was glad we had a good few months to plan and look forward to it.

It was August now, and the school summer holidays were stretching before us. I had a full week's work lined up at a surf trade show in Bristol, where I was part of a team putting on a paramedic show. I took the job on because it was well paid, the boys could tag along with me for some parts of the week, and it was local. It would pay for a little summer holiday, too, and I'd arranged to stay at the Highlands End Holiday Park in Eype, West Dorset, with my dad and stepmum later in the month. It was a convenient spot, as I had another job lined up just along the coast, this time doing something quite unusual.

I'd been asked to assist with the making of a promotional video linked to the Disney film *The Voyage of the Dawn Treader*, because it involved escorting *The Matthew* down the coast. Over the past few months *4 Saints* had become *The Matthew*'s unofficial safety boat, and that's how the opportunity arose. I was really chuffed about it. My plan was to drop the boys off with their other grandparents nearby after the caravan stay with my dad and stepmum, so I could take the job while the boys continued their holiday.

'Are we going to be in the movie?' Finn asked excitedly. He'd heard me on the phone to the organizer of the trip, Chris, and was all ears.

'No, Finn, I'm going to help take *The Matthew* down the coast so it can be used to make a DVD.'

'Are you going to be in the DVD?' he asked.

'No,' I said. 'It's a bit complicated to explain, but people from all over the world have won a competition about the film, and they are going to sail on *The Matthew*, which will be dressed up to look like the *Dawn Treader*. It's my job to help them sail safely to Land's End, where they'll be filmed doing lots of activities, like archery and knot-tying.'

'Oooh! Can we come?' Finn begged.

'No, Finn, I'm afraid you can't. You and Reef are staying with your grandparents, but I'll take lots of pictures and tell you all about it.'

It was my first big commercial job with *4 Saints*, and I was pleased to start recouping some of her costs, but I accepted the work mainly for the sheer thrill and fun of it. It also worked out perfectly that the boys could stay with their grandparents while I zipped off along the coast for a few days.

I was telling Ruth my holiday plans one night when she popped over for a cup of tea.

'You're so lucky,' she said. 'Lots of single parents have a real struggle coping with the kids during the school holidays. It's great you can take them to work with you sometimes, and you have plenty of help.'

I hadn't really thought about the benefits of my job because that's how it had always been. When Kate was alive I always worked flexible hours to accommodate her office job and the boys' school holidays, and when Reef was ill I managed to juggle work around hospital appointments and visits, with Kate's parents helping out a great deal too, of course. But Ruth was right, as usual.

'You're spot on,' I told her, acknowledging what she said. 'But having a flexible job isn't everything, is it?'

'What d'you mean?' she asked.

'I mean there's a lot more to being a successful single parent than coping with work.'

'Of course,' Ruth said, nodding wisely as I carried on.

'Everyone keeps telling me I'm doing great, but I'm far from perfect. I have good days and bad days, you know. Sometimes I just feel like crying. I wonder if I'm doing as good a job as Kate would have done.'

What I said was unplanned, but it came from the heart.

'Singe, you try your best with the boys every day,' Ruth said. 'Kate would be delighted. They're thriving. As long as you keep telling them what's happening in their lives, so they don't get upset or confused, you mustn't worry about leading your own life too. I've found that as long as children know what's going on, and you are always on time for them and you stick to arrangements, things work out fine.'

I could imagine Kate saying the same things. No wonder she and Ruth were such good mates, I thought. They shared the same thought patterns in many ways.

'I didn't think I would be saying this so soon, but I'm starting to see that Kate was right,' I added cautiously.

'In what way?' Ruth asked, her lips stretching into a smile. I think she was already one step ahead of me.

'The boys do need a female influence. I think it's impossible to be Mum *and* Dad.'

'I'm glad you feel like that, Singe,' Ruth said happily. 'It's normal. Don't feel guilty. It's what Kate wanted, and it'll happen when the time is right. Now go on and enjoy your holidays!'

I couldn't believe we were packing up and going on our third caravan holiday of the year. If Kate was on a cloud looking down I was sure she must be doubled up laughing at me.

Chapter 8

'Kiss goodbye even if leaving for a short time'

'Where are you going, Daddy?' Finn asked.

'I'm going to do some filming with the boat, remember I told you?' I replied.

His eyes widened. 'I forgot. Can I come?'

'No, Finn, you can't come with me this time, but I'll tell you all about it when I get back.'

It was the last week of the school holidays. We'd had a good time with my dad and stepmum at the caravan park, despite a few glitches in the system.

When we arrived at the van the boys were beside themselves with excitement.

'Yippee! There's our little house!' Finn squealed. Both he and Reef couldn't get through the door quick enough, zipping round like livewires, deciding who was sleeping where. Kate used to encourage them when they behaved like that, no doubt remembering her own exciting childhood trips to caravan parks. It drove me nuts, as I preferred to unpack and get settled in peace before starting to relax. I used to leave Kate to deal with the boys while I lugged in the bags and supplies, and this time I decided I'd just try to work around them. It was a big mistake. They were like wasps at a barbecue, buzzing in my face every five minutes.

‘Where’s the bag I asked you to put in the car – the one with the pyjamas and toothbrushes?’

‘It’s in my bedroom,’ Reef said.

‘Which bedroom – the one in the van?’

‘No, my bedroom at home!’

‘Reef, I don’t believe this! What good are they at home? It’s the only thing I asked you to do.’

Reef was upset at being told off and sulked, while Finn didn’t seem to care about anything but bouncing on the beds and getting under my feet.

I swear I had hot steam coming out of my nostrils by the time I’d unpacked. Kate would have double-checked the bags and Kate would have run round like an excited little girl, instead of simmering with tension like me. Ruth had been very kind when she told me I was coping so well as a single parent, but was it true? How could I possibly give the boys as good an upbringing as Kate and I would have done together? That day, I felt like I had one hand tied behind my back, and I couldn’t see how I was going to pull it free.

I did eventually manage to relax that week, cooking barbecues and swimming and canoeing with the boys, but I realized it was perhaps good timing that I was going to escape on my own for a few days with *The Matthew*.

When we left the caravan I delivered the boys to my mum and stepdad in Devon and said my goodbyes, kissing both boys twice.

‘I won’t be away for long, be good now for Nanny and Brian,’ I told them.

‘Tell us *everything* when you get back!’ Reef said.

‘Of course I will. I’ll take photos too, and you do the same.’

The Matthew looked fantastic, with *Narnia* emblazoned in purple on the sail, a huge dragon's head constructed on the bow and a swishing tail attached to the stern. The plan was to sail round Land's End to St Michael's Mount and Falmouth, making stops on the way at Padstow, Tintagel, Lundy and the Scillies, where the competition winners would carry out a series of outdoor pursuit challenges.

As well as having *4 Saints* as an escort vessel, we also had the *Mabel Alice* lifeboat accompanying us, as the safety of the guests was paramount. The initial journey threading our way between Steep Holm and Flat Holm down the Bristol Channel was pretty horrendous. The weather wasn't too bad, but the waters were incredibly choppy, and certainly not what we were hoping for in late August. Conditions were getting steadily worse, and it was decided we'd head to Ilfracombe and wait in the safety of the port rather than continue our journey down to Land's End.

Unfortunately, as the tide went out that evening *The Matthew* rolled on to a moored steel ferry called the *Oldenburg*, causing some minor damage to *The Matthew*'s wooden superstructure. We had to attach a rope from my rib to the top of *The Matthew*'s mast to pull her free, and everybody panicked for a good few hours until the tide finally came back in and *The Matthew* was able to set sail again at around 10.30 p.m.

I'd been awake for almost twenty-four hours by this point, and decided I ought to get some sleep below deck on the *Mabel Alice*. I didn't feel very comfortable with the arrangements. Both boats had volunteers among their crew, some very young and inexperienced, and if I hadn't been so tired I'm sure I wouldn't have slept a wink.

I was crammed into a small bunk, and it took some time for me to actually fall asleep. My mind was ticking over, worrying about what tomorrow might bring. I tried to think about the boys and what adventure stories we might be able to swap at the end of the week. It was lonely on the lifeboat in the dark, and I eventually drifted off thinking about Kate, imagining what she would make of this trip.

I thought about her instruction to '*Make scrapbook of your adventures*' and I reckoned she would approve. I pictured her making her own scrapbooks, sticking in airline tickets and restaurant receipts amongst the captioned photographs of us smiling on foreign beaches.

I could see Kate's girly handwriting, and I imagined one of her old love letters coming to life in my sleepy head. I saw it floating towards me on the water, like a message in a bottle, except there was no bottle.

Kate wrote it when she was on a family holiday to Switzerland with her parents. It was 1987; I could see the date written neatly in black fountain pen. 'I dreamed about you last night,' she is saying. Kate is reading the words to me; I can feel her warm breath on my ear.

I see a teenage Katie lying on her own in a single bed in a hotel room. 'Another night down, twelve to go,' she is whispering in the dark as she writes to me. 'It rained most of the day with a few thunderstorms. I am missing you so much. I am dreaming of you. Please make sure we are together forever one day. I love you, I love you, I love you, I love you . . .'

I see Kate blow three kisses to me as she draws them on the end of the letter. 'I have to go now, I love you acres and acres, love Katie xxx' She starts to float away, and in my dream I am jumping off the side of the boat and searching for her in the water, trying to swim to her fading face and body as fast as I can, before she vanishes from view.

The moon above is a giant Disney-style clock, and each stroke I swim in the cold, dark water seems to turn the hands anti-clockwise. I am trying to swim to Switzerland, trying to turn back time. There are sharks circling the waters around me.

'Watch out!' someone screams.

It sounds like Kate.

'Sharks don't sleep at night!' the voice shouts.

'Watch out! Help! What's happening?'

It's not Kate's voice any more, and the screams are piercing. Something is wrong, and I am in danger. I see the giant dragon's head of the *Dawn Treader* staring at me in close-up. I panic, my heart thumping. Another voice starts shouting, and then another.

'Look out! Oi! Be careful – what's going on?'

I can feel my brain slosh from side to side in my skull as I'm pushed by the waves. Kate is in danger! I have to get to Kate or she might slip away from me for ever! I snap open my eyes in panic to look for her and immediately realize I am all alone, lying in a bunk in the darkness, on board the *Mabel Alice*.

My dream is over, but the voices are still screaming. Confused, I jumped out of bed in my shorts and ran to the deck to find out what all the fuss was about.

'Anchor's slipped,' I heard the lifeguard shout. 'We're colliding with *The Matthew*!'

My heart sank like a stone and I watched, helpless, as

the *Mabel Alice* struck the side of *The Matthew*. It felt like another minor collision, thank goodness, but it had caused a huge commotion.

'Don't panic,' I said to some of the assembled crew and passengers who were shouting and upset, but it was 4 a.m., and it clearly wasn't the best time for people to keep their heads. Seconds later, I felt the *Mabel Alice* speed unexpectedly into reverse. With the best of intentions, the captain had tried to limit the damage by getting the lifeboat well away from *The Matthew* as quickly as possible.

The trouble was, he forgot *4 Saints* was on the back of the lifeboat, and he reversed into my rib with a deafening smash. I watched in absolute horror as my damaged boat bobbed free of the stern, adrift. I slid aboard *4 Saints* from the *Mabel Alice* to survey the mess. The console and windscreen were smashed to pieces and I just about managed to get her started so I could limp away and utter a few choice words in the darkness, out of earshot. I looked up at the sky. Kate would have been spitting tacks too, but she would have told me to stay calm. It could all be fixed on the insurance. I knew that, but I was absolutely devastated about how the boys would react.

I replayed in my head that moment when Reef first spotted the boat. 'I'd *love* a boat like that!' I could hear him saying it, and I could see both boys grinning like Cheshire cats when I told them the rib was ours. We'd had *4 Saints* for just five months, and now we'd be without her for months on end while she went away for repair. The boat was the boys' pride and joy, and I was absolutely gutted for them.

I spent a miserable, difficult three hours scuba diving to

help cut the *Mabel Alice* free, as my bow line had been wound around her propeller in the accident, crippling her.

The Matthew had continued her journey, taking all my kit, including my phone and wallet, with her. I eventually caught her, even though *4 Saints* was limping along, and once I'd retrieved my belongings I had to arrange for my dad to collect me and *4 Saints*, so he could take the battered rib home while I travelled overland to meet *The Matthew* in Padstow.

When I finally rejoined the group and we reached Tintagel Castle later that morning, I'd managed to cheer up a bit. I taught a group of children archery and gave them a snorkelling lesson at Rock. They did some filming for the DVD, which all went smoothly, and most of the youngsters were oblivious to the drama that had played out in the early hours, which was exactly as it should be. 'All's well that ends well,' I thought.

Driving back to pick up the boys, I couldn't stop thinking about what had happened and I found myself dwelling on Kate's wish, *'Kiss goodbye even if leaving for a short time.'* What if things had gone really badly wrong, and something had happened to me? I felt a pang of deep-seated worry. It reminded me of the day Kate died, when I told the boys Mummy was dead. I remembered the overwhelming sense of responsibility I felt as a single parent, and that same feeling flooded my body again.

I thought about Kate kissing the boys for the very last time. She hugged them tight as she lay in her hospital bed the day before she died, not knowing if it would be the last chance she would ever have to kiss them. Still, she kissed them as she always did, with joy and affection, and love in her heart, making them feel like the most special little people in the world. The boys had no idea it could be, would be the last time. Their brave mum looked into their eyes and smiled like she had done so many times before.

'I'm going to have my hand prints put on to a canvas,' she told them. Pausing to pull in some breath from her oxygen mask, she added: 'I thought it would be nice if we all did it, and made a family hand-print picture.'

'What colour can mine be?' Reef asked.

'You can choose,' Kate said.

'I want green,' Finn said.

'I would like red and blue,' Kate said.

I took a photograph, not realizing it would be the last one of Kate and the boys together. Only Kate knew that; at least, I think she did.

Now I had a very powerful feeling that you never really know what's round the corner. Anything could happen, at any time. Reef's cancer could come back, or I could be run over by a bus on Clevedon High Street tomorrow. Who knows? All we can do is try to live each day as if it's our last.

I wasn't looking forward to delivering the bad news about the boat to the boys, but it certainly wasn't the worst news I'd ever delivered, and when the moment came I just told them straight.

'Look, boys, I am really sorry,' I said. 'The boat got hit by a lifeboat, and it's a bit smashed up. It was an accident, and it can be repaired . . .'

Reef burst into tears on the spot, while Finn shrugged his little shoulders and stomped off in a sulk.

'When can we have it back?' Reef sobbed. He was absolutely distraught, and I felt tears pricking the backs of my eyes as I looked at him like that.

'Reef, we'll get it fixed as soon as we can. I can't say exactly how long it will take because there's a lot of damage to be fixed, but I promise you we'll get it back, and when we do it'll be better than new.'

'How can it be better than new?' Reef asked, reasonably.

'I'm going to get extra gadgets put on it, like radar reflectors and a radio, to make it safer in future,' I explained.

Finn reappeared a couple of minutes later and gave me a little cuddle, which helped lift my mood.

'Don't get too upset,' I told them both. 'It really isn't the end of the world. I'm cross and upset too, but there's no point in us all being cross and upset for ages and ages, is there?'

They both looked at me and shook their heads, and I vowed to myself to draw a line under the whole sorry business there and then. Finn was starting school in less than a fortnight, and we had plenty to do back home in preparation for the new term. I reminded the boys of this as we said our goodbyes to the grandparents and headed home. Finn was all ears as I told him we still had a few items of uniform to buy and needed to go shopping for school shoes.

'It'll be good having you at my school,' Reef said, slipping his hand into Finn's hot little palm. I seemed to have succeeded in pacifying the boys and changing the subject, but deep down I was still gutted about losing the boat myself. It was a gift from Kate, bought on her birthday, the day we now called Mum's Day. It symbolized a new chapter in my life with the boys, and now it was all smashed up.

I felt sorry for myself if I'm honest, and once the boys were in bed that night I started rooting around my bedroom for memories, not quite sure if I was trying to cheer myself up or indulge in a bit of self-pity. Most of Kate's things had gone now. I'd packed up all the clothes and shoes I didn't want to keep or give to friends and sent them off to the charity shop. Her old make-up and cosmetics were gone, except for her last bottle of Charlie Red perfume, which I still sprayed on my pillow at night to help me get to sleep.

The room looked a lot more like a bachelor's bedroom now, I realized. There were no soft, floaty skirts and tops peeping out of wardrobes, no sweet-smelling lotions and potions on the dressing table and no dangly earrings discarded on the bedside table. This was my room now, not our room.

I looked at the bed and thought about how even that was mine and mine alone. Kate had ordered it when she got ill, when our waterbed was too soft to support her sore back. She wanted it to be her nest, somewhere the boys could snuggle in with her when she was too weak to get up. I imagined us making love in the new bed when Kate was better. We had to wait weeks for delivery, and in the meantime Kate had to use her grandmother's old electric bed that had a memory foam mattress. When the new bed eventually arrived, Kate was in hospital, never to return. She never slept in it, not once. If she was looking down on me now, I could imagine her thinking the timing was a blessing. I didn't have to lie alone in a bed we'd made love on.

At the foot of the bed stood the treasure chests stuffed full of memories. Recently, Kate's mum Christine had handed me copies of an email diary she kept during Kate's treatment, which she used to inform close friends and family of her daughter's progress. I'd been asked to do another newspaper interview, following on from the coverage of Reef's birthday party, and Christine thought the detail in her diary might help. I hadn't wanted to read it until this point, but I guess I was in the mood for a good cry that night. I took the printed A4 sheets from their envelope and looked at the top page. The date on the first entry jumped out at me. It was written exactly two years before.

20 August 2008
I am sorry to have to pass on some unpleasant news – Kate has been diagnosed with breast cancer and is having a mastectomy next Wednesday, 27 August. She has two lumps in the same breast, one 1.9 cms and one 4 mm so a lumpectomy is not an option.

This has all happened so swiftly and she is having the op at Weston General. Reconstruction at a later date and no knowledge of chemo or radiotherapy until biopsies done from the operation. At the moment they are not up to communicating with anybody, but the little boys are fine. Kate is very positive about it all and thinks: 'It's just a nuisance and if Reef didn't cry, I won't either!' It's been found early so fingers crossed.

27 August 2008
Katie is as amazing as ever and is sat up in bed as though she has only had a wart removed. She reckons the small boob she had taken away was only about the size of Reef's tumour, so what the heck! She consumed soup and two rolls and has been up and out of bed a bit. Her main discomfort at the moment are the cannulas (little tubes) inserted in her hand.

Any ideas as to the answer to Reef's questions: 'How will I recognize if you're my mummy if you don't have your hair?' I would suspect the boys will be busy on her head with yellow felt tip pens!

Singe has survived his side of the ordeal and stayed with her all day. Reef went off to the zoo with Lynne, his Disabled Team carer, and had a lovely time. Finn stayed at home with us and enjoyed playing with Reef's toys whilst he had the chance

29 August 2008
Katie is being discharged from hospital today and is hoping (!!!) for lots of rest. She will be attending a clinic Monday week for results and future treatments.

31 August 2008
Katie is being so positive and even went to a birthday party with Reef on Saturday!!! She has good movement in her arm and is managing without painkillers at the moment. All she wants to do is get on with life and bugger what she looks like!

I stared at the page in disbelief. It reminded me how hopeful we were at the start, how we fully expected Kate's treatment to work and for her to emerge out of the other end of it with a breast reconstruction.

'Who'd have thought this was how I'd get bigger boobs?' she laughed wearily. 'Remember when I was a teenager and I kept thinking they'd get bigger? They never did, did they!'

Despite the fact Kate had always been flat-chested

and the removal of her breast really didn't look that obvious, she was very self-conscious after the mastectomy.

'I don't feel like a real woman,' she told me afterwards.

'Don't be silly,' I soothed. 'You're still sex on legs!'

'No, Singe, I've lost a part of my femininity and I need to put it back,' she replied.

I told her I loved her however she looked, but Kate wasn't comfortable in her skin, even when she had healed. If I touched her where her breast had been, she moved my hand away.

'It feels kind of exposed and sensitive,' she said. 'It's weird seeing my ribs closer to the surface.'

Inevitably, I suppose, our love life suffered. The passion of the past had already been sidelined by the stress and exhaustion of parenthood and caring for a sick child, and I missed the intimacy.

'It won't be like this for ever,' she said.

'That's good, because I'll love you for ever,' I said.

8 September 2008

Kate has been told she has Stage 2, Grade 3 cancer and is now classified as 'common'! Thank goodness she found it early! The prognosis is 80 per cent survival for ten years, but improving all the time. It had only spread to one lymph node. She will have chemo and radiotherapy, starting in one to two weeks' time. Reef started school this week and had a wonderful time. He likes using the 'pewter' (computer to you and me).

15 September 2008

Kate at last got to see the consultant. Her cancer is triple negative, which means it is not responsive to the easier hormone treatments and she will need to have the full whammy of strong chemotherapy and then radiotherapy. She may also participate in a clinical trial for the drug Avastin, which they hope could reduce the likelihood of reoccurrence, but it docs have to be taken three times a week for a year. Tough times ahead!!

23 September 2008
Kate has been undergoing ECGs, echoes, blood tests etc at Weston and Bristol Hospitals to see if she is acceptable for the clinical trial of Avastin. At least she is able to drive again now following her operation and her arm movement is almost 100 per cent, so the school runs are a little easier. The boys have settled into school happily now that they have got used to being split up at different schools, with Finn at the Montessori nursery. Although they are different personalities they get on well together – Reef is more thoughtful and imaginative than his hooligan little brother! Chemotherapy starts in a couple of weeks and I am not sure that the long blonde wig Singe fancies won't make Kate look like a Barbie Doll. Roll on next summer!

16 October 2008
Katie had her first chemotherapy today and had no problems. As she has been allocated the new Avastin drug as well as three different chemotherapy drugs, it took quite a long time. She arrived at 9.30 a.m. and left at 4 p.m., but hopefully it will take an hour or so less on following visits. Staff nurse Jamie who was on Children's Ward 34 all

the time Reef was on treatment popped up to see and reassure her, which was very kind.

Katie will probably have a special cannula inserted in her upper arm next time for administering the chemotherapy, which will remain permanently in place for a year.

Reef had a satisfactory check-up with his professor too today and came out with a special sticker for being a good boy. We then took him to the museum to see the dinosaur bones. Finn was at nursery in the morning and then went to Puxton Park Play Barn with the disabled team care worker.

Katie came home feeling tired and a bit woozy but ate a hearty tea (homemade special lasagne – thank you, Ruth!). She has an armoury of tablets to counteract all manner of side effects from chemo, but fingers crossed she won't need them too often.

Taking Reef for hospital appointments while Kate was still undergoing treatment brought it home to me how incredibly unlucky we had been, both then and now. When Kate was first diagnosed we debated how to tell the boys without frightening them.

'I suppose in a way we're lucky,' Kate said, with astonishing good grace. 'I mean, we can tell them Mummy has a lump just like Reef had a lump, and that mine will be taken away just like his, and I'll have the same nasty medicines he had, and then, hopefully, I'll get better like he has.'

I agreed, even though in my heart I was thinking that, although I had every faith that Kate would survive, I was still scared stiff that Reef's cancer might come back some day. His initial prognosis was much worse than hers, and he had still not been given the official 'all clear'.

One of the cancer charities gave us a colourful story book called *Mummy's Lump*, which was really helpful. The illustrated family looked a bit like ours, and they even had a dog and went to the beach, so the story was easy to identify with. When Kate lost her hair we looked at the mummy in the book, who had also lost her blonde hair, and it helped us explain things to Reef and Finn. Reef barely remembered losing his own hair, bless him, which fell out when it was still baby hair. When Kate's hair got so thin and wispy she was almost bald, she asked me to shave her head.

'I feel terrible doing this,' I told her, as I wrapped a towel around her shoulders and got to work with an electric shaver.

'Why? I want you to. I'm fed up of all these bits of hair falling out all over the place. I'm moulting more than the dog! It looks a mess as it is, I'd rather get rid of the lot.'

'OK, whatever you want, Madam,' I said jokily, but I still had a bad taste in my mouth. I adored Kate's blonde hair. It was a part of her, and being a part of taking it away felt wrong.

'Can I try on Mummy's wig?' Finn asked a few weeks later.

Kate overheard him. 'Course you can,' she said.

She had agreed to have a wig made to match her own hairstyle as much as possible, but it looked a bit synthetic and made her head sweat and itch, and she never really got on with it. She'd decided against cold cap treatment, reasoning that the ice-cold treatment that could potentially save some of her hair follicles was painful and had no guarantee of success. She figured she already had enough treatment to cope with, without volunteering for more, and I fully supported her decision.

Both boys tried on the wig, giggling their heads off while I snapped away taking photographs. Kate's brother Ben turned up in the middle of the photo session, and he tried the wig on too.

'What d'you think?' he said, flicking his head back.

We all screamed.

'Take it off, you look exactly like Kate!' I said.

Kate had hysterics. I think that was the only good thing about the wig, in fact. It gave us all a much-needed laugh. That night the boys had a bubble bath together, and I found them making wigs for each other by piling up the bubbles on top of their heads, then knocking them off.

'I've got an idea,' I said, winking at Kate. The boys had a big plastic toy called an Airzooka which fired out a really strong blast of air. The next time they had the bubbles piled high on their heads, I darted in the bathroom and fired the Airzooka at them, completely obliterating their bubble wigs in the blink of an eye.

Kate had tears rolling down her cheeks as she took photos on my phone.

I could see my old Kate standing there. It didn't matter that she had lost a breast and lost her hair. She was still my giggling, vivacious Kate; cancer could not take that away.

> 18 December 2008
>
> Katie had her fourth treatment today in spite of a nasty cough and is feeling rather sick and poorly. Reef and

Finn are on antibiotics too with chesty coughs. Kate managed to see Reef as a 'king' in the school nativity play and was delighted at his new-found confidence. No such problems with Finn who is always up at the front! Fingers crossed that Kate will not be in hospital for Christmas.

21 December 2008

We took Reef and Finn to a big family do at Tortworth today and they had a super time, especially seeing Father Christmas whom they assured that they had been good boys. They stayed the night with us to give Kate a rest (a 'sleepover' as they now call it!) and luckily didn't wake up until 7.30 a.m. They then chatted and ran around ALL DAY – who says children around keep you young – we are worn out!

Poor Kate is trashed at the moment following last Thursday's treatment but at least we know it is doing the business. Her chemo gives her bad aches all over and the usual sickness. Hopefully she will be back on her feet for Christmas Day but if not we will drop them off a picnic lunch. We are going to the pantomime on 2 January, blood counts permitting.

5 January 2009

Katie managed to have Christmas at home in spite of having to dash into hospital twice over the festive period with high temperatures. She will be having her 5th chemotherapy session this Thursday.

Reef is having an MRI scan on 19 January, followed the next week by a consultant's clinic.

We all enjoyed the Bristol Hippodrome Pantomime Cinderella, especially Reef!

14 January 2009
The Disabled Children's Team is chasing for an additional carer for Reef at school, especially at dinner times, as he seems to be falling quite a lot during the usual rough and tumble of the playground. Other than that the little boys are in fine fettle and full of mischief!

Kate's last full treatment is on 28 January (the same day as Reef's MRI results), followed by nine months of three-weekly intravenous treatments of Avastin. Her five weeks of daily radiotherapy are programmed to start on 26 February.

3 March 2009
Kate is doing fine on her radiotherapy. The worst part is getting two boys off to school and struggling through the traffic into Bristol every day for 10 a.m. Weather here is disgusting – wet, windy and cold.

24 March 2009
Kate's last radiotherapy will be Wednesday of next week. She has kept fairly well – just a bit tired and achey. She has another session of Avastin Thursday of next week. Her hair is showing signs of re-growing, although her eyebrows have now disappeared.

The date of that entry caught my eye. Both my birthday and Kate's birthday had been and gone the week before, and were completely overshadowed by Kate's treatment. I remembered vowing to make our thirteenth wedding anniversary, on 31 March, as special as possible.

On the way home from work, I went shopping and bought Kate a lovely card and a beautiful big bunch of flowers containing some of her favourites; ivory roses and gypsophila. I also picked up a huge box of chocolates, a bottle of champagne and the ingredients to make her favourite steak dinner with pepper sauce, using an old family recipe of mine she absolutely adored.

When I pulled up at the house I decided to back into the drive and ask her to come out and help me get the shopping in, so she would see all the goodies at once and enjoy the surprise.

'I'm home,' I called, turning my key in the lock. 'Come and help me, Kate,' I shouted. 'I've got some shopping to carry in.'

I stuck my head around the living room door to see Kate lying on the sofa looking tired and nursing a bandaged arm. I could see her dad in the adjoining kitchen, washing up at the sink. Kate didn't move.

'Come on, Kate, give me a hand,' I said chirpily.

'Are you stupid?' she hissed, still refusing to move and looking anxiously towards her dad. 'Are you looking for a row?'

'Of course not! I just want you to help me with the shopping. Please Kate, give me a hand?'

I pulled her gently up off the sofa as she continued to protest, and I could feel Martin, always the protective dad, giving me a disapproving glare as I ushered Kate outside. I threw open the boot of the car as quickly as possible and watched Kate's face light up.

'Singe!' she shrieked, throwing her good arm up and covering her gaping mouth with her hand. 'You bastard! Look at all this! It's amazing!'

I gave her the card, which she opened immediately.

'I love you acres and acres too,' she beamed. 'I'm sorry . . . I didn't even remember it was our anniversary . . . and I'm sorry about . . .'

I kissed her to shut her up and stop her apologizing any more and I smiled when I realized she had lifted one foot off the ground when I kissed her, which was one of her little habits. She was still my same old Kate, cancer or not.

'You don't have to say sorry,' I said.

12 May 2009

Kate is still OK and has had 8 of the 15 three-weekly doses of Avastin. One of the children's charities, Make a Wish, has offered them a Florida Disney World trip for November time when her treatment is finished.

Reef's recent X-ray check has indicated that the growth plate on his affected leg is showing signs of recovery which will mean his disability may be less than originally thought, and major surgery in his teens may be avoided.

28 June 2009

There is an article about Kate in the *Sunday People* today, under the headline: 'My Son Reef had chemo . . . Then he pulled ME through it.' Here are some of the things Kate told the newspaper:

Although I had sympathy and support from everyone, Reef became my rock because he had been through it all before. He knew when I was aching and he would hold my hand and say, 'It's OK, Mummy, I'll look after you.' He was caring beyond his years.

He's been in a medical environment so much that it rubbed off on him. He knows that when someone is unwell you need to hold their hand and look after them and that's what he did for me.

The worst part of it was feeling first hand what Reef had been put through. After the CT scan I cried and cried. It was horrible, it was uncomfortable and gave me hot flushes.

But I didn't cry because of how it made me feel, I cried because we'd put Reef through that and he'd gone through it with a smile on his face. I knew because he had been through it and been brave I had to do it and be there at the end for him, and for Finn. Both boys have been brilliant.

Reading this, I had a vivid image of four-year-old Reef playing on the floor with his toy Bakugans. His head was down and he was totally engrossed in the little magnetic warriors that sprang into life when they hit anything metal. I watched as he flicked a glance up to Kate on the sofa and suddenly left his toys exactly as they were and walked over to her. 'I love you, Mummy,' he said and climbed up on the sofa for a snuggle. Minutes later he got down again, trundled back across the carpet and picked up his game where he had left off, leaving Kate with a wistful but contented look on her face.

'Reef seems to have a sixth sense,' Kate said to me. 'It tears me apart to think about him having gone through this treatment. It's bad enough for an adult, but for a tiny little boy it must have been so frightening. I can't bear to think about him worrying about me now, knowing what I'm going through.'

I cuddled her and told her not to let herself go too far down that road.

'I think he was so little he was oblivious to some of what was going on,' I said. 'That has to be a blessing.'

'I hope you're right,' Kate said. 'I really do.'

I desperately hoped I was right too. I remembered Reef screaming in the night in pain. I remembered the black rings around his eyes, the red holes in his skin from needles and drips, how I'd have to untie him in the night when he tossed and turned and wrapped himself up in all his tubes in his hospital bed. I would never forget having to pinch him, just as Kate did so many times too, when we needed to make him cry so he would inhale the anaesthetic and fall unconscious for his scans. That has to be one of the most horrific tasks a parent can be asked to perform. I remembered each of the sixty times Reef was given a general anaesthetic, and each and every one of the thirty lots of radiotherapy and forty rounds of chemotherapy he endured. The numbers sound mind-boggling now, but at the time we just got on with it, signing off more and more treatment in the hope it would save Reef's life.

I cried like a child myself when he suffered side effects, and so did Kate. Reef lost his soft baby hair, his mouth was riddled with ulcers, he had dreadful diarrhoea and he had to be fed though tubes. At one point he had eight different tubes going into his frail body, including a nasal gastric tube injecting milk though his nose to his stomach. He was so ill he was in bed 24/7 and had observations every single hour, with doctors and nurses prodding and examining him as the equipment that was keeping him alive pumped and beeped alarmingly all around him.

When he had chemo, Reef's nappies were radioactive. We were warned to wear disposable rubber gloves to change him, as the drugs had made his urine so toxic it could burn our skin. Kate had to be extra careful, as she often alternated between changing Reef and expressing breast milk into bottles for Finn, which would then be driven across town to feed him.

It was beyond horrendous. Other parents of toddlers were obsessing about organic food or worrying about whether to give in to the odd chip or scoop of ice cream, in case their child overdosed on salt or sugar. Here we were blasting Reef with as many toxic chemicals as he could physically endure. The rest of his little body had to take the rap, because killing the cancer came first, second and third.

'I can't wait for my treatment to end,' Kate said, just as she had wished for Reef's to end, month after month, year after year. 'I just want us to be a normal family again. It's not that much to ask, is it?'

'No,' I said. 'It really isn't. You just have to keep going as you are. You're flying through the treatment, you really are. It won't be like this for ever. Remember how Reef's treatment seemed to go on for ever? It was two years of hell, but we got through it, didn't we? Look at him now, doing so well. It won't be long for you now.'

9 August 2009
We went to a local animal farm with the grandsons for Reef's fifth birthday and had a good time in spite of the showers.

Kate came with us to a posh family wedding at Sonning at the weekend and everyone was delighted to see Katie looking so bonny now she has some hair.

I went with her for her chemo this week and she admitted she was at the point of asking to miss her last four treatments as she is so full of aches and pains. The consultant says this is probably just an after effect of the radiotherapy and Kate says she now feels able to go through with the remaining three treatments. Roll on 8 October.

Reef can now ride his bike without stabilizers – wow – I can only just do that!

16 September 2009

The doctors are concerned about some of the levels in Katie's blood and are doing more tests. Her back is extremely painful which may have been due to the radiotherapy or one of the drugs she has taken, or could just be the way she has been holding herself since her operation. She has been seeing Martin's chiropractor who seems to be helping to bring back movement. We are very proud of the way she keeps cheerful and brave with so many worries.

Reef is back at school and loves it to bits. He was full of beans at his latest hospital check up this week, wanting to know how much he has grown and having his chest X-rays like a good 'un. His MRI scans are now every six months and he is doing well. His leg growth seems to be coming along nicely and he is amazing on his two-wheeler bicycle. He is also having swimming lessons, which he loves. His reading and writing is coming along nicely.

Young Finn is still a hoot – full of energy and chat.

They were ready to go back to school and nursery after the summer holidays. Finn managed to sneak into Reef's queue going into 'big school' and Katie had a job extracting him to go to nursery.

8 October 2009
We cannot believe that on the day of Katie's last chemo treatment they have found two worrying lymph node swellings in Reef's groin and he will be having urgent investigations tomorrow.

16 October 2009
Reef's consultant is satisfied that his 'lumps' were caused by an infection following a recent fall on his bad leg. Kate still has problems with her back, cough and blood results but is soldiering on as usual. She may have a bronchostomy to take lung samples to source her discomfort. The consultant has confirmed her bones and liver are cancer free. Life is a roller coaster!

8 November 2009
I was at Kate's when the doorbell rang and a big parcel addressed to Reef from the 'Make a Wish Foundation' was delivered. Reef's eyes nearly popped out when he opened it. It contained all the information about their trip to Disney World on 20 November. He didn't know anything about it beforehand and he just hugged his mum and said: 'We can all go and you and Daddy don't have to find the pennies!'

Everything is paid for – hotels, flight tickets, car hire, entry tickets and they even get spending money. When

Singe came home Reef told him: 'I've got lots of money now – 16 quid,' and we all laughed, thinking the holiday was worth rather a lot more than that. Don't they all deserve it?

I smiled when I read that, thinking of one of the highlights of our trip to America, when we went swimming with the dolphins at Discovery Cove.

'You deserve this so much,' I said to Kate, kissing her.

I can see Finn now, literally nose to nose with a dolphin while Reef, Kate and I huddle in as close as we can around him in the water. Kate has her arms wrapped protectively around Finn as she drinks in the wonderful scene, and we all have big smiles on our faces. We are packed tightly together in our wet suits and life jackets, a family 'tight knit', as Kate would say.

'I'd have flown to America just for that moment,' Kate said afterwards. 'Wasn't that amazing?'

'Awesome,' I said. 'I will never, ever forget it.'

Kate's eyes were shining out of her face, which had a healthy, pink colour in it for the first time in ages. Her treatment was over, and even though she was still weak, I was convinced the worst was behind us.

'You really do deserve this trip so much, Kate,' I said, giving her another kiss, and another. 'Look at you – you are amazing.'

In typical style, Kate was up for milking the most out of every moment of our time in America, and she didn't let her tiredness or frailty stand in the way. We stayed in the Give Kids the World Village, which was absolutely overwhelming. It's like a miniature Disney World with Disney characters strolling around and pizza and ice cream on tap 24/7.

Our accommodations looked like a cartoon-style fantasy house a child might draw, painted in bright blue and orange. Kate got very emotional and started to cry when she saw it, and the boys buzzed around like maniacs.

'What are you crying for?' I asked Kate when I noticed the tears starting to well up in her eyes.

'It's just so incredible,' she said. 'We're just so lucky.'

We both cried in each other's arms. I was convinced this really was the turning point I'd been longing for. A line had been drawn in the sand with this trip. It marked the end of cancer in our lives, I felt sure.

A six-foot-tall rabbit called Mayor Clayton and his wife, Ms Merry, welcomed us to the village and asked Kate and I if we would like Mayor Clayton to do a surprise 'tuck-in' for the boys later that evening. We agreed, giggling to ourselves, and when the time came for Mayor Clayton to appear, Reef and Finn didn't suspect a thing. They were both ready for bed in their pyjamas, with teeth cleaned and hair combed as usual, when there was a loud knock on the door of our apartment.

'I wonder who that can be,' Kate said, sounding like a children's TV presenter as she played along enthusiastically.

'I'll go!' Finn volunteered. Both boys had cottoned on to the fact that only good things happened in this resort, and Reef's eyes were dancing like sparklers as he watched his brother bolt to the door. Finn threw the door boldly open, only to step back open-mouthed, amazed at the sight of the giant fluffy rabbit on the doorstep, who was waving merrily and wearing a night cap and pyjamas.

Finn ran for his life, heading towards Reef who was

legging it to the bedroom, and Mayor Clayton gave chase. The boys didn't know whether to laugh or scream.

'Thanks for coming, Mayor Clayton,' Kate said brightly, enjoying the moment. 'Have you come to say goodnight to the boys? That's great! How kind! Into bed now, boys!'

I've never seen the pair of them scamper into bed so quickly, and I was giggling so much the video camera was shaking as I filmed the scene unfolding. Mayor Clayton tucked the astonished but delighted boys into bed and gave them each their cuddly toy before waving them goodnight and giving Kate and me a hug each.

'Night-night, Mayor Clayton,' Kate said, giving him a big kiss, which left a large lipstick mark on his plastic nose. We both burst out laughing as we waved Mr Clayton off, and Reef and Finn hugged their cuddly toys tight as they eventually fell into a contented sleep.

Kate and I were on a real high, and that night we cuddled up tight together in bed. For so long now Kate had been either recovering from surgery or going through treatment, which hadn't made it easy for us to get close. For the first time in ages it felt almost like the old days, with Kate lying comfortably in my arms. Happiness, not worry, hung in the air as we drifted off to sleep.

Nobody who saw us on that holiday could have guessed what we'd gone through. Over the next week we felt like movie stars as we blasted out all of our favourite music in our huge, hired American people carrier, heading to Animal Kingdom and the Epcot Centre. Kate looked stunning in shades and shorts, enjoying the feeling of the wind blowing through her newly grown hair as she sang along to Abba, the Clash and the Undertones. The boys joined in, learning the words to 'SOS', 'Should I Stay or Should I Go?' and 'Teenage Kicks'.

I remember how full of life Kate looked as she strolled down Main Street, smiling from ear to ear as she lapped up the carnival atmosphere in Disney World. When we stopped to watch a parade I felt choked with emotion. I looked at my family, all happy and excited, and felt totally convinced Kate had beaten cancer and was going to survive, just like Reef.

I took out my video camera to capture the moment and caught little Finn in the viewfinder, pulling urgently on Kate's arm. He was pointing at the larger-than-life cartoon characters strolling down Main Street, and at first Kate thought he was just excited about the whole parade and didn't realize why he was getting so animated. A moment later the penny dropped, as Kate realized Finn had spotted Mr Incredible travelling on a float, waving in our direction. Finn wanted his mum to see Mr Incredible, as he knew friends called us 'The Incredibles'

That's when I had that moment all over again, the one I'd had when I lay on the beach with Kate after Reef's treatment had ended. Back then, the boys looked like they didn't have a care in the world. Watching them scampering on the shore that day pushed the bad memories of Finn in an incubator and Reef on a cancer ward deep back in time. Then, Kate was as fit and well as ever, or at least we thought she was. We were both flooded with relief and optimism about our future, about sharing so many more happy times with our two lively little boys. Now, it was just me looking at the rest of my incredible family, marvelling again at how they'd all survived against the odds, Kate included this time.

It was a miracle how we had survived together as a family too, in the face of so much pain and stress.

'Look, Daddy, it's *Mr Incredible*!' Finn shrieked, turning to give me a big grin as he pointed at the character.

'I know, he looks brilliant!' I said. Kate turned and flashed me a smile too. With the big-band music pumping and the street-party atmosphere swirling all around, I felt invigorated. It had to be a good omen, I thought. Baddies couldn't destroy my family. Cancer had been defeated, and The Incredibles were back in town.

30 November 2009

Although Kate and Reef are not quite out of the woods yet, it is lovely to know they had such a marvellous time in Disney World and swam with the dolphins in Florida. They will not be at the family Christmas meal at Tortworth as they are flying off to Lapland that day, returning Christmas Eve.

29 December 2009

Christmas was a non-event for us as we had to take poor Kate to A & E at Weston Hospital, extremely ill on Christmas Day. It resulted in her having fluid drained from her lung and loads of blood tests. She has also had a bad allergy rash from too many antibiotics and has lost a stone in weight.

She stayed in Boxing Day too and came home late in the evening. After 27 December at home in bed we had to return her to hospital again on 28 December, very poorly again. Humbug!

Poor thing has been in bed today and has to go back

into hospital for a bronchostomy to have lung samples taken tomorrow. They suspect that chemo and radiotherapy have damaged her lung/back and made her very susceptible to infections/fungus and they need to find out exactly what is causing the trouble.

It was Finn's fourth birthday but it wasn't much of a day for him, although we did manage to get a cake and blow out candles.

Roll on 2010!

30 December 2009

Kate had her bronchostomy today and is back home tucked up in bed. She has had the nod that nothing 'C'nister was visible, but there was a lot of inflammation of unknown cause. She is still coughing and they took away some more fluid today.

Kate needs complete rest and relaxation (fat chance with three 'boys' in the house, a dog and four guinea pigs!). We are asking the family support team to take the boys to school in the mornings and hopefully the doctors can sort Kate out after her appointment with the lung consultant on Tuesday.

5 January 2009

Not the news we were hoping for – Kate's cancer has spread to her lungs and bones and she is now on palliative care.

We are devastated.

9 January 2009

After the shocking news of last week, Kate is now at

home in bed on permanent oxygen awaiting a full body MRI, CT and heart scans next week to see whether it has spread to any other organs. The results will decide what holding options might work. They are considering using one of the chemicals Reef was given.

Katie finds it fairly difficult to talk on the phone. The boys are still home from school with the snow, but the Disabled Team who they know well are assisting. The boys are getting used to their mum not participating that much, although she is determined to go to the Snow White pantomime at the Bristol Hippodrome tomorrow – oxygen tanks, wheelchair and all!

She didn't deserve this!

11 January 2009

The panto trip went well, but Kate is tired out.

Big furniture moving round at their house today. The waterbed has been sold and removed as it was not supportive enough for her. Kate is using Nan's electric bed which has a memory foam mattress until their new 'megabed' arrives soon.

Reef is back at school and Finn back to nursery tomorrow, weather permitting. Singe is getting almost nimble on the stairs! Katie very weak.

12 January 2009

Katie, with enormous effort, had her full body MRI done. She couldn't have her oxygen tube for forty minutes and came back exhausted. Singe could hold her foot through the scanner. Both boys enjoyed school.

13 January 2009
Katie stayed in bed today as her breathing is so difficult. She is hardly eating or drinking and is very fed up. She felt a bit better after a shower. Reef's teacher came to have a chat with her. We had six inches of snow and difficulty getting up our hill today.

16 January 2009
Kate was a smidgen improved today and managed a smile and a giggle when she saw her brother. She is now in Berrow Ward at Weston General Hospital and having moisturized oxygen, which seems to be beneficial. Reef and Finn came in for a short visit and a cuddle, which cheered her up. She is enjoying receiving texts, although it's difficult for her to reply as her right arm is full of cannulas. She managed a mouthful or two of food and a cup of tea but her breathing and talking are still terrible, and she is wearing the oxygen mask most of the time. She took it off and smiled for a photograph with the boys – a mum's joy!

19 January 2009
Kate has been moved to a single side room and is more comfortable with a rumble bed. She brightened up a bit this afternoon and was looking forward to seeing the boys, who have been at school today. She will be having two chemo tablets twice a day for two weeks and then a week's break. Her prognosis is poor. If the lung drain can be removed later she may be moved to a hospice. Boys OK – us spaced out.

20 January 2009
Sorry to be the bearer of bad news – but we lost Katie at 5.15 a.m. this morning. Singe, Martin and I were with her and she saw the boys yesterday evening.

It was peaceful and we knew she couldn't struggle on any longer.

Life can be very cruel. She was only 38.

I cried uncontrollably when I got to that last line. I think I'd been reading and reminiscing for two or three hours, I'd lost track of time. Even though it was unbearably sad, and I knew the terrible ending, I had been unable to stop myself reading the next entry, and then the next.

I was struck by the medical detail Christine had recorded. It was shocking to see it in black and white, to see how quickly Kate declined. Even in her last weeks I still thought she would make it, I really did. Losing her was absolutely unthinkable. Reading the bald facts about her failing health made me realize how desperate I was for Kate to survive, because I didn't let those facts stand in the way of my love-fuelled, blind hope.

I was grateful to Christine for her diary, as I would never have remembered so much specific information, and I was very touched by some of the memories it brought back of our everyday routines. It was amazing to remember how, somehow, ordinary life carried on as cancer ran amok through our lives. I smiled at how Christine kept her sense of humour, managing to have a cheeky little dig at my size and weight when she called me 'nimble' on the stairs as I was zipping up and down so often, tending to Kate in her final days. Treatment was slotted in around school, work, day trips and normal family life – or at least it was in the beginning. Somewhere along the line, and I couldn't remember where or when, Kate and the boys and I had to fit in around cancer, as it grew and spread and seized control.

I realized there were countless elements missing from the diary, and it is very much Christine's version of events, but that pleased me. There was no mention of Mum's List, for example, because this was something Kate and I did alone, and I am glad some memories are unashamedly ours and ours alone.

Through both Reef and Kate's illnesses, we inevitably lost some privacy and control of our family life. We needed so much help we had to throw open our doors. Family and friends had been unbelievably supportive, and I could never have coped without Christine and Martin, but it wasn't the way life was meant to be.

Time had moved on now, and boundaries had been gradually redrawn. Finn was about to start school. On a practical level, life would be more manageable. I could take both boys to school together and then go to work. I could ask their grandparents for help as and when I needed it instead of having to rely on them, which is how it should be. I also had Kirsty to babysit, and the Disabled Team on hand for extra help.

I realized I was looking forward to this new chapter, and to taking back full control of my life.

Chapter 9

'Always help them if they ask'

Finn was beside himself with excitement. It was 6 September, the long-awaited day when he was starting 'big school' with Reef. He'd tried on his grey trousers and red jumper half a dozen times already, and had even decided exactly how he was going to gel his hair, with a bit of a quiff in the front so he looked 'really cool'.

'Come on, Daddy!' he said, jumping on my bed and pulling me up. 'Get up now!'

I squinted at the clock. It was only just 7 a.m., and we had bags of time to get ready, but I dutifully got up and joined in the excitement. Reef was awake too, and the whole house felt incredibly alive and vibrant for such an early hour on a cold September morning.

'Your hair looks like a hedgehog!' Reef said to Finn, who was already busy with the hair gel.

'Yours looks like a *dead* hedgehog!' Finn replied, giggling a wicked giggle.

I thanked my lucky stars, grateful Finn was so happy and full of optimism. The drive to All Saints School was an absolute pleasure as I listened to Reef rattling off all sorts of tips and advice. It was good for his confidence to play the big brother, and Finn was listening intently, lapping up every last word.

'Mr Webber is really nice,' Reef said with authority.

'I know, silly!' Finn laughed. 'I've met him LOADS of times.'

This was true. Kate asked: *'Go to as many school activities as possible – praise assemblies etc.,'* and I promised I would. Praise assemblies are held on a Friday at the end of the school day, and Mr Webber hands out certificates and awards to deserving children.

Finn used to come with me after nursery, often clapping and cheering enthusiastically, and Mr Webber had told him many times he looked forward to him joining Reef at school. Now the day had come, and as we walked up to the school gate I spotted Mr Webber striding towards us through the bright, crisp morning air. Finn was striding too, looking every inch the 'Mr Confident'.

'Good morning, Mr Webber,' Finn called out, raising his hand to give his new headmaster a 'high five'.

Gamely, a rather surprised Mr Webber gave Finn a 'high five', then looked at me with a wide smile on his face.

'I don't think I'm going to have any problems there,' Mr Webber said, and I had to agree.

I had a big grin on my face too. The way the boys had coped without their mum was incredibly impressive. To sail through a milestone like this so happily, I thought, was a minor miracle. It was less than nine months since that terrible day when I had driven the boys to the beach to tell them Mummy had died, yet here they were, as bright and confident as any parent could hope for.

Of course, it was a tragedy Kate couldn't share the occasion, but I didn't let it spoil the mood, which was overwhelmingly happy. Lots of thoughtful parents made a point of asking me how I was, and I genuinely replied: 'I'm fine. It's just brilliant to see Finn start school,' because it was.

I liked the boys being together at school, and it also meant we could establish a more regular routine. I was working Tuesday to Thursday, Reef was about to start Beavers on a Wednesday night, and both boys were having swimming lessons on a Friday after school, plus rugby practice at the weekend.

Kate's parents, as ever, were willing to help out as much as they could, and sometimes had the boys for sleepovers as well as helping with school runs and taking the boys on trips, though I didn't want to put upon them too much. I asked Kirsty to babysit every Wednesday night, regardless of whether I was going out or not. It gave me a chance to catch up on chores in the house, get paperwork done or nip to Tesco's if need be.

Occasionally I had another 'date', typically with a friend of a friend, or even a friend of a friend of a friend. We'd meet for a drink or a bite to eat, and I always enjoyed swapping life stories and having a few laughs. I realized after the first two or three encounters that I was not the only one with 'baggage', which was a relief. It was a bit of an eye-opener, to tell the truth, to realize that some people have such dreadful marriages. I'd kind of assumed that if a marriage wasn't working people got divorced, and that most marriages were as loving and passionate as mine and Kate's. I thought every man idolized his wife, and I imagined every wife was besotted by her husband, and that they naturally fancied the pants off each other. From what

I was hearing, though, our marriage seemed pretty exceptional.

'How did it go?' Kirsty always asked afterwards.

'Great time. No snogging though!' I always replied.

I felt comfortable talking about seeing other women. Kirsty was a really good friend of Kate's, but I didn't feel guilty at all discussing the dates, which surprised me. I guess it's because Kirsty knew all about Kate's wishes.

'It's really good for you to get out and do something unconnected to the boys and the house,' Kirsty said one night.

'I know,' I said. 'It's very weird doing this whole single bloke thing again, but I'm not hung up about it like I was at the start. It's just socializing really, isn't it?'

'Yes,' Kirsty agreed. 'And you're good at that! You're doing well.'

One Wednesday I was sorting out some photographs to dot around the house when Kirsty arrived. With the new school term and our new routine established, I could sense life moving forward quickly as we headed towards the end of 2010. I was worried the boys would start to forget Kate, and I wanted to keep her memory very much alive in the house.

We had a large photo frame on the landing, filled with wedding photographs, and it pained me to look at it every day.

'It just makes me too sad,' I explained to Kirsty, as I replaced the wedding pictures with up-to-date ones of Kate and the boys. I did the same in the office and the lounge.

'I think this will help the boys remember Kate more, because they were actually there with her when the pictures were taken,' I said. 'But do you think it's too much . . . and do you think if I ever bring a girlfriend here one day it might put her off?'

Kirsty shook her head. 'Kate wasn't just your wife, she was Reef and Finn's mum. Anyone who cares about you would appreciate that.'

'I hope you're right. Do you think the boys are starting to forget?' I asked.

'No!' Kirsty laughed. 'Only the other day I was reaching back in the car to help them with their seatbelts when Reef piped up: "Mummy must have had longer arms than you because she could reach the back." I don't think a week goes by when the boys don't say something about Kate. Last week we went past the dry ski centre and Reef said: "That's where we went skiing when Mummy was alive."'

'What about Finn? I asked, enjoying the chance to explore my fears so comfortably.

'Reef usually brings Finn into the conversation – you've seen him,' she said.

I nodded. I was worrying too much, and it was good to hear that from someone else. Recently Finn had pointed to someone in the audience on their Blue Man DVD and said: 'Look, there's Mummy!' I knew he meant the blonde-haired lady in the crowd just looked like Mummy, and I didn't correct him. I was just quietly pleased Kate's image and memory lived on.

Work took an exciting twist later on in September when I received an unexpected phone call from Pete Miles, an old friend of mine who is a stuntman.

'Fancy being an extra in a film I'm working on?' he asked.

'Too right!' I replied. 'Tell me more!'

I knew it would be big. Pete had worked on lots of Harry Potter and James Bond movies, so I was all ears.

'It's the new Steven Spielberg movie, *War Horse*,' he said. 'Fancy it?'

'Count me in,' I said, not having a clue what sort of extra I might be.

Pete explained that scenes for the period film were being shot in picturesque Castle Combe in Wiltshire, which had been transformed into a traditional First World War village for the occasion. They needed about 300 extras for various scenes, and as an experienced and respected member of the crew, Pete would be able to get me in to claim one of the prized places. It was a great opportunity to work on the set of a real Hollywood blockbuster, and I would even get paid for it. I couldn't wait.

A few days later I drove excitedly to the village and, as promised by Pete, was checked through security and straight into a vast costume hangar. Pete had fixed it for me to be a German chef, but the grin slid off my face when I saw the other extras who were being kitted out, and the outfits. The other men were playing cavalry soldiers and were all very fit and young. All the costumes were clearly designed for trim young blokes like them, including my chef's outfit.

After an embarrassing few minutes when I tried to squeeze into several different shirts and jackets that were bursting at the seams, I was unceremoniously dismissed for being too fat. I scuttled back to the car feeling like a bit of a chump and phoned Pete to tell him what had happened.

'Sorry about that, mate. Leave it with me, I'll call you back,' he said optimistically.

I sat there stewing for what felt like ages. I needed to lose weight, and this was a bit of a wake-up call. Kate didn't like it when I piled on the pounds and she made that clear, but she never really nagged me it about it. My weight had crept up while we had far more serious things on our minds, and I always blamed the hospital food and the takeaways we relied on for so many years when Reef and Kate were ill. There were times when the only home-cooked meal we ate all week was a Sunday roast at my dad's, because we simply didn't have the time or energy to shop and cook on top of everything else.

That day, I added 'lose weight' to my own mental 'to-do' list. When the boys went swimming on a Friday night, I would swim too instead of sitting on the side and watching. At least that would be a start. My phone rang.

'Forget the cook,' Pete said. 'I've got you a job as a gaffer – an auctioneer's assistant.'

'Are you sure, Pete? I don't want to cause you any hassle.'

'No trouble, Singe. It's worked out for the best. This scene involves horses, and I know you can ride and handle horses. You'll be with some of the stunt team.'

I followed Pete's instructions and went to a separate unit, where I was dressed in a flat cap, hobnail boots and a big coat and black waistcoat, which thankfully fitted well and really made me look the part. I couldn't wait to get on the set.

The whole of Castle Combe was surrounded by smoke machines, so you couldn't see anything of the village from the costume hangars outside. Several checkpoints later, I was finally allowed through the last cloud-shrouded security gate and on to the film set. When the mist cleared and I emerged on the other side I couldn't believe my eyes. I was instantly transported back nearly a hundred years. The set was stunning, decked out with market stalls and banks of delphiniums and wisteria to make it look like springtime in a typical English village in the First World War.

On the right hand side of the set I was astonished to see Steven Spielberg himself, sitting in his director's chair. Wandering across the road, I noticed the actor who played the werewolf character in Harry Potter. 'David Thewlis!' I heard another extra whisper excitedly as he nudged his mate.

Several of us 'gaffers' were asked to walk some horses across the set, and I was eventually chosen to perform a little sequence with a huge Clydesdale, where I had to run into the camera and grab the neighing horse. I secretly smiled to myself, thinking my size was actually a bonus now, as this was certainly not a job for a small man. The horse was enormous, and it took all my strength to control him and lead him away exactly as Steven Spielberg directed. In the end I performed the same sequence about ten times before the great director was satisfied.

'Good job, Singe,' he called over a few minutes later in his great American drawl, much to my delight.

My very first thought was: 'I can't wait to tell Kate!' Her number was still listed as my favourite contact in my phone, and I desperately wanted to ring her or text her and tell her my exciting news. I took out my phone and suddenly felt deflated, like bubbles were bursting around my heart. I clicked through her old texts, many of which contained items she wanted me to add to the list. *'Sort out fish tank, pebble chess set, netball centre,'* I saw. It was the last item added to her list, I remembered. Kate would be so sad the tank had crashed, but so pleased I was planning on installing a bigger and better one in the extension.

I found a quiet spot to sit and think. The pebble chess set was a job for the future, I thought. I could do that when the building work was finished and we had our garden back. I had started teaching Reef to play chess when he was in hospital, and one day Kate had picked up a perfect, shiny black pebble and a shiny white one on the beach. 'We could paint pebbles and make our own chess set for the garden,' she had said, but we had never got round to it when she was alive.

I looked at 'netball centre' and thought what an awful irony it was that they were the very last two words on Kate's list. She played the position of centre in netball when she was younger, as she could run like the wind and was extremely skilful. She wanted the boys to know she was a good team player, to set an example to them, and to remind them she was not always bed-bound and tired out, breathing through an oxygen tube.

I wanted to contact Kate so badly I very nearly pressed 'reply' to her text as I stared at it. I wrapped my fingers around the phone and could feel them trembling.

'You OK, mate?' one of the other extras asked.

'Yes, yes, I am,' I said, meaning it. I'd just had the most incredible experience, and even though I felt Kate's loss very acutely, I realized my shaking hands had as much to do with my excitement as anything else. I knew Kate would have been delighted for me, and I couldn't wait to share the experience with the boys.

'Why did you do that?' Finn asked, looking rather bemused when I got home and described my adventure on set. 'Why couldn't you do a Disney one again, like Narnia?'

'Well, I didn't have a choice about the film,' I said. 'I was very, very lucky to get the chance to go on this set, and sometimes you just have to take the opportunities you are given.'

'Why? What do you mean?'

'What I mean, Finn, is that when you get the chance to do something exciting and different, you should take it.'

'Always?' he asked, screwing up his forehead.

'Er, not always,' I said.

Reef was listening now, and I saw an opportunity.

'If it was something dangerous, like riding a motorbike, then no,' I said. 'Mummy didn't want you to ride motorbikes or scooters because you could have an accident, especially on the road. Neither of us want you to do that. But with things that are safe, that aren't going to hurt you or other people, you should always have a go. It makes life fun!'

Unbelievably, within the hour I took an unexpected phone call from the local press agency, South West News Service, which had distributed several stories on both Reef and Kate's cancer in the past. They wanted to do a 'follow-up' now Finn was at school, to report on how we were coping as a family of three.

'I think it's a lovely idea,' I said. I could hardly refuse, after what I'd just said to the boys, though I did wonder whether anyone would really be interested, so long after Kate's death.

'I suppose I could talk you through Mum's List, and tell you what I've done and what I plan to do.'

There was a momentary pause before the journalist asked: 'What's Mum's List?'

'Oh, you know, Kate scribbled down a load of things she wanted me to do with the boys, stuff she wanted them to know about her, a few rules she wanted me to keep – normal mum stuff. It all started when I asked her, "What if you leave me?" She started coming out with so many things that I said she'd better write them down, so I didn't forget.'

Now there was a longer pause, during which I wondered if it might have sounded a bit strange to describe it as 'normal mum stuff' when what had happened to Kate was actually quite out of the ordinary, and so sad.

'I think it's a lovely idea, too,' the reporter said, sounding more animated. 'In fact it sounds really special. When can I come round?'

I gave a long interview the next day, during which I broke down several times as I was asked to recap on events of the previous nine months. I gave the reporter a copy of Mum's List, which Christine had kindly typed up for me, and I agreed it could be reproduced in the article, which would be sent out to both the local and national media along with a selection of family photos.

'If anyone prints it, I'll be able to put the stories in the memory boxes,' I said. 'Mind you, I won't hold my breath! I can't imagine why anyone would be that interested in me and Kate.'

The reporter smiled. 'You might just be surprised,' she said. 'I'll keep you posted.'

A few days later I had to take the boys for their holiday jabs so they'd be ready for Egypt. I wasn't looking forward to it. This was the sort of job Kate and I would have done together, so we could look after one child each. We always went as a family whenever the boys had the dentist or anything like that, just to make things easier.

'I need you to be really good boys,' I told Reef and Finn. 'You have to have these injections so you'll be safe when we go to Egypt. It might hurt a tiny bit, but it'll be over in a flash. I know you're both brave enough to do it.'

'I've had lots of injections before, remember, Daddy,' Reef said. There was a slight questioning tone in his voice.

'Yes, Reef, I do remember,' I said, thinking to myself: 'How could I ever forget?'

Reef put his arm around Finn's shoulder. 'It's not that bad, you'll be fine,' he said, throwing in a serious little nod and a narrowing of the eyes.

It was a relief to find two nurses waiting for us at the surgery. The boys needed one injection in each arm, so the plan was to inject both arms simultaneously, one child at a time. Despite his brave words, Reef looked nervous, and so Finn, in typical bombastic style, volunteered to go first. Sitting on my lap, he boldly rolled up his sleeves and stuck out both arms, looking as confident as he did when he 'high-fived' Mr Webber.

Seconds later, the efficient nurses having performed their job perfectly, Finn let out a loud scream and looked at Reef in horror.

'They stuck nails in my arms!' he wailed in disgust.

He turned to look at me, tears spilling down his cheeks.

'It *really* hurts,' he said accusingly. 'Reef, it *really really* hurts. They are going to stick nails in your arms!'

Finn's little face was so full of outrage and his reaction was so dramatic I found myself trying not to laugh. Thankfully, Reef barely had a chance to respond before the nurses had swiftly administered his jabs too, and the ordeal was over. By now Finn was walking round hugging himself, rubbing his upper arms as if he'd been attacked with six-inch nails, and Reef was as white as a sheet but was saying unconvincingly: 'It wasn't *that* bad.' Kate would have done the mummy bit now, kissing their arms better and offering words of comfort, and no doubt giving me a look to warn me to stop laughing.

'Come on, lads,' I said. 'You're both tough guys, well done. Now put your jumpers back on and let's go. You can have some chewing gum in the car.'

I wasn't Kate and couldn't do what she would have done. There are just some things mums do better than dads, and I had to accept that, even though I felt pangs of regret thinking that way.

I jumped in the driver's seat, and, with their sore arms, both boys struggled to buckle themselves into their booster seats in the back. It was a job I'd taught them to do, and something they'd done hundreds of times before.

'Can't do it!' Finn sulked.

'Daddy, *you* have to do it,' Reef whined.

'No, boys. It's not that difficult. You have to do it yourselves,' I said.

It would have been quicker for me to get out of my seat and do it for them, but I was making a point. They were four and six years old, well capable of clicking a seatbelt into place, even with aching arms. I wanted to bring them up to be self-sufficient and, besides, as a single parent I needed them to do as much as possible for themselves. It was a full five minutes before both buckles were finally clicked into place, and when I caught a glimpse of the boys' cross little faces in the rear-view mirror, I wondered if I'd been a bit hard.

'Here you are, boys, here's a piece of chewing gum each,' I said cheerfully.

They brightened up, but it reminded me of the first time they'd had chewing gum, after I told them Mummy was dead. Just like then, Finn had tear-stained cheeks and the smell of sweet strawberry flavouring hung in the cold, damp air. Treating grief with gum suddenly seemed like putting a sticking plaster on a shark bite. I then had a horrible jolt, thinking that I'd failed to do something Kate had asked. *'Always help them if they ask,'* she had said.

Was I too tough on the boys? Should I do things differently? Was Kate right to put that on the list? I'd have a chat with Ruth and ask her opinion tonight, I decided. I'd had a few missed calls on my phone while we'd been at the surgery, and when I got home I was surprised to see the answerphone flashing too. I dialled my voicemail, and to my delight it was the reporter from South West News Service.

'We've had quite a lot of interest in your story from the national press,' she said. 'You could be in a few national papers tomorrow, give me a ring.'

It turned out that almost every national newspaper in the country was planning to use our story, complete with family photos. I phoned Ruth excitedly to tell her the news.

'Wow!' she said, adding in typical frank style, 'I'm not sure Kate would have loved it though, Singe.'

'She'd be absolutely gobsmacked, I know I am,' I said. 'But I know she wouldn't mind, or I wouldn't do it. By the way, Ruth, can I run something past you?'

I explained all about the scene with the seatbelts and asked Ruth straight whether she thought I was too hard on the boys.

'Absolutely not,' she said without a moment's hesitation. 'They know you love them and care for them, and you'd be doing them a disservice if you pampered them.'

'Yes, but I can't do the mummy stuff like Kate did . . .' I said.

'Singe, nobody expects you to,' Ruth replied. 'The boys are a credit to you. How many times have people complimented you on how well-mannered and poised they are for their ages? It's all down to the way you and Kate brought them up together, and how you've carried on bringing them up without her. Kate wouldn't want you to change. You are a great dad. Sometimes saying "no" is a way of helping your children.'

I was very grateful to Ruth. I knew she would tell me straight if I was making mistakes and wouldn't just tell me what I wanted to hear. I remembered how she stood toe to toe with me once when Kate was ill and I was finding it tough dealing with relatives. I lost my temper with some of them when I was desperately short of sleep, but even though I was going through such a difficult time Ruth cut me no slack. 'You're out of order,' she told me. 'Calm yourself down, you're making things ten times worse.' With hindsight she was right, as she always is.

'Thanks, Ruth, you're a great mate,' I told her. 'I'll call you tomorrow.'

As soon as I put the phone down it rang again. It was the news agency, asking if I would appear on Sky News, the BBC and ITN the next day to talk about Mum's List.

'Of course,' I said eagerly. 'I wasn't banking on having film footage for the memory boxes too, but bring it on!'

1 October turned into quite a surreal day. I'd agreed that the local BBC News could film the boys going into school, but when the reality of it dawned as we went about our normal morning routine, I wondered what I'd let us all in for.

'Why are the television people filming us?' Reef asked, completely bemused.

'Because they want to do a story about the list Mummy left for us.'

'Why?'

'Because, well, because it's quite unusual for a mummy to do that.'

'Why did Mummy do it?'

'Because she was extra special.'

'OK, then. Can we go now?'

Finn was thrilled by the excitement of it all, enjoying his fifteen minutes of fame as the film crew followed both boys walking up the little path into school. My mobile rang before it was my turn to be interviewed. Unusually for that time of the morning, it was my old friend Nathan.

'Singe, I'm on the train,' he said. 'And I've just nearly fallen off the seat. You're splashed across *The Times*!'

I roared with laughter. 'I think it's great,' I told him. 'I'm thrilled to bits.'

When the camera turned to me, I must admit I felt a

bit like a rabbit caught in headlights. This was weird and totally unexpected, though undeniably exhilarating too. Once I got going I relished the opportunity to sing Kate's praises and explain what an amazing wife and mother she had been, and what a wonderful life we had had together.

Mum's List was the icing on the cake, I explained. It was over and above what any mum might be expected to do in her dying days, but that was Kate all over. I'd got so used to living with Mum's List I was surprised it was causing such a stir, and I said that too.

The BBC journalist told me we were indeed featured in all the big daily newspapers. As well as *The Times*, there were huge articles in the *Telegraph*, *Daily Mail*, *Mirror*, *Sun*, *Express* and *Guardian*. Now Radio Five also wanted me to do an interview with them.

'Are you happy with everything?' the reporter from South West News Service asked tentatively.

'Yes,' I said. 'I'm not sure Kate would have relished all this attention, but I think it's a brilliant tribute to her.'

My phone never stopped ringing throughout the day, with friends from all over the country phoning me to say they'd seen me in a newspaper or on the news. Journalists from as far afield as Spain and Japan wanted to cover the story too.

I arranged for ITN and Sky to do their interviews once I'd brought Reef and Finn home from school in the afternoon, and I'll never forget the look on the boys' faces when we drove into our cul-de-sac. The house was completely surrounded by TV vans topped with satellite dishes, and people with clipboards and phones were milling all around.

It's just as well the neighbours know us so well, I thought, because save for a strip of yellow police tape it looked like a major crime had been committed.

'Can we go in the trucks?' Reef and Finn asked, having no trouble unbuckling themselves swiftly and bouncing excitedly out of the car.

The journalists and crew were fantastic, showing them all the equipment before we started the interviews in our lounge. I had no qualms about letting the boys be filmed. It was an extraordinary experience for them, and they both took it in their stride.

'Not many young boys have an opportunity to talk on the news,' I told them. 'Make the most of it!'

'Is it really exciting to have the television cameras here?' one journalist asked them.

'Yes,' said Finn. 'Daddy does silly things all the time!'

I just shrugged and smiled; that was music to my ears.

The media interest continued over the weekend and then dispersed just about as quickly as it had arrived. I'd found it cathartic talking about Kate, and I don't think it did the boys any harm at all to talk about how lovely their mummy was, and to have a bit of fun along the way. They told the reporters she was very kind and she always played with them, and they missed her. They did Kate proud, and they looked as cute as anything too.

A couple of days later I overheard one of Finn's classmates asking why he had been on telly. ''Cos my mummy was very special,' Finn said before skipping off.

When we got home that night there were two packets of seeds pushed through the letterbox, with an anonymous note explaining they were for the boys to grow clovers and sunflowers in memory of Kate. More arrived the next day, and the day after that, and I told the boys we would plant the clovers around Mummy's grave and grow the sunflowers at home when the weather was warmer. They nodded and didn't question the unusual gifts; I guess nothing was quite as surprising, or exciting, as being besieged by film crews and reporters.

The following week Reef's teacher told me he had stood up in the class and talked very eloquently about losing his mummy. I was very moved to hear how he told the other children he missed her a lot but is happy because he has a nice daddy and brother, and they all stick together when they feel sad. Reef volunteered to do it because another little boy in the class lost his mum to cancer too, which was an unbelievably sad coincidence.

'I was very impressed by Reef's maturity,' the teacher said. 'But I must admit I had to blink back tears as he spoke.'

I was thrilled Reef had the confidence to stand up in front of the class, let alone talk about his loss. His confidence was growing daily, and that was a great achievement.

There was another piece of good news from the school. I had been elected Chair of Governors, which would allow me to have an even greater input into the boys' education. It would mean quite a commitment in terms of my time, but what could be more worthwhile? I'd be asked to help shape school policy and would sit in on interview panels for new appointments as well as being involved in all the fun things like fundraisers, 'wow' activities and parties.

The fact I was only working part-time made this possible. I know there was not one dad in the playground who would swap places with me, but this was something undeniably positive to come out of the tragedy of losing Kate. Not only that, I'd exceeded her expectations. When she wrote, *'Help All Saints School and try to get Reef extra help,'* I think she had something less ambitious in mind.

'You made a great Father Christmas,' Kate smiled at me as she scribbled that entry on her list. 'You should do more things like that at school. You're so good with the kids.'

It had been just weeks before Kate's death, in the last few weeks of term before we flew to Lapland for Christmas, when I'd dressed up as Santa. Hilariously, the costume was so good neither Reef nor Finn recognized me when they visited the school's grotto. I delighted in all the 'ho-ho-ho-ing' and wound Kate up by encouraging a couple of the yummy mummies to be Santa's helpers and sit on my lap. Kate got the last laugh, though, as usual, when we got to see the real Santa in Lapland.

'Oooh, he's much better than the one at school!' Finn said.

'That's 'cos he's *real*, silly,' Reef said.

Kate pulled her scarf up over her mouth so they couldn't see her giggling.

'You're just a second-rate fake,' she whispered in my ear. 'But I still love you.'

I remembered that day so well, and was reminded of it every day when I saw the Lapland souvenir photograph on the shelf in the boys' room. It was difficult to believe it was not far off a year since that picture was taken.

It was November now, and the temperature outside was dropping. One afternoon I had a meeting to attend at the school, to discuss performance management with the head teacher. It was a bright day but bitingly cold, and I shivered as I walked across the churchyard, thinking how glad I was that we had Egypt to look forward to. It would be lovely to escape to the sun, I thought.

The meeting was in a room with no windows in a converted loft space at the back of the church attached to the school. I heard someone say that it had just started snowing, but I imagined a few flakes and didn't give it a second thought. The meeting went on for a good couple of hours, and when I finally stepped outside I couldn't believe my eyes. Everything had turned white. It must have snowed solidly from the moment I'd gone inside, because the snow was really thick on the ground.

I was completely taken aback. I had a similar feeling to the one I'd had when I stepped through the clouds of smoke and into the *War Horse* film set at Castle Combe. Going out into the whiteness was like stepping back in time, except now I felt unnerved rather than excited. I wasn't entering a recreation of a past I never knew; I was going back into my own past, my past with Kate.

I looked down at my feet as I took a step forward. The crunch of my shoe in the snow sent a shockwave shooting through my body. I was back in Lapland. The noise reminded me of walking hand in hand through the snow with Kate. Everything reminded me of Lapland, of Kate, of our last holiday together. I saw her surrounded by white, just as I was now. I felt the same bone-chilling cold I felt back then. I'd forgotten how cold it was in the snow, how the sound of snow underfoot can squeak and crunch like fine gravel. I normally love that sound. I loved it in

Lapland, because it was accompanied by the sound of laughter. I loved it in Austria too, on my and Kate's first ever holiday together.

'I can't believe we're here!' the teenage Kate shrieked as she bounded through the snow like an excited kitten. 'I love skiing!' she declared. 'And I love you, Singe, with all my heart!'

I could picture her spinning round to me and saying those words, blonde ponytail dancing in her wake. The snow was romantic. It made the roses in Kate's cheeks blossom even more. She had taken her first flight with me, the first of many more, and she was the most gorgeous girl in the world.

A few years later, when I proposed in Wengen, Switzerland, the snow made everything seem magical. I had spent half a year's wages on a stunning aquamarine engagement ring, because it was Kate's March birthstone as well as mine, and it matched the blue of her eyes. Kate's eyes changed colour from very light blue to an even paler, icy blue when she was angry and emotional, and I loved the way the stone changed colour in different lights too. The ring was perfect, and it was burning a hole in my rucksack from the second we stepped foot in the ski resort. I couldn't wait to put it on Kate's finger, but the moment also had to be absolutely perfect.

I designed the ring myself, asking a jeweller friend of mine to keep a lookout for exactly the right stone. As luck would have it he sourced a beautiful teardrop shaped gem in Switzerland, and I got him to set it in a pretty wishbone-shaped white gold band with little diamonds on either side. Next, I spoke to Kate's boss and arranged for her to have time off work, without her knowing. When she came home on the Friday night and saw her ski boots and skis in the hall, she screamed and cried.

'Singe! I can't believe we're going skiing,' she said, hugging me. 'This is just amazing! I thought my boss was trying to make me redundant, winding down my hours! This is just brilliant!'

I had to bite my tongue. I wanted to tell her she wasn't just getting a holiday, but a proposal too, but I had to wait for that magic moment. I'd chosen Wengen because it is chocolate-box stunning with views of the north face of the Eiger. I wanted to propose in one of the most beautiful places on the planet, and this was it.

Kate was enthralled. I'd booked first-class rail tickets that took us from the airport to Wengen station.

'There are no cars in Wengen,' I explained to Kate. 'It's too pretty for cars.'

'Singe, I love you!' she said a million times.

She hugged me and kissed me the whole way there.

'Thank you so much, Singe. I keep thinking this is a dream and I'm going to wake up. It's like a fairytale.'

I wanted to get down on my knees and propose to her right there and then in the railway carriage, but I didn't. It had to happen in the snow. Kate's excitement grew when we arrived at the Hotel Edelweiss. It was like stepping into a painting of an idyllic Alpine scene, and the views of the Eiger knocked her out.

'We're not far from where they filmed that James Bond stunt with the revolving restaurant at the top of the mountain,' I told her. 'Tomorrow we'll go on the clockwork railway, which hooks up to the highest railway in Europe.

We'll also see the horse-drawn sleighs that carry the ski equipment around the valley.'

Kate started giggling and couldn't stop. 'I don't think I could be any happier,' she told me.

The next day we found our ski legs on part of the famous Lauterbrunnen downhill slope, and I left Kate catching her breath and enjoying a hot chocolate while I darted off to the supermarket. Heart pounding, I bought a punnet of strawberries, a bottle of champagne, some salami and some freshly baked crusty rolls, hiding the lot in my rucksack.

The ring was in my pocket now, and I suggested we should go right to the top of the mountain on the railway, ski halfway down and find a good spot for lunch.

'Singe, whatever you say!' Kate laughed. 'I'm in your hands, which is exactly where I want to be.'

The views were incredibly spectacular as we rode up the mountain. I was nervously excited about the proposal, but Kate was too busy drinking in the stunning scenery to suspect a thing.

'This is just breathtaking,' she said over and over again. The view of her face, aglow with happiness, was breathtaking too. How would she react to the proposal, when she was already on a massive high?

'Here we go!' Kate yelled excitedly as we set off downhill.

I was tingling with anticipation now. My heart was aching to tell her how much I loved her, how much I wanted to marry her. I just couldn't wait to see her face when I pulled out the ring. I spent every second of the ski run scouring the landscape for the perfect spot to stop, and suddenly I saw it.

We turned a corner and a vast expanse of empty snow

opened up in front of us. There was a bench in the distance with a snowdrift banked up to the side, and there wasn't another person in sight. I let Kate go in front of me, and as she skied close to the drifted snow I zipped in behind her and took out one of her bindings. She ploughed headlong into a deep pile of powdery snow, shrieking as she performed the perfect wipe-out. Before she could come up for breath I piled in behind her and pulled the ring out of my pocket.

'Will you marry me?' I said.

'What? Yes! Yes, of course I will!' she gasped ecstatically, wiping snow from her face to reveal tear-loaded eyes.

I kissed her passionately as I pulled off her ski glove and placed the ring on her finger. It fitted perfectly. Everything was perfect in the world, absolutely everything. We walked to the bench to crack open the champagne, crunching in the snow. I remember the crunch. It was crisp and clean, and it made me feel so alive. I can still taste the champagne on Kate's lips, and I can smell the ripe strawberries and the fresh crusty bread. The combination was delicious and dizzying, but most of all I remember the sound of crunching snow, connecting me to our beautiful planet. I was marrying the girl of my dreams and I was so alive.

The crunch grated on me now. I was alive, but Kate was dead, like so many others buried around me in this churchyard. The white brightness made me blink, and my eyes stung. It was very quiet all around me, as if the normal sounds of the street and the traffic had been frozen into the snow. I was all alone.

I quickened my pace. I could feel the warmth of my

blood in my cheeks, and they were burning and stinging in the cold. My breath was short and shallow. I wanted to get inside my car, where I could breathe normally and escape from the snow. I almost threw myself into the driver's seat, slamming the door sharply behind me. It made an eerie echo sound and a curtain of snow dropped heavily from the driver's window beside me, landing with a muted thud on the ground outside. I gulped in the stale air of the car, and tears started falling from my eyes.

I had a very deep feeling of loss; but it took me a few moments to realize it wasn't my own loss I was lamenting, it was Kate's.

'She's missed it,' I thought. 'Kate won't see snow again, not ever. She won't see anything, ever again.'

I felt so sorry for her, missing out on so much. I turned on the engine, but the noise only gave me a cover to cry harder and louder, uninhibited by the quiet whiteness around me. I was bawling my eyes out now, and I had no control over my tears. I didn't like feeling so powerless, so beholden to my emotions, and I tried to tell myself off.

'Just have a big cry, you bloody idiot,' I said in my head. 'And then pull yourself together and drive the car, for goodness' sake.'

My body wouldn't listen to my brain. I felt physically wounded, like I'd been cut or beaten. My stomach was tied in tight knots that pinched and twisted deep inside me, trapping my breath uncomfortably in my throat and guts. The pain felt so raw I had a job trying to convince myself I wasn't actually injured.

I don't know how long it took for the hurt and pain to subside. When my eyes finally dried, I looked across the car park and saw footprints in the snow. There were lots of them, running in every direction. The perfect whiteness was just a moment in time, and the sounds of the street had thawed and dripped back into the atmosphere. Life goes on, I thought, for everybody except Kate.

I drove to the supermarket, wondering what to make for tea. The only meal I could think of was our favourite steak in pepper sauce. The boys love it now too, and I had started to teach them how to make it. Kate had wanted me to make it for the boys, because she loved it so much, and she had even put it on Mum's List: *'Singe's pepper sauce.'* I smiled when she wrote that, telling her my grandfather would be thrilled his old family recipe was being preserved in such a way. 'It deserves to be,' she said. 'It's delicious.' I felt gutted she would never eat it again, but I vowed to make sure the boys did.

I pushed the trolley down the aisles in a bit of daze, picking up fillet steak, peppercorns and sea salt, double cream and brown sugar. I knew the recipe so well and it seemed a good idea to cook it tonight. I know I eat when I'm depressed, and I thought it would be something to cheer me up. When Kate needed cheering up I often bought her favourite Tesco Finest chocolate and caramel éclairs. I was surprised she hadn't put those on her list of 'likes', alongside orange Club biscuits and lemon curd, or Walnut Whips and strawberry cheesecake. Then again, there were so many things she liked, too many to list.

I could easily tell the boys what else Mummy liked, I thought, because I knew Kate's favourites so well. I didn't need a list for everything, and to prove it I ran through a mental shopping list of Kate's likes. Crème brûlée, strawberries, chicken korma, Chinese duck pancakes, crispy shredded beef (no chillis), chicken tikka, ham and pineapple pizza, Turkish delight, my dad's Sunday roasts, spaghetti Bolognese, Cadbury's Flake (straight from the fridge), salad with celery, nuts and apple, fresh profiteroles and Double Decker chocolate bars. Kate ate Double Deckers in a funny way, always saving the nougat layer until last. I could see her eating one, nibbling the nugget like a little squirrel. The image was so clear it was like a video flickering away in my head.

I can't remember paying at the checkout and I can barely remember driving home. When I unpacked the groceries I wasn't entirely sure what I'd find.

'What's for tea?' Reef asked.

'Daddy's world famous pepper steaks,' I announced, pulling the ingredients from the shopping bags.

'Yummy!' Reef said. 'Can I help you smash up the salt?'

'Of course!' I said. 'Remember what I told you?'

'You have to beat the living daylights out of it!' Reef said.

'Correct!'

'Have we got pudding?' Finn asked.

'Let me see,' I replied, rummaging through the bags. 'We've got some fruit yoghurts,' I said.

Thankfully I hadn't indulged in éclairs or strawberry cheesecake or Double Deckers. I liked them too, but not as much as Kate did.

I looked out of the front window and thought back to the footprints in the snow I'd seen earlier in the afternoon at the churchyard. Now I could see that the boys and I had left three sets of deep footprints in our driveway. It was still snowing heavily, and it wouldn't be long before our footprints were covered over, I thought.

'Can we play in the snow after tea?' Finn asked.

'Of course you can,' I said. 'Only if I can play too.'

I didn't really want to go back out in the snow, but we were a family of three now, moving forward together, and it was the right thing to do. We would go outside and make plenty more footprints, because we could.

Chapter 10

'Go to Egypt and snorkel in the Red Sea'

'We'll have to cancel, again,' Kate said flatly. 'I'm sorry, Singe.'

It was our third attempt at taking the boys snorkelling in Egypt, and the third time we'd had to cancel the holiday because of Kate's illness.

It was the spring of 2009, and she still had six months of treatment to get through.

'Don't you dare apologize; we'll get there in the end,' I said, holding her gently in my arms.

Kate felt smaller than ever, like a little bird, and I was afraid to hug her too tightly for fear of hurting her slight frame. She rarely complained and seemed to be soaring through her treatment plan, but the surgery, the trial drug, the chemo and now the radiotherapy had stolen so much from Kate.

It wasn't just the obvious things that had been taken from her. While we were absorbed by the sudden loss of Kate's breast and then the gradual disappearance of her hair and eyebrows, cancer had been slowly siphoning the colour from her lips and skimming the soft curves from her hips and thighs. It was a sneak thief, still prowling in the shadows long after its initial smash and grab on Kate's body. It took cancelling the holiday again to trigger the burglar alarm in my head, and I realized that I'd only just started taking stock of cancer's huge and merciless haul.

I kissed Kate's forehead, then her small hands. Cancer had sapped the moisture from her skin and stripped the sheen from her nails. It had helped itself to bags and bags of Kate's energy and left bucketloads of sickness, nausea and tiredness as its calling card. It couldn't steal Kate's spirit, I thought. It could never take the spark from her eyes or the fire from her belly. It could never take away the hope in her heart.

'Egypt can wait,' I whispered. 'The most important thing is to get you well. We can rebook it when you're better, and we'll have something fantastic to look forward to.'

'I know,' she said softly. 'You're right, Singe. There'd be no point in going anyway if I couldn't even snorkel with the boys.'

Her pale lips curled into a soft smile, and I knew she was imagining that great moment when Reef and Finn would swim amongst the fish and the coral in the Red Sea. Her eyes glimmered, like fluorescent strip lights flickering into life, then flooding the room with light.

We'd looked forward to this trip so much. Both boys could snorkel by the age of two, and they were swimming by the time they were three. I'd lost count of the number of times we'd said: 'I can't wait for them to snorkel in the Red Sea.'

Reef and Finn would be completely bowled over by the sight of the tropical fish and the sea creatures and anemones, and Kate and I couldn't wait to share the experience with them. It was a dream I tried to keep alive for month after month throughout Kate's treatment, when first her mastectomy and then her chemotherapy and radiotherapy forced us to cancel.

When we eventually booked up the holidays to Florida and Lapland later in 2009 I thought we'd turned a corner, and I told her Egypt would be next on the list, because I firmly believed it would be. 'We'll go in the New Year,' I said. I wasn't saying it just to try and cheer her up; I had absolutely no doubt in my mind.

'We'll finally get there in 2010,' I told Kate. 'You'll see, it'll be worth the wait.'

'I know,' she said 'Let's hope so.'

Eventually, as time ticked by, Kate started to just say: 'Fingers crossed' whenever I mentioned it. I thought she was being cautious, to avoid the disappointment of cancelling the holiday yet again, but now I can see that she must have feared long before I did that she might never make it.

I will never forget the forlorn look on her face when she wrote on her list: *'Go to Egypt and snorkel in the Red Sea.'* We'd been working on the list well into the early hours by that point, and she was very weak and tired. It must have been agonizing for her to write those words. I could almost feel her pain and disappointment hanging off the page.

'Of course we will,' I said. My words stuck in my throat, and I began to cry.

Those words, Kate's instruction to me, said that I had a future, and Kate didn't. All she could plan was her death, while I had my life with the boys stretching before me. I couldn't quite believe it, because I didn't want to believe it. Until then the word 'we' always meant me and Kate, or me, Kate and the boys. Now 'we' was going to mean just me,

Reef and Finn. 'Of course we will, and we'll think of you when we do.'

Kate cried. 'Hold me,' she said, and I took her in my arms. She was her smallest ever, a fragile shell of herself. She sobbed and apologized and told me to promise her the three of us would have the most wonderful time.

'We will,' I said, choking on the words and still not quite believing what I was saying. I would believe it when it happened, I thought, in case it never had to happen that way. Even with Kate on her deathbed, I clung to hope.

I had the same choked-up feeling in my throat when our flight took off for Egypt just before Christmas 2010. I was surrounded by members of my family, who'd made the trip as promised, and Reef and Finn were incredibly excited, which was good to see. It was just as well they had to wear safety belts, I thought, or they'd be bouncing up and down on the plane all the way there.

It was a relief to finally be jetting off, ticking off something huge on Kate's list, and I was very glad to be escaping the prospect of a cold, dark Christmas at home. Despite all the positives, I couldn't fight off sad thoughts, though. I really thought Kate would recover and be beside me on this holiday. Even when she put Egypt on her list, I still held on to a thread of hope, as crazy as that now seemed.

Now there was no hope. This was the reality, and even though I felt like crying I told myself to get a grip, keep my promise to Kate and have a fantastic time with the boys.

'Will we get bitten by a shark?' Finn asked.

'No, you're not tasty enough,' I told him.

If Kate were there she would have rolled her eyes and

told me off for being silly. Then she would no doubt have relayed the story to my family about how I told her all the sharks were sleeping on that night dive we did in the Maldives, when she crash-landed on top of that white tip and scared the living daylights out of it.

'Don't listen to Daddy,' she'd have told the boys. 'He's just a teaser.'

In actual fact, a tourist had been killed in a shark attack in the Red Sea a few weeks earlier, and several divers had been hurt. There was a bathing ban still in place, and I was very worried we wouldn't be allowed to snorkel, which would defeat the whole object of the holiday.

'Daddy, what if we can't swim in the sea?' Reef asked. He'd heard the adults talking.

'Not much gets past you, does it, Reef?' I teased. 'Seriously, don't worry about things that might not happen.'

'But what if?' he said.

'Reef, we'll just have to wait and see. Whatever happens we'll have a good time. We won't let it spoil the holiday.'

He nodded, not looking too convinced.

'Now then, what shall we do?' I continued. 'How about a few jokes?'

Both boys pricked up their ears. Finn had won a joke competition organized by the cabin crew on our flight to Lapland and fancies himself as a bit of a comedian.

'Knock knock,' I said.

'Who's there?' the boys replied in unison.

'Boo hoo.'

'Boo hoo who?'

'Don't cry, it's Christmas!'

Reef and Finn killed themselves laughing as they passed the joke on and began telling a string of their own. I was laughing too. It was holiday time now, and I was slowly beginning to relax. I was very grateful to have so many family members all around me. Being in a large group created a constant backdrop of bustle and busyness, which was just what I needed.

It was quite chaotic getting everybody from the airport to the hotel in Sharm El Sheik, then checking in and arranging when to meet for dinner. The boys were beside themselves when they spotted room service menus.

'Can we order pizzas?' Finn asked.

'Oooh, and lots of puddings!' Reef drooled.

'No, you can't!' I said.

'Pleeease, Daddy,' they begged.

'No, you can't,' I replied. 'We don't need it, we're going out to eat. Now, stop nagging!'

The boys' bickering and chatter was non-stop. There was no time for me to think, let alone get sad, and that was a blessing, I suppose.

Preparing for the trip had been a real eye-opener about just how much Kate did for us. I always considered myself a hands-on dad, but Kate was the one who ultimately organized everything, double-checked arrangements and made sure we all had what we needed. On holiday she was always like Mary Poppins with her magic bag, producing wet wipes, snacks, plasters or colouring books effortlessly on demand. Even when she was ill she somehow managed to keep all the plates spinning, in every part of her life, and she always had whatever the boys needed to hand.

Over the previous few weeks I'd been flat out buying

Christmas presents and sun cream, sorting out dog care, exchanging money and packing the suitcases. That was on top of trying to run the house and keep my work and school governor duties running smoothly. There was so much to do I actually wondered if I'd get through it.

One night I was so tired I could barely bring myself to unpack the boys' school bags, but I was so glad I did. Inside Reef's was the first official school photo of the two brothers posing confidently together in their neat red jumpers. '*Would like school photos bought every year.*' Kate would have adored it, and I immediately filled in the slip, ordering several copies.

The photo brought things back into focus for me. I felt some of my stress evaporate as I looked at it, because it told me why I'd been running around like a headless chicken these past few weeks. It was a joy and a privilege to be a dad, even if it was bloody exhausting too.

When we finally unpacked and settled into our hotel I felt shattered but fulfilled. We'd made it at last, and it felt like a massive achievement. The boys, of course, were raring to go, and I knew that however tired I felt I had to 'do a Kate' and keep the show on the road as best I could.

'When are we snorkelling in the sea?' Finn asked.

He was so excited he was jumping up and down on the spot.

'As soon as you've done some good practice in the swimming pool, Diddy,' I answered. 'Or should I call you Tigger?'

'When are we seeing the pyramids?' Reef asked. 'Will we see a mummy?'

'No, silly, Mummy isn't here,' Finn said, clearly not intending to make a joke.

Reef cracked up laughing. 'I mean an Egyptian mummy, ones wrapped up in bandages!' he roared.

I had to laugh; it was either that or burst into tears of despair.

It was a few days into the holiday before we were finally ready to venture into the Red Sea for our long-awaited snorkelling experience in the reef. Thankfully, the shark scare had passed, and there were no bathing restrictions. Nothing was standing in our way now, and I didn't want any sorrow to spoil the moment either.

'Enjoy it,' I told myself. 'Enjoy the moment, you can't repeat it.'

My brother Matt offered to come with me to help, as I'd decided to take a taxi to a beautiful nature reserve, which was a little bit of a trek away. Reef and Finn nicknamed our taxi driver 'Mario' after their favourite Mario Kart character on their DS games, and we all had a giggle as we travelled along the hot desert road. On the way we passed Dreams Beach, where Kate and I stayed when we brought the boys to Egypt when they were very small. It was Christmas then, too, and I wanted to say: 'Look, remember that?' but I stopped myself, because I was the only one among us who would remember.

Instead I thought of my and Kate's favourite saying: 'If you're not living on the edge you're a waste of space,' and I put my energies into getting the boys' adrenaline pumping as we pulled up at the nature reserve. I told them all about the types of fish they might see and asked them to look out for the funny clownfish that Mummy liked to tease.

'This is going to blow your socks off!' I said. 'You won't believe your eyes! Let the adventure begin!'

The boys, who were already excited, really rose to the occasion and were brimming with anticipation, which made me double my efforts to make this an overwhelmingly happy experience.

I smiled, but I had to take a deep breath as I helped the boys pull on their wetsuits, masks and snorkels. Kate would have done this job, and I would have taken photos, capturing the delighted look on her face as she did so. Now I was doing both jobs, feeling like a one-man production line as I got the boys equipped and ready to pose in turn for a picture. 'I didn't know you could multitask,' Kate teased. Her voice was so distant it sounded ghost-like in my head.

I looked up at the sky. It was dense blue. If she ever was on a cloud, she wasn't there now. There wasn't a whisper of cloud in the entire sky. Kate had gone, and I was going to enjoy this moment with the boys without her, in her memory. I was very glad Matt had come with me. He was a great moral support, and he also agreed to have Reef on his back while I took Finn, as it was too soon after the shark attacks for me to feel comfortable letting them swim alone. Matt's a big six-foot lifeguard, and the boys adore him, so it couldn't have worked out better.

Watching Reef dip expectantly into the Red Sea on Matt's back was heartbreaking and heart-warming all at once. I could feel Finn's grip tighten around my neck as we entered the water too moments later. It was cold after being in the hot taxi, and both boys squealed and wriggled.

I was delighted to spot angelfish and clownfish swimming towards us almost immediately. Kate adored both of those types of fish, and they were a welcome, familiar sight. That said, it was also like seeing them for the first time, because I was sharing the boys' excitement at this new experience. I loved it.

A blue-spotted stingray, a Picasso Trigger fish and some parrot fish darted in and out of the pink, blue and green coral. It was breathtakingly beautiful, but the big excitement came when the boys spotted regal tangs and yellow tangs like the ones we have in the tank at home, named Dory and Bubbles after the characters in *Finding Nemo.* Finn was wriggling like a little fish himself he was so excited, and I could see Reef drinking in the moving spectacle, eyes everywhere.

The grand finale was seeing several large shoals of fusiliers turn from dazzling blue to sunshine yellow right before our eyes, an amazing stunt they pull to confuse predators. It was magical, and I didn't want the show to end, but I couldn't wait to hear what the boys had to say either.

When we eventually headed back to the shallows and took off our masks, both Reef and Finn were gabbling ten to the dozen, throwing out questions excitedly. 'Can we get firefish and damsons for our tank? Can we get a tank that makes the fish look like that? How do the yellow ones turn blue? Is it magic?' I could feel both their little hearts beating wildly as I helped them out of their gear and answered their questions. Their eyes were glistening and twinkling in the sun, but Reef suddenly went quiet.

'Why did some people walk on the corals?' he asked solemnly.

'Well, either they don't know any better, or they are just very careless and selfish,' I said.

'They'll hurt them,' he said, looking very upset. 'I don't want the corals to get hurt. They might die.'

I gave him a hug. Reef was wise beyond his years at times, and I was moved that he had such respect for living things. I couldn't be sad at a time like this, though. It was an overwhelmingly wonderful event in the boys' life, and I didn't want Reef to focus on hurt and dying.

'Mummy was always very protective over the coral,' I told him. 'You're a little star, just like she was. She'd be very glad you care so much.'

'Thank you, Daddy,' Reef said, giving me a brave smile.

Driving back, we had a different taxi driver, who turned out to be the brother-in-law of the one who'd brought us to the reef.

'It's not Mario!' Finn said, disappointed.

'Must be Luigi,' Reef joked, and Matt and I burst out laughing before politely trying to explain to the driver how the boys love to race Mario against Luigi on their DS games.

I talked to Matt about how I couldn't wait to go scuba diving with the boys one day, when they were both old enough to be fully trained. Reef had already had a few lessons in my friend Ken's swimming pool back home. He was only five years old the first time he tried it and was the youngest person I had ever taught. He went down eight foot with a cylinder on his back, and gave big, triumphant 'OK' hand signals under water, which was a real achievement at such a young age.

'Bet you can't wait to have a go,' Matt said to Finn.

'Done it already!' Finn bragged, and I explained how, not to be outdone, Finn had swapped his snorkel for a regulator and tank that day. He floated on the surface, pretending to dive too, while Kate fell about laughing on the side of the pool.

'Typical Finn!' Matt said, and he was right.

It was a funny memory, but I also remember that Kate had a few tears on the poolside that day too. I thought it was because she had wanted to give Reef his first dive lesson, but wasn't able to go in the water because she still had tubes sticking out of her arms. Now, I thought, there was probably more to it than that. She could see what she would be missing, if the worst happened. Or maybe she actually sensed or knew the worst was going to happen, but I truly hope not, not six months before her death.

By Christmas Day all thirteen members of our party had arrived in Egypt. We all chipped in to hire a private boat from one of the dive centres at Na'ama Bay. To our delight, the boat was absolutely massive and included a crew and instructors, all for just £40 a head. We were all in a good mood as we headed for Tiran Island, catching a huge tuna on the way, which was cooked for us and served in a delicious hot salad for lunch. I really enjoyed myself and managed to unwind.

It didn't really feel like Christmas Day, but that was a blessing. Santa visited the boys, of course, and all the family and friends swapped presents, but it felt pretty much like any other day of the holiday really. There was precious little time to think, let alone dwell on Christmases past.

On Boxing Day I helped the boys practise snorkelling in the swimming pool and then swam a hundred lengths in another delicioiusly cold pool, trying to improve my fitness and lose a bit of weight. It was a daily routine I established on the holiday, while other members of the family kept an eye on Reef and Finn for me.

It was a bit tough in the evenings at times, to be honest. Some of the younger ones in our group went out to clubs and bars, which I'd have loved to do but couldn't because of the boys. Had Kate been there I'd have been very happy to stay at the hotel and have a quiet drink in the bar, but it wasn't like that now, and the holiday provided a sharp reminder of the difficulties of being a single parent.

Even though I was surrounded by close family, it wasn't their responsibility to babysit while I went out and let my hair down. They all wanted a good holiday on their own terms, of course. I understood that completely, but it didn't stop me feeling a bit sorry for myself from time to time. The weather didn't help, and on 29 December it started to absolutely pour down.

'It's the first time we've had so much rain for many, many years,' the waiter told me merrily. 'Normally it rains just a little, about three days in a year. We're all very excited about it. It's such a very unusual event.'

'Great,' I thought. 'That's all we need.'

It was Finn's fifth birthday, and I was hoping to spend the day snorkelling, swimming and playing on the beach in the sunshine.

'Am I having a party?' he asked.

'No, Finn, not out here,' I told him.

'But Reef had a giant massive big party. It's not fair!'

'I know, but I've had a brilliant idea,' I told him, pulling him close.

'What?' he said suspiciously.

'Well, it's not great having a birthday so close to Christmas, is it?' I said.

'S'pose not.'

'It means you get all your presents at once, and then nothing happens until next year.'

He nodded. 'What's the idea then?'

'How about if we celebrate your birthday again in the spring, when the weather is better? All the family will celebrate your real birthday, but you can have a giant massive party with your friends in March, near my birthday and Mum's Day.'

'Yes, deal.' Finn smirked, immediately asking: 'How many sleeps is it? Can I have a cinema party?'

'It's lots of sleeps, and yes you can,' I said. 'We'll hire the whole cinema, just like we did for Reef, and we'll call it "Finn's unofficial birthday party".'

He gave me a high five and bounded off happily to tell Reef, but this didn't solve the problem of how I was going to keep the boys entertained today, and my nerves were beginning to snap a little. The rain was getting heavier by the minute and was battering on the window of our hotel room, while rivers of water were running down the paths outside.

I desperately wanted to get out in the sea, but there was no chance of that.

'When will the rain stop, Daddy?' Reef whined. 'I'm bored.'

'Hopefully soon,' I said.

'How soon?'

'I don't know, Reef. How can I possibly know?'

He started playing with the buttons on the hotel phone, and Finn tried to jump from one bed to the next.

'Stop it, both of you!' I said. 'You're going to break something.'

Bang on cue, Finn toppled off the end of his bed and fell awkwardly against a chest of drawers, hurting his back.

'I'm all right,' he said bravely, wincing and biting his lip to hold back his tears.

Seconds later he was zooming round the room again, while Reef had turned his attention to a tube of sun cream, which he managed to squirt across the bed clothes.

'Boys, give me a break!' I shouted. 'Can't you just play nicely together with one of Finn's new toys or something?'

'Boorriing!' Reef muttered.

'When can we go outside, Daddy?' Finn nagged.

'Not yet,' I said. 'Please both play quietly on your DSs while I have a shower and get five minutes' peace!'

They grumbled but did as I asked, sitting on my bed with their games. I'd been in the shower for less than five minutes when there was a loud, urgent knock at the door. I couldn't believe it, and I wrapped myself in a towel and stormed to the door, dripping wet and fuming.

In front of me on the balconied passageway stood an immaculately dressed waiter who was wearing a starched white apron and holding an enormous tray containing a large chocolate cake, a selection of biscuits and a steaming pot of tea. He was framed in the doorway by an angry black sky, even though it was the middle of the morning.

'For your boy, sir,' he said, giving a nervous smile.

At that very moment a tremendous flash of lightning hit the tennis courts behind him, lighting him up like a Christmas tree. The cake had a large sheet of tin foil swirled flamboyantly around the top, and I looked at it in terror, suddenly seeing a giant lightning conductor instead of a chocolate sponge. Rain was pelting down like bullets, ricocheting off the pavements, and electric zigzags of lightning were zipping across the sky, leaving purple, flashing clouds in their wake. There was an irritating smell in the air; a cloying mixture of smoke and disturbed dust which caught in my nostrils. I could feel hot blood rising up the veins in my neck and I let rip.

'Reef! Finn!' I bellowed. 'Which one of you two has ordered room service? I told you not to touch the phone!'

I turned and saw their two little heads poking out from under the covers of my bed, four blue eyes looking very sheepishly at me.

'You're both in so much trouble I can't tell you! Have you any idea how much this is going to cost?'

The pair of them came slinking over to me, looking worried and confused.

'I knew I shouldn't have let you watch those *Home Alone* DVDs. Is that where you got the idea from. Well, is it?'

They looked at me blankly.

'Er, there is no cost, sir,' the young waiter explained delicately. 'This is a birthday cake for your boy, Finn, compliments of the manager. It is a happy birthday cake.'

I noticed the waiter's thin smile had completely disappeared, and he was looking extremely worried. I could feel my blood rising again, but this time it wasn't bubbling up in temper, it was filling my cheeks with the glow of shame.

'I am *so* sorry,' I said, finally taking the tray off him.

'It's quite all right, sir, but please can I come inside for a moment?' He had a note of urgency in his voice, and his hands were trembling. I suddenly realized he wasn't in the slightest bit upset by my outburst, but was absolutely terrified of the storm. 'I have never seen a storm before,' he explained, his voice quaking now. 'Two palm trees on the complex have been hit by lightning. Their roots are on fire. It is like nothing I have seen in my life. Normally we do not have rain.'

'I can't apologize enough for the confusion,' I said, ushering him in. 'Please come in. And boys, I owe you an apology. Come on, you two, have a piece of cake.'

Reef gave me a rather unimpressed look, and even Finn needed a few moments to get over the mix-up.

'We all make mistakes,' I told them. 'But don't hold a grudge, boys. It's best to accept an apology, shake hands or have a cuddle and get on with it.'

Finn nodded silently and wrapped his little arms around me, and Reef quickly followed suit. It was the fastest cuddle on record as the gooey chocolate cake was beckoning, but I was glad of it.

'Happy birthday, Finn,' I said. 'I think it could be one you will never forget.'

When the waiter finally plucked up courage to venture back outside, the rain had turned to giant hailstones. I was amazed to see they were practically as big as pound coins. I'd seen plenty of storms, but never one as dramatic as this.

I looked up into the sky and shook my head. It's just as well I didn't really believe in the afterlife, I thought. If I did, this was most definitely Kate's doing. She was venting her rage at not being allowed to share Finn's birthday; at least that's what some people might have thought. Either that or the crash of thunder was Kate falling off her cloud, laughing her head off at me making such a prat of myself. I didn't believe those things, not really, but the timing was weird enough to make me think twice.

The next morning the sky was blue again. I somehow knew it would be. The sun was shining brightly, and there was a clean smell in the calm, still air. It was a fresh start to the holiday, and we could go back to what we did best: making the most of it. While my brother entertained the boys with a morning game of water polo, I wandered off to sit on the beach.

The calmness in the air was a little unnerving. I saw the burned roots of the palm trees that had been struck by lightning and I couldn't stop thinking of the same phrase over and over again: 'the calm after the storm'. This definitely felt like the calm after the storm, but I'd been caught out by that feeling before, and I didn't trust it. I hoped to God there wasn't another one coming.

I sat on the sand and looked at the empty space beside me. Never in a million years did I think Kate would die so young. Thirty-eight was no age at all. It was ridiculously young. She didn't deserve to have her life cut so short. My mind wandered once again to the day Kate and I sat on the beach back home when Reef's treatment was finally over, and he was thriving, against the odds. 'We made it!' Kate said, and we really thought we had. We'd survived the lightning bolts and put out so many fires for so many years. Doctors had stopped the spread of Reef's cancer with drugs and surgery, and we were all enjoying the calmness we craved. We didn't realize that it was the calm before another storm; the bloody great electric thunderstorm of Kate's cancer. What if there was yet another clap of thunder or crack of lightning waiting to strike? Would I be able to cope with another blow on my own?

I lay back and closed my eyes. 'What if?' was a stupid question, I thought. Anything could happen, I told myself. I'd told Reef there was no point in 'what ifs', and I knew I was right to teach him that. It was a negative and unnecessary way to think. Far better to hope for the best, and wait and see.

All I could be sure of was what had already happened, not what might happen. It was almost twelve months since Kate's death, and plenty had happened. Life had moved on, and I was both shocked and comforted by that thought. It was right that life had moved on, even though in the beginning there were times when I simply couldn't fathom how it could. I wasn't quite sure how or when I'd started moving on because it was a gradual, delicate shift; a softening of raw, screaming grief into tender, aching mourning.

The first anniversary of Kate's death was just a few weeks away, and I thought about how, in the year without her, so many good things had happened to make my bereavement more bearable. I let my mind wander through the months and the seasons.

The freezing cold winter that hung heavy around Kate's funeral had thawed a little by the time we bought the boat and set off on new adventures. I didn't expect plain sailing, but I hoped for some happiness, at least. We'd had plenty, I thought.

I enjoyed the warmth of the sun on my forehead as happy memories gathered in my mind. I could see Reef and Finn eating a picnic at Priddy and scampering off to hunt for bugs and butterflies. I saw their delighted little faces as they took the steering wheel of *4 Saints* and chanted, 'Faster, faster!' with the wind in their hair. I had a clear, vivid memory of the three of us dressed as pirates, posing for a photograph on Reef's birthday, happy as sand boys in the sunshine, all three of us.

I thought sadly about how sometimes, even on bright, sunny days, the sky turned grey seemingly at the flick of a switch, when clouds of grief gathered overhead, overshadowing everything. I never had any bereavement counselling, but I knew that this was normal, and that nobody goes through neatly organized stages of grief. You never know when it's going to get you, when it's going to make the memories or the tears flow.

I had a pang of regret about how I'd handled the Easter caravan holiday, when I couldn't help feeling out of sorts. I'm sure I could have tried a bit harder. I also winced at the memory of *4 Saints* being smashed to smithereens, and having to tell the boys she would be out of action for ages and ages, too many sleeps to calculate.

Without warning, I felt an icy knot in my stomach when I thought about the lumpy nodes in Reef's belly. Without a doubt, discovering them was the low point of the entire year since Kate's death, and finding out they were harmless was the best moment ever. Thinking about it pushed all other thoughts from my head, and I had a very clear, lucid thought.

Having two happy, healthy children was Kate's dream, and that's what I had right now. When she wrote Mum's List, that was her motivation. The little snippets about herself, the pointers for me and the instructions to the boys were really all saying the same thing. 'Be happy, appreciate life, have lots of fun,' they said. 'And be kind and safe along the way.' Between the lines Kate was also saying: 'Don't forget me, but please move on and make the most of every day.' She said those things in so many different ways as we talked for hours and cried and cuddled while she scribbled away, compiling Mum's List.

Would Kate approve of what I'd achieved so far? Would she think I was doing all right? I wished I could magic her back, if just for a minute, so I could ask her exactly what she thought, and get just a little bit more of her precious advice and feedback. She was great at organizing, and she'd be able to tell me in a flash what was what.

Nobody is perfect, and I knew I hadn't done everything she had asked, while some of the things I'd actually ticked off the list weren't perfect either. Moving on with someone else was the toughest request of all. I knew it would be, from the very second Kate told me to find another woman. Her request was so unthinkable back then it took my breath away. My wife was dying, but she would always be my soul mate. How could I ever find another woman, or another mother for the boys?

I sat up on the beach and looked out over the Red Sea, mulling over this thought. Instinctively, the fingers of my right hand reached across to my left hand, feeling for my ring finger. Over the months I'd developed a habit of twiddling the lovers' knot band I wore in place of my wedding ring. It was an almost subconscious ritual, something I now realize I did when I thought about Kate, and especially when I thought about Kate telling me to find another woman. To my surprise there was nothing but a smooth groove of flesh where I expected to feel the band. I stared at my bare hand for several minutes, registering the blank, white space on my finger and working out what had happened to my substitute wedding ring.

The band had been looking a bit frayed and thin lately, and I realized it must have finally split apart, and perhaps drifted off in the sea without me noticing. I guess it was bound to happen, yet I had done nothing to strengthen the fibres on the cord when I noticed it sagging and tearing. No doubt it had floated silently away from me when I was snorkelling with the boys, and I'd been too engrossed in watching them marvel at the fish to notice.

I was moved and a little saddened, but not shocked. Finding another woman actually wasn't unthinkable any more, and I didn't feel uncomfortable acknowledging that. I found myself studying the horizon, wondering what was out there beyond the thin indigo line separating sea from sky. I wasn't afraid or daunted as I had been in the early months after Kate was gone. I was ready to take a closer look and go exploring. I'd already moved on, perhaps much further than I knew, and I realized I felt strangely expectant about the future. I still didn't believe I would ever find another soul mate, because Kate was simply irreplaceable. But for the first time in a long time I could envisage a good life, perhaps a great life, beyond bereavement and loss and the endless painful milestones.

If I'd had the power I'd have jumped up on to the horizon, prised apart the sea and sky and peeped into my new world right there and then. I was ready for it. I would never,

ever forget Kate and I would make sure the boys remembered their mum as much as they possibly could. But something had shifted, and it hadn't just happened that day. Time had been slowly nursing my heart. It had worked away in secret under my skin, silently stitching cuts and soothing bruises. There was still plenty of work to be done, but the wounds of grief were no longer raw and bleeding.

This was my calm after my storm. The worst was over, I was sure. The sun really was shining, and Kate was smiling down on me.

Chapter 11

'Would like dining room table so you can have family meals once a week at least'

Seven months have slipped by since Egypt, and it's July 2011. The building work is finally finished, and our brand new dining table arrives this morning. I'm sitting on my bed, having just written out a shopping list for Tesco's, and I'm going to cook a meal tonight. The boys are at school, and I have the day to myself. I feel it's time to start writing the final chapter of my book, and I'm looking back through this year's diary.

On 20 January 2011, the first anniversary of Kate's death, Reef had a routine hospital appointment, to check his cancer was still in remission. As I look at my diary entry I almost want to pinch myself when I'm reminded of the words the doctor said to me that day. I'd held Reef's hand as he went through his familiar barrage of scans and blood tests. After last year's good news and the reassurances we received about the nodes in his groin being harmless, I was quietly optimistic. As well as joining Beavers and thoroughly enjoying all the activities he did with them, Reef was also doing well with his tag rugby at weekends. I marvelled at what an awesome little player he was, despite being unbalanced on his weak leg.

In his very first match he managed to avoid being

tagged and made a dash of about ten yards right through the opposition. He also has an amazing little pass on him, and I watched enthralled as he made the ball spiral through the air brilliantly. Standing on the touchline that day, I was transported back to the incredible moment, three days after doctors had told us Reef might never walk again, when he pushed a pram across the hospital playroom. Kate and I had looked at each other in stunned amazement. 'Oooh, you shouldn't be able to do that!' Kate had said to eighteen-month-old Reef, before collapsing in incredulous, delighted giggles. We couldn't believe our eyes, and the doctors had to see it with their own eyes before they believed it too. We knew the femoral nerve in Reef's leg had been attacked by his cancer and we had been warned that it would be further damaged by all the chemo and radiotherapy he was due to have, but we hadn't even begun to come to terms with the dreadful prognosis that he might never walk again. Seeing him push the pram that day, it was obvious that somehow the signals were still getting through from his brain to his leg, despite the aggressive cancer he had. It was a miracle, and even today the doctors don't fully understand how he pulled it off.

Now, every time I watch Reef play rugby I'm filled with incredible pride because it's such an outstanding achievement for him just being on the pitch. Finn, too, goes like a little train at rugby practice, and it's a delight to watch them both play. It takes me back to my own playing days, when I was a scrum half for a Bristol team. Kate was my biggest fan and would come and watch even when it was bitterly cold.

Once, when we were playing against a team from Bath University, the opposition supporters were screaming all sorts of abuse at me, oblivious to the fact my girlfriend was standing among them on the sidelines. Little Kate, wrapped up like an Eskimo in a hat and scarf against the sleet and howling wind, listened in silence for ages while they called me a 'ginger-haired git' and goaded their players to take me out of the game. She waited for the perfect moment, after I scored a try, before making her allegiance known and bursting into loud, enthusiastic cries of: 'Well done, Singe!'

'Who are you with, then?' one of the opposing fans asked.

'The ginger-haired git,' she replied with a big grin on her face, watching him turn redder than my hair before apologizing profusely for the comments he had made.

The memory made me smile to myself as I looked back at my diary, and read out the words I'd written under '20 January 2011: Reef, hospital appointment.'

'Fantastic, amazing, awesome news. Doctors delighted with Reef. All tests good. Told he now has same chance as anyone else of getting cancer!'

I could hardly believe my ears when Professor Stevens told me that. It was the best news I had heard in years and years, and I wished I could share it with Kate. It was the news she had waited so long for, the news we had been told never to dare expect. It was an absolute miracle.

I took both boys up to Kate's grave after the hospital appointment, explaining to them it was exactly a year to the day since Mummy died, and it would be nice to deliver some great news along with some fresh flowers for her gravestone.

The friendly robin who lives in the churchyard sang a beautiful song while we placed white roses around her, and I quietly told Kate Reef's incredible news. I allowed myself to imagine her ecstatic reaction. 'If we were only allowed one piece of luck, I'm so glad Reef got it,' she said.

When the boys were out of earshot I explained that I was trying to get tickets for the Ireland v. England Rugby International in Dublin in March. 'That was an easy one, Kate, telling me to take the boys to see an international rugby match!' I whispered while the boys pottered along the hedgerow, peering out to sea. 'I'm sure that can be arranged.'

The boys waved goodbye to Mummy as we left, just as if they were waving to her across the playground as they did so many times when she was alive. There were no tears, and I felt no tightening in my chest or throat as I had done on so many previous visits to Kate's grave. It was freezing cold, but the air felt light, and the boys looked carefree. We had visited Kate's grave so regularly over the past twelve months it had become a normal part of our lives, and it always would be. When we climbed back in the car Reef and Finn gave me a lovely little smile each, which melted my heart.

Focusing back on my diary, I saw there were plenty of other noteworthy dates and anniversaries in the first few months of 2011. We finally got *4 Saints* back at the end of January and went for a string of celebratory days out on the Bristol Channel, inviting any friends who were brave enough to endure the bitterly cold winds to join us.

Valentine's Day was easier than last year, I remembered. I ignored it again, and the page was blank in my diary, but this year it was a whole lot easier to ignore. I'd learned, to my relief, that once you've survived one painful date or anniversary, it gets a lot easier to cope with the next one.

I had started to go out on dates more frequently, still with women who were a friend of a friend, one way or another. They were not serious in terms of romance, but I always enjoyed chatting and going out to dinner or seeing a film. Just having some uninterrupted adult conversation did me the power of good.

One of my dates asked me very directly: 'How are you coping with your loss?' We were sitting in a pub overlooking the coast at Clevedon. She'd been very open about her own life, and her problematic divorce, and I found myself giving a very frank, florid answer which came straight from the heart.

'This is exactly how I would describe it,' I said, flicking my eyes between her and the sea. 'When Kate first died it was like I was standing on a beach, being hit constantly with wave after wave of grief. The waves knocked my feet out from under me, and I was taken by the surf every time. Some days it felt like I'd never be able to get back on my feet, or even come up for air. As time's moved on, I still get hit by the waves and my footing is still unstable, but now I always manage to climb halfway up the beach and sometimes I even get a bit further. Does that answer your question?'

I grinned, feeling quite pleased with my self-analysis.

'I think you're doing brilliantly,' she said, staring at me through watery eyes.

'That's kind of you to say,' I replied jovially. 'But what

choice do I have? It's sink or swim. I have two little boys to bring up and I have simply got to cope, I have got to get through.'

'Yes, but not everybody manages it as well as you,' she said.

'Not everybody has two cracking little boys like I do, and I'm lucky,' I said. 'A smile, a wave, or an "I love you, Daddy" from the boys keeps me going, no question, but I'm only human and I still have moments when the grief comes up and bites me.'

She nodded kindly and didn't probe. I wasn't going to tell her that I still went on Kate's Facebook page from time to time to read condolence messages from friends and family, and that I couldn't bear to take her account down. Nor was I going to mention the fact I still sprayed Kate's perfume on my pillow to help me sleep at night, or that a simple, unexpected remark from the boys could completely break me, even now.

'In the early days I had moments when I couldn't even make a cup of tea,' I added simply. 'It's not like that now. It gets easier.'

There was disappointment over the rugby tickets in March. The game was a sell-out, and despite my best efforts to get to Dublin with the boys, we had to admit defeat and watch the match at the local rugby club in Clevedon. England lost, and from a supporter's point of view it wasn't a great match. I can only imagine how much Guinness was drunk in commiseration and celebration.

'You know what?' I said to my brother afterwards. 'I think it was meant to be that me and the boys didn't get to go to Ireland.'

'What, because England lost?' Matt replied.

'No, not for that reason. The boys really enjoyed watching the match at the club with me, waving their flags and wearing their rugby tops. They're probably too little to really appreciate a big international game. It's something I can look forward to doing with them when they're older, and they'll get more out of it.'

'Er, but what about the list?' Matt asked tentatively. 'I thought the main reason to go was because of Kate's list?'

'It was,' I replied. 'And if this had happened this time last year I would have been much more cut up about it, but things have changed. I can take as long as I like working though the list. It's there to help me, not to put me under pressure. Kate didn't set time limits.'

Matt nodded. 'I'm glad you're so cool about it,' he said. 'You've changed. That's good.'

I kind of ignored my own birthday. I turned forty-five on 18 March and stayed in with the boys, who made me a card and a little paper pot to keep my pens in. This was hardly in keeping with Kate's instruction to '*Celebrate birthdays big time*', but I didn't think she meant mine. Besides, as I'd promised Finn, he was having an unofficial birthday party the same week, when we'd also celebrate 'Mum's Day' on what would have been Kate's fortieth birthday on 22 March.

I hired the old Curzon cinema in Clevedon again, inviting more than 200 friends and family, including both Reef and Finn's classmates, to a private screening of *Yogi Bear*.

'Look, Daddy!' Finn shrieked excitedly as we walked in. The cinema screen was filled with the words 'Happy Unofficial Birthday, Finn!'

'How did you do that?' Finn asked me, open-mouthed.

'Magic,' I told him, and he smiled all afternoon as he bounced around with his 'I am FIVE!' birthday badge pinned to his chest, asking me to perform 'more magic, Daddy!' by doing his favourite tricks with disappearing coins, which I enjoyed as much as him. We tucked in to cream buns after the film and had a wonderful time. The staff of the Curzon, all volunteers, had gone to an enormous amount of trouble to make the day extra special, and I was very grateful to them.

At bedtime that night I asked the boys if I could measure them again on their doorframe. It was ages since we'd done it, and they were both delighted to see they'd gained an inch or two in height, though Reef was still not much taller than his brother.

'You'll both be catching me up soon,' I joked.

'Mummy was small,' Reef said, looking at the little marker reminding us Kate was a petite five foot one. 'We'll catch her first!'

I took the opportunity to remind the boys about Mum's Day, as in the excitement of Finn's party it had barely been mentioned.

'Do you remember last year when we got the boat on Mum's Day?' I asked.

They both nodded obediently, but I wasn't convinced they remembered the connection.

'Well, it's a whole year since then. It's Mum's Day again – hasn't time flown?'

'When are we getting our big bedroom and secret passage?' Finn asked.

'Very, very soon,' I told him. 'After the Easter break and

before the end of summer. It's quite a lot of sleeps but I reckon the time will fly.'

'Can we keep our height chart on the door frame?' asked Reef earnestly.

'We certainly can,' I told him, making a mental note to remind the builders not to damage it. Good old Reef, I thought. Not much escaped his logical brain.

I kissed the boys two times and said goodnight. 'Mind the bed bugs don't bite!' I added, to which the boys replied: 'Especially the daddy ones!' I don't know when we started saying that, but it had become part of our routine before we said 'acres and acres'.

I closed their bedroom door and walked across the landing alone. I've done the same thing hundreds of times, but somewhere along the line I'd lost the aching, empty pang that used to descend on me immediately after the boys went to bed.

Now, sitting on my bed alone with my diary, I remembered the lonely first nights after Kate's death, and I felt relieved they were a memory. I still felt lonely, don't get me wrong, but it was a far less painful type of loneliness. I'd learned to cope with it, I guess, even though I still didn't like being on my own.

There had been another gradual change in routine too. In the early days after losing Kate, friends and family made a point of phoning me after 8 p.m., knowing that's when I would be on my own and in need of a chat and some moral support. Nowadays, after 8 p.m. was the time I exchanged texts or calls with dates. It was a relief to swap the: 'How are you feeling?' conversations for some light-hearted flirting and a bit of saucy banter.

With the extension getting underway I had a lot to do to keep me busy in March, which was a blessing. The conservatory and the loft both needed emptying before the builders could start work, and my diary reminded me that I decided to tackle the conservatory on the eve of Finn's party.

It was completely cluttered with toys and books, sports equipment and knickknacks we'd accumulated over the years. Kate would have had a clear system here: '"Charity shop/give to friends" over here, "keep" pile here, "rubbish" over there,' she would have said, handing out bin bags and storage boxes as she whipped through the room efficiently. I tried to copy her system but didn't get very far before I was sidetracked and then swamped by memories. In between a pile of books I found a Valentine message that Kate had placed for me in a local paper I don't know how many years before. Inside a heart shape, which she'd carefully cut out, it said: 'Singe, I love you acres and acres. Forever yours, Katie.'

I took it to the bedroom and put it in one of our boxes of love letters for safe keeping, wondering wryly if the 'keep' pile in the conservatory was going to tower above the 'charity' and 'rubbish' piles. While I was there I couldn't resist picking out a few old love letters and having a quick read, knowing that whatever Kate wrote was flattering and heart-warming, and usually gave my ego a massage, both then and now.

'I love you Singe and I want you in the end. I don't think another couple could be as good as we are,' she wrote in the first one I looked at. 'I will always be by your side. I will trust you, ring you, marry you, even wash your socks!' she promised in another, writing with a fancy silver pen. The next letter I chose was clearly written when we had to spend time apart. 'God, I am cold. I would love to have you here to warm me up,' Kate said. 'God, I miss you. I've lost my human hot water bottle. Let's hope I don't get a chill.'

I exhaled deeply and felt goose bumps prickle my arms. I'd been looking for a sentimental boost, but I'd got a shot of tragic irony instead.

'Serves you right, Singe,' I scolded myself gently, knowing I should put the letters away now, but not being able to resist reading one last page.

'My urge for letter writing is dying, but my urge for you is not dying,' Kate had written.

I kissed the lipstick kiss she'd put on the end next to her name and put the box away, feeling saddened and a little stung by the experience. I hadn't expected to see the word 'dying' in Kate's teenage handwriting, or to be left with an uncomfortable ache in my chest.

While I was upstairs I decided I'd better have a scout around in the loft to get an idea of the scale of the decluttering job up there. Nearly everything stored in the loft would have to be cleared out to make way for the secret passage leading from my old office into the boys' play den that would be built up there.

I climbed the loft ladder and began picking through boxes and boxes piled high with old baby bottles and breast pumps, rattles and tiny baby clothes. I felt sorry for Kate, keeping all this stuff, hoping we might have another baby. I wish we'd had another baby too, a little girl like Kate. She would have had her mum's good looks and contagious giggles, I could just see her. She would have been the icing on the cake for us. I hadn't known that Kate had kept so much, and I felt a lump rise in my throat as I realized she must have been the last person to touch these things. One large white box had 'Singe and Katie!' daubed jauntily on the side, telling me instantly it contained souvenirs from our youth. I pulled out two dusty flying jackets we wore when Kate was in her teens and I was in my early twenties. We'd written our names on the back in bright bubble-gum pink to personalize them for a fancy dress party, and I had a sudden flashback of us posing in matching chinos and baseball caps at a Butlins holiday camp party, sharing a joke with lifeguard colleagues of mine as we showed off our jackets.

I enjoyed the memory but I have to be honest, I was also wondering what on earth I was going to do with all this stuff. Under the jackets I found albums and box sets signed by the 1980s groups King, AHA and Adam and the Ants, and beneath the records was a large stash of Kate's old college work. What was I meant to do with that?

I put it all back and ventured deeper into the loft. Propped upright in the very far corner, away from the clutter, I spotted a box I recognized immediately. It was a beautiful big cream display box, and in it was Kate's carefully packaged wedding dress. Believe it or not, seeing the box actually made me feel better, as I knew immediately what to do with it. I had to keep the dress; there was no doubt about that. The boys might want their bride to wear it when they got married, or they might just want to keep it themselves to remember their mum. At the very least I could show it to them and tell them all about our wonderful wedding day, when Kate looked so exquisite and elated.

Climbing down from the loft, I decided I would throw

out the baby stuff and ask Kate's mum if she wanted any of her old college things, and I'd keep a couple of our teenage mementos for old times' sake. The rest would have to go before the builders got cracking. I felt very emotional as my mind ticked over, but in more of a nostalgic than a sad way. It wasn't a pleasant job, and if it wasn't for the extension I certainly wouldn't have been in a hurry to do it, but it felt kind of liberating to make a start.

The last week in March was incredibly busy, I noted. I had the boys christened on 31 March, our wedding anniversary, as I'd planned. Noel agreed to do the ceremony at All Saints and asked me who the godparents were. I hesitated. 'I haven't chosen them yet,' I said cautiously.

'Is there a problem?' he asked intuitively.

'Not really,' I replied. 'It's just that Kate and I talked about this at length, when she was writing her list. She didn't want to be too controlling, and she told me it was my choice as she wouldn't be here, but she did tell me who she would be happy to have as the boys' godparents. I'm just having a job making up my mind.'

I wanted to keep the service personal and low-key, so I invited a very small group of close friends and family.

'Who have you decided on as godparents?' Noel asked.

'Are you ready for this,' I laughed. 'Kate's brother Ben, my brother Matthew, my sisters Kaye and Lucinda, Kate's cousin Ian, my good mates Ken and Nathan, my best mate James, Kate's best mate Ruth, and finally Jayne, a good friend who Kate met at the boys' Montessori nursery.'

Noel raised an eyebrow and smiled. 'Excellent,' he said. When the godparents were asked to step forward in the church, they made up more than half the congregation and everybody laughed.

'How could I choose between you?' I joked.

Noel got the next laugh when he invited the boys to 'step up to the gallows', as the font is raised up so high they needed a little stepladder to reach it. It was a lovely, personal service, and I knew Kate would have enjoyed it. She wasn't overtly religious and she knew I wasn't, but she wanted the boys to be christened so they would have the right to be married in church, which she hoped they would do one day.

'*Would be good if they settled down sooner rather than later so you get to see grandchildren,*' Kate wrote on her list.

'I can't believe you're thinking that far ahead,' I said in surprise when she came out with that one. Her words really brought it home to me just how much she would miss out on, how much we would both miss out on sharing together. Kate had only lived half a life, and I remember how I felt panicked, imagining decades and decades stretching ahead without her by my side.

'I have to,' she said, weeping but trying to give me an encouraging smile. 'I can only think about it, I can't do anything else now, can I?'

The boys didn't question why they were being christened on a dull Thursday afternoon in March while all their friends went home from school. They were quite happy with the explanation that I wanted their christening to be on the same date I married Mummy fifteen years earlier, which I thought was enough information for the time being.

So many unusual things had happened in their short lives that I think they had both become very used to going with the flow. Looking at them that day, posing for photographs and not fully understanding the wider significance of the date in that it had also been the date of Kate's interment last year, I couldn't help returning to thoughts of the list.

I really wanted to slow down now, I realized. It was a gut instinct that I felt quite acutely. I wanted the boys to enjoy ticking off some items on the list with me, and to fully appreciate Mum's List. The extension would fulfil several of Kate's big wishes, and after that I'd go with the flow a bit more too, I decided. I didn't have to rush into anything, not now. It felt like a good decision as I stood there in the churchyard, feeling the sun making a late break through the clouds.

My diary reminded me that Mother's Day fell in early April. Having made cards at school for their nannies the previous year, the boys didn't appear to worry about doing the same this year while other children wrote to their mummies. It was definitely easier second time around, and I knew it would be easier again next year.

The weather was improving daily, and I thought it might be a good time to plant some sunflower seeds, even though by now the builders had dismantled the old conservatory and filled the back garden with machinery and supplies. As well as having seeds pushed through my letterbox by people who must have known us, several packets had also arrived in the post from strangers who had heard about Kate and somehow tracked us down. I wanted to plant them while they were fresh and spring was arriving.

'Grow a sunflower every now and again,' Kate had requested. That was a typical Kate request, and I smiled every time I

saw it on the list. I got the boys to help me press several sunflower seeds into little pots, which we propped up in the sunniest spots around the house and in the front garden, and one bright afternoon we cycled up to the graveyard and planted a few around Kate too. We also sprinkled some four-leaf clover seeds that came in a packet marked 'Grow Your Own Luck' around her gravestone, using a piece of bleached coral to dig the ground and cover them over with soil.

'I hope they grow big,' Finn said. 'Mummy would like that.'

'So do I,' I said. 'But don't be sad if they don't. 'They're not the easiest things to grow, but we'll do our best.'

'OK,' Finn replied. 'That's all we can do, isn't it, Daddy?'

On many occasions, when we'd walked the dog by the river behind the house, I'd mentioned to the boys that Mummy used to find four-leaf clovers there, but they didn't really hunt very hard and we never had any luck. I didn't let it bother me, because at least we'd tried, and that's all you can do, as I'd told the boys often. Finn, bless him, had picked that phrase up and taken it to heart, and I was very glad he had.

I looked though the rest of April and then into May and June in my diary. I took the boys caravanning again over Easter with my dad and stepmum, and at home we had loads of great days out on the boat and jet-ski with the boys at the helm. Reef reached 55 mph on *4 Saints* and thought he was the bee's knees, which was a joy to see, and he and Finn both delighted in taking their little girlfriends from school out on the water and showing off their skills.

They were about the most exciting things to happen, and I realized that, despite the major upheaval going on in the house with the building work, we'd had the quietest and most ordinary few months since Kate's death. Work was busy, and I was spending a lot of time helping at the school, but that was normal day-to-day stuff. Besides writing this book, the 'Kate-related' events had petered out, and that was fine by me. It felt right to settle into a more regular routine, away from the unavoidable ceremony and aftermath of death.

'How's things?' the pretty blonde woman in the grocery shop asked one day, giving me a sunny smile.

'All the better for seeing you,' I replied cheekily. I noticed her cheeks went a little pink, and there was a hint of a twinkle in her green eyes. I'm an 'eye' person and I always notice eyes. Hers were lovely. We'd been sharing a bit of banter on and off for months, and I always enjoyed bumping into her as I did my shopping.

'You're such a flirt, Singe,' she laughed.

'I know, I can't help myself,' I replied, adding spontaneously: 'You bring out the flirt in me.'

Now she was crimson, and I could feel myself blushing a bit too.

'In that case we'll have to stop meeting like this!' she giggled as she filled a carrier bag with bread and milk.

'We will,' I replied. 'We should go for a drink instead. Do you fancy it?'

'Yes,' she said, sounding surprised but pleased. 'Why not? I'd love to.'

I drove home with her number stored in my phone under 'Ali', feeling quite chuffed with myself. All the other dates I'd been on had been fixed up by my friends, but I'd actually arranged this one all by myself, and it had all happened almost without me having to think about it. Perhaps dating in your forties wasn't that bad after all, I thought.

We arranged to go for a drink in a quiet pub the following Wednesday, when Kirsty was babysitting. I didn't stress about what to wear or what to say, I just looked forward to spending a few hours in the company of someone I quite fancied, who seemed to feel the same way about me, and appeared to be easy going and up for a giggle.

I wondered if Ali liked boats, and I really hoped she did. I couldn't be with someone who didn't share my passion for the sea, and for adventure. 'Calm down, Singe,' I told myself. 'It's just a drink. You are not looking for a new wife!'

It was early July by now, and the building work was almost complete. Dressed for my date, I walked around the house feeling like the king of the castle, knowing Kate would love what I'd done, what I'd been able to do because of her.

Downstairs, the new kitchen was really taking shape, and I'd chosen an eye-catching granite with a stunning pebble design. The spotlights in the ceiling picked out the stones and made them look like pebbles scattered on the beach. Dividing the kitchen from the living room, we had the most spectacular fish tank ever, which the boys could peer into from any angle. They'd chosen to fill it with red candy-striped cleaner shrimps and regal and yellow tangs, because of the characters in *Finding Nemo*, as well as firefish and electric blue damsons like the ones they'd seen in the Red Sea, plus sand sifting gobies, crimson hawkfish, maroon clownfish, hermit crabs, starfish and finally some algae-eating turbo snails to help keep the tank clean.

'Sort out fish tank,' Kate asked, and we'd certainly done

that, and more. I'd even kept the old tank, planning to install it in the boys' playroom in the loft eventually.

Outside, despite the large, two-storey extension, we still had enough room for Reef and Finn to play, and now the builders were nearly finished the boys could throw balls and bounce on the trampoline again, which they loved. Creating a climbing wall was still outstanding on the list, but that is a project we will have fun working on together, as well as planting some more flowers and making the garden look pretty. None of our sunflowers or clovers had grown, either at home or at Kate's grave, and I looked forward to trying again and perhaps planting wild flowers too, to attract butterflies. Kate adored butterflies, and I loved to remember her pregnant with Reef in the garden, chasing after them in the sunshine.

Upstairs, the boys' double bedroom was almost complete, kitted out with matching cabin beds and pirate-themed lamps, storage chests and curtains. It was exactly as I'd envisaged it. In prime position on a special shelf was the fantastic photo of the boys with Kate and me, swimming with the dolphins in Florida, plus one of us posing with Father Christmas in Lapland. *'Pictures of us in boys' room.'*

The secret passage led from what had been my old office up to the new playroom in the loft. As this book was being completed at the same time as the extension, I got a designer to copy the cover of Mum's List and recreate the image on the doorway leading to the secret passage. The idea is to make it look like a giant book on a shelf, and when you push the book and go through the doorway you feel like a character entering a secret world of adventures, which the boys are totally thrilled about. Kate would have been tickled pink by the whole thing, and I am too.

Eventually we'll kit the loft out as a chill-out space with beanbags and books and computer games for the boys, and no doubt one day it will be their teenage den, when all their toys are gone. It makes far better use of the space than before, and I know Kate would not have wanted me to keep the loft stuffed with our dusty old belongings. I stowed a few precious mementos, including Kate's wedding dress, in one smaller, storage section of the loft, and that was all I needed. My memories are mostly in my head and in my heart, where there will always be plenty of room for them.

My date with Ali went well, in a funny kind of way. It turned out she knew quite a lot about me already, having read a few stories in the local press and remembering seeing me and the boys on TV. I was glad I didn't have to start at the beginning and tell her all about Kate, and we were soon chatting like we'd known each other for ages.

I was pleased when she told me she quite enjoyed jet-skiing, though as a single mum she didn't get the chance to do it often. She also had a good sense of humour, which really put me at my ease and made me warm to her. When she asked me, after a couple of drinks, 'Are you glad Kate wrote the list?' I wasn't in the least bit put out.

'Yes,' I replied, feeling glad I could correct what I realized was a common misconception – that Kate had written the list on her own and presented it to me on her deathbed. 'We wrote it together, actually,' I told Ali, taking a deep breath. 'We did it in a time of extreme stress and, looking back, we could have added more. I thought she'd make it. I was convinced we wouldn't need it. If I'd had a reality check it would be even more comprehensive. I think everyone should write a list.'

'Why?' Ali asked, her emerald eyes full of questions.

'Well, it's been such a help and support to me,' I said. 'It gave me a reference point when I was lost in grief, and I've enjoyed doing lots of the things Kate asked me to do, even if I haven't done them perfectly. Reef's birthday party was amazing, for example, and Kate would have been gobsmacked at how I organized and delivered it. The caravan holidays she wanted me to do I can do better with practice, but I'm glad I've done them. Having the list to turn to has kept me going, and made me feel less alone.'

Ali smiled but looked slightly perturbed, and I found myself reassuring her that the list in no way held me back.

'I'm not clinging to the past,' I explained. 'I've already changed in some ways since losing Kate. The list helps me deal with the present, and the future.'

Ali looked at me expectantly.

'How have you changed?' she asked.

I thought about that question for a moment, and then I told her I didn't take things to heart so much.

'I used to get upset by criticism,' I said. 'But now I shrug and think: "It's my life." I've become a bit harder and I don't suffer fools gladly . . . but then again some things haven't changed at all. I'm still a big softy at heart, and I'm still amazingly romantic.'

Ali smiled at that last point.

'Glad to hear it,' she teased. 'So where's my bunch of flowers?'

'You'll have to wait and be surprised,' I smirked. 'The

best romantic gestures are unexpected – and far better than a bunch of flowers.'

She told me she had a romantic streak too, and that she didn't like being on her own, but was kept very busy by her lively children.

'I can't say I'm lonely, because I never have a minute to myself,' she laughed. 'But chasing round after the kids isn't the same as being whisked off your feet, is it?'

'I know exactly what you mean,' I said. 'I'm coming to terms with being on my own, but being a single parent is bloody hard work.'

'How are the boys doing?' Ali asked, adding sensitively, 'if you don't mind me asking?'

'The boys are great, and I love talking about them,' I said. 'The house is going to be amazing for them when it's all finished, and they're very excited about it. They have a remarkable resilience, and I'm really proud of them. They're both cheeky and playful and we have giggles every day. They've got really close as far as brothers go, and Reef is becoming more and more confident.'

'So Finn is the naturally confident one?'

'You could say that,' I laughed. 'He is me all over. He is winding me up at the moment because he whines when he wants attention. I need to work out how to stop him doing it instead of letting it get to me. I suppose I should have more patience with him, being a bit of an attention-seeker myself . . . Reef is naturally quieter and more thoughtful. He's missing his mum at the moment. The trouble is he has started to mention her a lot at bed time, and I can't work out if he's being a bit cute and using it to delay lights out . . .'

I stopped talking, suddenly aware I was being very honest here and perhaps rambling on a bit, even though I was enjoying having the space to unload. Ali said nothing to fill the gap in the conversation. She just smiled and nodded, so I carried on.

'Both boys look after me as much as I look after them,' I said. 'They cheer me up and they sense when I'm upset.'

'Do you get upset a lot?' Ali ventured. 'I mean, I suppose what I'm asking is, are you getting over Kate . . . will you ever get over Kate?'

'That's the million-dollar question,' I said, blowing out a long, deep breath. 'The saying that time is a healer is apt. In time you improvise and adapt to overcome the difficulties of being on your own, of being bereaved. You've got to let your grief come out, and I don't bottle things up. That said, there's a time and a place for tears and I've had to be careful not to cry too much in front of the boys, because they are so young and impressionable. I choose my moments to indulge in self-pity, but thankfully those moments are becoming fewer and further between.'

'That's good to hear,' Ali said kindly.

'Having Mum's List has helped me so much,' I added. 'Kate left so much of herself behind. Of course, she left Reef and Finn. But she also left bits of her heart sprinkled all over her list and all around our world, and that will never die.'

I noticed Ali had a tear in her eye and so I stopped talking again, realizing my own eyes were loaded with tears too.

'God, I'm so sorry,' I apologized. 'This is hardly what you want to hear on a first date!'

'A date?' Ali said with a question in her voice. 'Well, maybe it's just the start of a good friendship, who knows?'

I liked her attitude. She told me she was flattered I'd told her so much and asked if she could ask me one last question.

'Don't answer it if I'm being too nosy, though, Singe.'

'Fire away,' I said.

'OK, here goes. Do you think you could ever settle down again, as Kate wanted? I mean, it's tough enough after a divorce, I should know, let alone after losing the love of your life.'

'I can,' I said emphatically. 'I've thought about this long and hard and I do want to get married again one day. It surprises me to say that, but it's true. Kate was my soul mate and she lives on through her list, but life goes on without her. Maybe I'll be lucky enough to find another soul mate one day.'

I'd learned quite a lot about Ali that evening, and I enjoyed her company and straight-talking manner. Our unexpectedly deep conversation also helped me learn a lot about where I was, too.

'Shall we do this again sometime?' I asked, hoping I hadn't put her off.

'I'd love to,' she smiled genuinely, and we said our goodbyes, promising to fix up a day to go out on the boat or for a walk on the beach when the weather was good.

A few weeks slipped by, and I was swamped with chores at home. The builders were putting the finishing touches to the house, and I was spending all my spare time organizing the decorating, putting up shelves and pictures and installing furniture and carpets.

I spoke to Ali quite a few times on the phone in the evenings, and I enjoyed hearing about her adventures with her kids and her busy lifestyle. She had her hands full too with one thing and another, and we hadn't got round to fixing up another date.

'I tell you what, why don't you just pop round for a cup of tea after work one night?' I suggested. 'I could show you the house, you can meet the boys, and we can catch up.'

'Sounds great, thanks,' she said. 'I don't know which night is best yet, but I'll text you.'

That was last week. I turned another page in my diary and saw the words 'dining table arrives!!!' under today's date. It was the final big piece of the puzzle to fit into the house, and I'd been looking forward to its arrival. I'd chosen a massive solid oak six-seater with matching chairs, exactly like one Kate had pointed out in a magazine.

'I want a table like that,' Kate said dreamily. 'I want it to be at the heart of our home. I want us to eat together as a family as much as possible.'

I loved it when she said that. Her words tickled my heart, making it flutter with love for her. She was still my surf chick and my mini-mermaid, but she was also the fantastic mother of my children. Being a good mum and running a happy family home meant the world to Kate, and she lived by basic, old-fashioned values. She adored me, too. I felt incredibly lucky to be at the centre of her world, the man she wanted to sit at the head of her table.

'*Would like dining room table so you can have family meals once a week at least,*' Kate said quietly as she added that item to her list.

I felt so moved by her words.

'We can do that, no problem,' I told her.

It was such a simple wish, one I hoped we could fulfil together. In my mind, as Kate lay in bed, I was already shifting furniture out of the old conservatory, making way for a temporary table before we could build a proper dining area. I was trying to picture Kate breathing without her oxygen cylinder, serving up a home-cooked lasagne, telling us to tuck in and reminding the boys to use their knives and forks correctly. Of course, that never happened. Kate was never well enough to eat another square meal, let alone cook and sit around a dinner table with me, Reef and Finn.

When the new table was finally unwrapped and installed later that morning, I stared at it in what can only be described as awe. It looked absolutely stunning. Sunlight was streaming through the windows of the extension, making the oak glisten like warm sand. With the bubbling fish tank on one side and the glinting pebble granite on the other, the table could not have fitted in more perfectly.

After school I cooked a spaghetti Bolognese for me and the boys, looking forward to the moment we would all sit down and eat together. Predictably, Reef and Finn were far less impressed by the table than by their secret passage, the playroom or the fish tank.

'Can't we watch telly while we eat?' Finn whinged as I set the table.

'No, Finn, we can all sit around the table together and have a chat about our day, and you can watch some TV afterwards if you eat up. Now please wash your hands and sit down.'

'Not fair!' he complained, folding his arms and scowling at me in protest.

Reef dutifully washed his hands and then circled the table suspiciously, eyeing the six seats.

'Why have we got six chairs when there are only three of us?' he asked.

'Because sometimes your friends might come for tea, or we might cook Sunday dinner for Grampy, to say thank you for all the Sunday dinners he has made for us, or Nanny and Gramps might come and eat with us, or Ruth or Matt or Ben . . .' I said, serving up the food.

'Mummy would like that, Daddy,' Reef said.

'Yes, she would,' I said.

Finn had sat down with us now and had stopped being cross. 'How many friends can we invite for tea?' he asked.

'Three, silly!' Reef replied, pointing at the three empty chairs.

'Three each?' Finn joked, slapping his thigh

'No,' Reef said, getting annoyed. 'That makes *nine*! We can only have one friend each!'

I decided not to explain to the boys how very important this table was to Mummy. Actions speak louder than words sometimes, I thought, as I watched Reef and Finn suck up their spaghetti. Just being here together was more important right now than explaining how and why we were all here, sitting round this table, in memory of Kate.

The boys were being a bit silly, letting the spaghetti splash sauce around their mouths, but they knew I had my eye on them and they didn't go too far. I didn't want to tell them off. It was such an enormous privilege to be able to sit here and share this moment with them, and I felt so grateful to Kate, for making this happen.

There was a knock on the door as we were finishing

our meal, and I was surprised to see Ali standing on the doorstep.

'Did you get my text?' she said.

'What text? No, I was cooking! Come in,' I replied.

I was really pleased to see her, and invited her to sit at the table while the boys polished off their food. They greeted her with cartoon-style smiles that looked painted on with tomato sauce, and Ali and I both laughed.

'Are you hungry? There's plenty to go round if you'd like some,' I offered.

'No, that's really kind, but I can't stay long,' Ali replied, pulling out a chair. 'Oh, this is comfortable – what a lovely table! A cup of tea would be great though, as long as I'm not intruding.'

I was about to tell her she certainly wasn't intruding and to introduce her to the boys properly, but they beat me to it, in their own way.

'Are you Daddy's friend?' Finn asked charmingly.

'Yes,' she smiled. 'You must be Finn, and I'm Ali.'

'Daddy is allowed one friend for tea,' Finn added approvingly. 'We have enough chairs now!'

'Just one friend?' Ali asked, giving a quizzical little frown.

'It's like this,' Reef said patiently. 'Now we have six chairs, and with me, Daddy and Finn that leaves three chairs extra. If Mummy was still here it would be four chairs taken and two left, and so Daddy couldn't have a friend, only me and Finn could. But Mummy isn't here now, and Mummy wanted Daddy and us to have a nice big table, and Mummy wanted Daddy to have a new friend, too.'

Ali looked at me, lost for words.

'I didn't know he knew so much, but he's absolutely right,' I said, rolling my eyes playfully and looking out of the window and up to the sky. 'Thanks, Kate,' I said out loud, adding silently in my head: 'Thank you for absolutely everything.'

Epilogue

Having urged so many people to write a list, I realized I ought to write my own.

In the early days after Kate was gone I was in no rush, as I had Mum's List, which reflected so much of my life as well as hers. Now, two years on, things have changed. When Rachel, my ghostwriter, asked me recently which holiday I planned to do next, I surprised her by saying: 'Las Vegas and the Grand Canyon.'

'But it's not on the list,' she said. 'I expected you to say Switzerland, or maybe Australia.'

'It's not on Kate's list,' I replied. 'But it's on mine. I want to explore America, let my hair down in Vegas, go target-shooting and ride bareback through the Grand Canyon. It's something I've always dreamed of doing.'

'Did Kate know about this?'

'No, it's not something we ever discussed. I know Kate would have come with me had I asked, and she would have enjoyed herself and got interested along the way, but it wasn't really her thing.'

'So . . . who will you go with?'

'I'll go on my own,' I answered confidently. 'I'll enjoy the freedom, and it'll give me time to think about the future.

At the moment I feel like I'm driving round a roundabout with loads of exits, not knowing which route to take. I want to build up my business; I still have loads more to do in the house; I want the boys to become more independent but I want to hold them close; I want to keep the family happy, and I don't want to make mistakes in my relationships. I have a lot of responsibility on my shoulders. I often wish I could ask Kate: "What should I do next?" I can hear her talking to me, telling me I have to make the right decisions, but I don't know what they are. I think it'll do me good to get away from it all before I plan my next move.'

I had the beginnings of a list in my head at that point, which was part 'to-do' for me and for the boys, and part 'to-remember'. Now it was time to put it in writing, for several reasons.

Of course, there are the practicalities of making provisions for Reef and Finn, should anything happen to me. I had to make my wishes known to my loved ones, and leave instructions about the boys' care and finances. That was the easy bit, and I will keep those details private.

My list also needed to be written because time is moving on quickly, and we have all grown, one way or another, since Kate's death. The boys are now aged six and seven, and I can already see them developing from two small, cheeky boys into poised, articulate and entertaining little lads. I turn forty-six in March this year (2012), and I feel the passage of time very acutely. I know how unexpectedly life can be cut short, and how important it is to stay on your toes and not let opportunities slip by. I can already envisage the boys as teenagers and young men, and I want my list to reflect that.

I am so proud of Reef and Finn and I want them to

know that I loved Mummy as much as she loved me, and that they are our greatest achievement.

Kate's death has made me want to do more with my life than ever before. I am so glad we had so many amazing, action-packed years together, but I wish we'd done more still. I wish we'd gone on more holidays, seen even more of the world and had more children. I can't live my life with Kate any longer, but I can still live my life to the full, and that's what I intend to do, while continuing to show Reef and Finn how to do the same.

Writing *Mum's List* has been a labour of love. I wrote it as a tribute to Kate and the wonderful life we shared, and I've thoroughly enjoyed doing it, despite blubbing my way through much of it. Finishing the book has been incredibly moving, as reaching the end has drawn an emotional line under the past. To me, it symbolizes the end of my life with Kate, and the start of my new one without her.

Kate, if you're watching over me, please look over my shoulder and read the words I'm about to write, as I know they will make you happy.

I will never forget you, Kate, and of course Mum's List will always be with me, wherever I go and whatever I do. Thank you so much for taking the trouble to write it when you were so very ill. The boys and I miss you very much and will be forever grateful for what you did for us, always.

I am on my own now, and I am doing well. I don't know what the future holds, but I am ready to explore with an open mind and with hope and excitement in my heart, as we always did together. Maybe I will be lucky enough to find another soul mate, and I promise I will try. When you make the most of every day, anything is possible.

Here is my list, but it is by no means complete. I will always keep adding to it, because you can never laugh too much, learn too much, care too much or love too much.

Dad's List

Life wishes

Want Reef and Finn to live as near as possible to both sets of family and for both sets of family to be fully involved in boys' lives

Reef and Finn to do Camp America, if possible

Both boys to be instructors in diving

Sailing and boating regularly

Want boys to go on regular family holidays. Mummy and Daddy had planned to explore so much more of the world, going back to New Zealand, Australia, Switzerland and the US and visiting Canada, Belize and Thailand

Daddy to do Las Vegas and Grand Canyon

Daddy to get fitter and thinner

Want all godparents to be involved in Reef and Finn's lives

When boys reach twenty-one they may like to live or work abroad, and that's OK

Dad's memories of Mum and the things we did together

Daddy used to love kissing Mummy and always gave her big hugs

Daddy loved the way Mummy used to lift her foot off the floor when she was kissed or hugged
Mummy and Daddy met on roller skates at the Robin Cousins Sports Centre
Both Mummy and Daddy loved looking at the stars in wild places, or miles from cities
Daddy and Mummy thought manners are really important
We believed in lots of cool rules to live by. These sayings will always be part of our relationship: 'Live life,' 'Do something every day to be proud of,' 'Live on the edge or you're a waste of space,' 'Don't go to sleep on an argument,' 'Smile and say hello to people you meet,' 'Don't be reckless with people's feelings,' 'If you are romantic, do it in style'
Mummy's first flight was with Daddy. We did lots of firsts together. Make a list of things to do and record your 'firsts' for when you are older
If you are lucky enough to find a soul mate, hold them tight and work together for those special moments which life has to offer
Daddy loved Mummy's eyes, her smile and her bum – especially in tight bleached jeans!
Daddy loved all kinds of magic and doing magic tricks, but the magic of life is the best
Daddy loved food and cooking. His favourites are strawberries, fish, prawns, shellfish, thick steaks and rum
Daddy called Mummy Kate or Katie, and Mummy always called Daddy Singe
Mummy was always helping Daddy do things, and we would often learn new things together

Try to respect nature and never be a litterbug. Mummy and Daddy would pick up litter in our favourite places

Daddy was helped to write a book about his life with Mummy. It is called *Mum's List.* It has been hard to write but worth it, as Daddy's memories of Mummy will never be forgotten, and that is very cool

Daddy is so proud that Mummy chose him to be her partner and he will always have you two boys to remind him how amazing she was